Éliphas Lévi and the Kabbalah

The Masonic and French Connection of the
American Mystery Tradition

by

Robert L. Uzzel

Éliphas Lévi and the Kabbalah

A Cornerstone Book
Published by Cornerstone Book Publishers
Copyright © 2006 by Robert L. Uzzel

All rights reserved under International and Pan-American Copyright Conventions. No part of this book may be reproduced in any manner without permission in writing from the copyright holder, except by a reviewer, who may quote brief passages in a review.

Cornerstone Book Publishers
Lafayette, Louisiana

Authors Photo: A Samuel E. Naive Photo

First Cornerstone Edition - 2006

www.cornerstonepublishers.com

ISBN: 1-887560-76-9
978-1-887560-76-4

MADE IN THE USA

Table of Contents

Acknowledgments vi

Dedication viii

CHAPTER I
Éliphas Lévi's Life and Approach to Kabbalah 1

CHAPTER II
The Influence of Éliphas Lévi in France
and Great Britain as a Prelude to the American Scene 41

CHAPTER III
Lévi in America: Albert Pike 68

CHAPTER IV
Lévi in America: Religious Movements 98

CHAPTER V
Éliphas Lévi within the *Zeitgeist* of the Nineteenth Century and
Its Relevance to the Twentieth and Twenty-First Centuries 145

Bibliography 169

Glossary 178

Index 181

About the Author 193

Acknowledgments

So many people helped to make the completion of this book a reality that it is hard to thank them all. At any rate, I intend to try.

I must first thank members of the faculty and staff of Baylor University for their encouragement and help during the process of research and writing what began as my doctoral dissertation. Dr. John N. Jonsson, my dissertation director, deserves special thanks for his enthusiasm regarding the subject matter, his expert supervision, and his friendship. Numerous visits to his office and home, marked by theological discussions over hot tea, inspired me with reassurance that I was moving in the right direction and with dedication to bring the project to fruition. I am very grateful to the words of encouragement, as well as constructive criticism, provided by Drs. James M. Kennedy and James E. Wood, Jr., respectively my second and third readers. My gratitude is also extended to Drs. James Breckenridge and Bruce Cresson, respectively my fourth and fifth readers, for their help at the end of the dissertation project. Much encouragement was also provided by Dr. Glenn O. Hilburn, chairman of the Department of Religion; and Dr. W. H. Bellinger, director of Graduate Studies in Religion. For this I am very grateful. I also appreciate the tremendous help provided by the staff of the Baylor University Moody Library, including the Circulation Department, the Interlibrary Loan Department, and the Computer Lab.

The completion of my dissertation in 1995 was facilitated by a Mellon Fellowship from the United Negro College Fund (UNCF). I am grateful to Dr. William Scott of Lehigh University, administrator of UNCF's Mellon programs; and Rev. William H. Gray, III, president of UNCF, for their encouragement in the application process. I am also grateful to Dr. Weldon J. Walton, vice-president for academic affairs at Paul Quinn College, for arranging for me a sabbatical in order to devote fulltime to the work on my dissertation during the 1994-95 academic year. After my dissertation was accepted for publication, I received invaluable help with scanning and editing from Henry Rodriquez of the Paul Quinn College Technology Department, to whom I extend my heartfelt thanks.

My research involved the mailing of over one hundred letters to various individuals and organizations. Most of the recipients of my letters did not respond. I am grateful to those who did. Very helpful information was provided by letter and/or telephone by the following persons: John Algeo of the Theosophical Society in America, Paul A. Clark of the Fraternity of the Hidden Light, D. W. Dalton of the International Order of Kabbalists, Soror Lucia Gorsch and Soror M. A. of Societas Rosicruciana in America,

Tarot scholar Dr. Cynthia Giles, Gloria Hayes of the Rosicrucian Fellowship, Bill Heidrick of the Order of the Temple of the Orient, Bishop Stephan A. Hoeller of Ecclesia Gnostica, Dr. Daniel Matt of the Center for Jewish Studies at the Graduate Theological Union, Luther Ray Montandon of the Church of Mercavah, Frances Adams Moore of the Meditation Groups for the New Age, Dr. Hilmar Moore and Barbara Richardson of the Anthroposophical Society, Shirley Nicholson of Krotona Institute, Dr. Gerald E. Poesnecker of the Rosicrucian Fraternity, Carroll R. Runyon, Jr. of the Order of the Temple of Astarte, Soror V of the Builders of the Adytum, Kirby Van Mater of the Theosophical Society (Pasadena), Rev. Victoria E. Vandertuin of the New Age World Religious and Scientific Research Foundation, and the staff of the United Lodge of Theosophists.

I am grateful to my fellow-Masonic writers who encouraged my research and/or whose works are cited here. Lt. Col. Harvey Newton Brown—who died in El Paso, Texas on 9 April 1998 at the age of 99—was the first person to tell me about Éliphas Lévi and the use of his writings by Albert Pike. I also feel greatly indebted to Joseph A. Walkes, Jr. (my mentor in Masonic writing), Rev. Forrest Haggard, Rev. William H. Stemper, Jr., Keith Arrington, Allen E. Roberts, Robert L. Dillard, Rev. Howard L. Woods, Robert A. Gilbert, Dr. John W. Boettjer, Dr. Rex R. Hutchens, and Rev. Donald W. Monson. When Dr. Boettjer, then editor of *The Scottish Rite Journal*, furnished me with copies of *A Glossary to Morals and Dogma* and *The Bible in Albert Pike's Morals and Dogma*, he greatly facilitated research on chapter three. I later had the pleasure of meeting the authors of these books—Bros. Hutchens and Monson—at a meeting of the Philalethes Society and Allied Masonic Degrees in Washington. D. C.

I am grateful to my family for tolerating the excessive demands on my time required by this project. Special thanks to my wife Debra for all of her love and support.

I thank our daughter Ericha who, on 13 May 1995, joined me in making history. Ericha received her baccalaureate in the same ceremony as I received my doctorate. I thank our daughter JoAnna; our sons Eric and Elton; and our grandchildren, Richard, Dominique, Alicia, Kendra, Davion, Kayla, and Eric, for their love.

Finally, I extend praise and thanksgiving to my Lord and Savior Jesus Christ, the new and eternal Solomon Who came not to destroy but to fulfill the secret tradition of the Jews and Who daily gives me strength to meet the challenges of life. Like Éliphas Lévi and John Henry Barrows, I see no conflict between being a Christian and being a seeker of universal religious truth. Like Lévi's heirs, I earnestly await the reign of the Paraclete.

Robert L. Uzzel
2006

Dedication

This book is dedicated to the memory of Carlos Santana, my friend, Christian bother, and fellow student of Kabbalah. A native of the Dominican Republic and a man of deep spirituality, Carlos spend twelve years on Texas' death row before he became a victim of state murder at the Walls Unit in Huntsville, Texas on 23 March 1993. His last words were: "Love is the answer, nor hatred. . . . I will see you in the state of heaven."

In *The Key of the Mysteries*, Éliphas Lévi wrote: "Every head that falls upon the scaffold may be honoured and praised as the head of a martyr." May the martyrdom of Carlos Santana serve as an inspiration to all who strive for peace, justice, and liberation!

Éliphas Lévi and the Kabbalah

CHAPTER 1

Éliphas Lévi's Life and Approach to Kabbalah

Alphonse Louis Constant was a noted French writer in the field of medieval Hebrew Kabbalah and other esoteric subjects. He will be referred to throughout this book by his pen name of "Éliphas Lévi." This decision was made, notwithstanding the fact that he did not choose to refer to himself by this title until 1853. He has been called "the last of the magi" and has been given much credit for the revival of interest in magic and mysticism where it featured in the nineteenth century.[1] One writer has observed that Lévi's life spanned the "heart years" of the nineteenth century and that he was in and out of most of the major movements and currents of his day.[2] His influence has continued in the twentieth and twenty-first centuries, especially in the area of occultism. It is probable that a great deal of modern occult terminology and practice is indebted to him.[3] In a very real sense, he can be described as the French connection of the American mystery tradition.

Many nineteenth and twentieth-century students of medieval Kabbalah have relied primarily on the writings of Éliphas Lévi. On this account, certain leading Kabbalistic scholars have been critical, contending that Lévi was guilty of hermeneutical distortions. According to Lévi, all esoteric systems are rooted in Kabbalah.[4] Arthur Edward Waite (1857-1942), the British mystic who translated a number of Lévi's works, contended that: "So far Éliphas Lévi, whose undeniable influence upon all modem occultism has done more than anything to exaggerate the true philosophical position of Jewish secret literature, and to place some of its expositors in a false light."[5] Gershom Scholem (1897-1982), who was probably the leading Hebraic authority on Kabbalah in the twentieth century, charged Lévi with "supreme charlatanism" in promoting "totally unrelated inventions such as the alleged kabbalistic origin of the Tarot cards."[6] Nevertheless, the fact remains that he has had extensive influence on the thinking of many religious circles.

To date, there has been no exhaustive study of Lévi's influence on American thought. The only three biographical works now extant relate to his influence in France. Paul Chacornac's *Éliphas Lévi, renovateur de l'occultisme en France, 1810-1875*[7] has never been translated into English. Neither Christopher McIntosh's *Éliphas Lévi and the French Occult Revival*[8] nor Thomas A. Williams' *Éliphas Lévi: Master of Occultism*[9] provides a treatment of his influence in America. Numerous books on American occultism make passing reference to Lévi, but none of them have provided an exhaustive treatment of him.

Alphonse Louis Constant / Éliphas Lévi Zahed

Éliphas Lévi's Early Involvement in the Christian Church

Éliphas Lévi was born on 8 February 1810. He was the son of a poor shoemaker named Jean-Joseph Constant and his wife Jeanne Agnes Constant. He was baptized as a Roman Catholic on 11 February 1810.[10] His family lived at 5 Rue de Fosses-Saint-Germain-des-Pres.[11] In an autobiographical essay, he wrote about the experience of his first Communion:

"Through the mysteries of Catholicism I had glimpsed the infinite; my heart became filled with passion for a God who sacrifices himself for his creatures and transforms himself into bread to nourish them. The gentle image of the immolated lamb brought tears to my eyes, and my heart throbbed at the tender name of Mary."[12] As a child, he was given more to meditation than to action. Early in life, he developed a marked talent for drawing and painting.[13] He was described as "the clever lad," and exhibited an aptitude for picking up stray bits of knowledge.[14]

At the age of fifteen, Lévi enrolled at the *petit séminaire* of Saint-Nicholas de Chardonnet. There he was influenced by Abbé Frére-Colonna, whom he described as "the most intelligent and sincerely pious priest I have ever known." This priest predicted a final golden era of mankind "in the shade of the apple trees of a New Eden." The abbé's teachings about a secular, historical realization of the Christian ideal of pure and selfless love in the structure of society influenced Lévi's inclination toward utopian thought. However, when the abbé was censured by the conservative church hierarchy, Lévi became disillusioned with the idea of Roman Catholicism as a great revolutionary force.[15] According to one of his biographers: "His Catholicism was too deeply ingrained for him ever to abandon it but he never lost his dislike for the authoritarian side of the Church."[16]

Eventually, Lévi left Saint-Nicholas to continue his studies at Saint Sulpice Seminary, in preparation for the priesthood.[17] There, he demonstrated much scholastic ability, including great proficiency in Latin, Greek, and Hebrew.[18] However, he had some problems with the theological instruction. He later recalled that the chief occupation of students and teachers seemed to be the "slow and painful learning of ignorance" and the main qualities required for success were "sufficient memory to retain the old arguments of the scholastics, a little old-fashioned subtlety in making them over again into the Gallican mold, and a tongue capable of repeating and twisting reason to conform to them."[19] Despite many negative experiences, he remained at Saint Sulpice. While there, he developed feelings of "great compassion for the church that had fallen into the hands of such of its children as these." He declared: "My soul by virtue of its love alone, sought to raise itself to the divine unity, to the great religion of the future, which will unite all beings in a single being, all sciences in a single idea, all hearts in a single love; in short, to the pantheism that men of bad faith would have us avoid as a monstrous error and that is, in reality, the last word of the sublime doctrine of Christ and his apostles."[20] For a long time, he wrestled with the problem of evil and finally concluded: "The dogma of Hell could no longer stand against my ardent love of God and humanity."[21] About this time, he was assigned to read *Golden Verses of Pythagoras*, a work he found to be very inspirational.[22]

On 19 December 1835, Lévi was ordained a deacon, taking a vow of celibacy.[23] He served for a brief period as professor at Petite Seminaire de Paris. About the same time, he was sent to a number of rural parishes, where he preached with great eloquence. However, the doctrines he preached were not always in accord with orthodox Catholic dogma.[24]

In May 1836, Lévi was scheduled to be ordained to the priesthood. However, he concluded that "I could not take my vows before the altar of a cold and egotistical cult without remorse."[25] It appears that his break with the church was precipitated by his assignment to prepare a class of young girls for their first Communion. He recalled: "I felt as if I were surrounded by my family, and I was not wrong. They listened to me, loved me and respected me as a father." He supervised this catechism class for a period of two years. One of his catechumens was Adéle Allenbach, the daughter of a poor woman who had been turned away by a number of priests. A close relationship developed. She called him "my little father" and he called her "my little girl" On the day of her first Communion, he wept as he prayed to God on her behalf. He saw her every day and had no fears of becoming too attached to her until the day he realized he could not do without her.[26] As the relationship developed, he recognized that it could create a barrier to his ordination as a priest. Thus, he recalled:

> I told my confessor about the childish but all-powerful affection that filled me and was changing my life so totally; he replied that I could not receive the episcopal benediction before purifying my heart.... As a matter of conscience, therefore, I turned away from the future for which I had prepared and left the seminary at the very moment when it seemed that I would attain the goal I had set for myself on coming there and toward which I had been so laboriously working during the last fifteen years of study and sacrifice.[27]

After leaving the seminary, Lévi experienced many crises. His mother committed suicide. Some believe that depression over her son's lost career contributed to this. For the time being at least, he no longer saw Adéle Allenbach.[28] He lived in the poor sections of Paris, where he found earning a living to be very difficult. For a year, he taught at a boarding school near Paris, but he did not get along well with the masters of this school. Thus, it turned out to be a very unhappy year.[29] By 1839, he had established a friendship with Alphonse Esquiros, author of a book called *The Magician*. Through Esquiros, he met a socialist prophet named Ganneau, who claimed to be a reincarnation of King Louis XVII who had "come back to earth for the fulfilment of a work of regeneration."[30] Lévi and Esquiros came to scoff and became disciples. Ganneau's combination of socialism and illuminism influenced Lévi's book *La Bible de la liberté*.[31]

Lévi made his first unsuccessful attempt to return to the Catholic Church at the Benedictine Abbey at Solemes. There, he spent much time in the library, studying the Gnostics, the Church Fathers, and the Christian mystics. He came under the influence of the seventeenth-century mystic and quietist Madame Guyon. He found her doctrine of universalism exhilarating and developed a vision of a utopian future for man, with the Virgin Mary as a bridge between the ministry of Jesus and the reign of the Holy Spirit, and a final experience of divine unity through love.[32] During his stay at the abbey, his first book, an anthology of hymns entitled *La Rosier de mai*, was published.[33] He went to work at College de Juilly, first as a tutor of backward students and later as a playground supervisor.[34] The position set the stage for another confrontation with church hierarchy.

Lévi's Transvaluation in His Perception of Religion

Lévi wrote *La Bible de la liberté* (Paris: A. Le Gallois, 1841) while at College de Juilly. In this book, he expressed a mystical, transcendental overview of man's historical struggles and spiritual growths, pointing out the relation between the two. He presented his visions of God's liberty, with charity and love as the breath of life and governments as servants of the people. His superiors at the college were very displeased with his plans for publication and even offered him a bribe to withhold publication. He responded that he was happy that he had finally done something—anything at all—that merited the attention of the church and the offer of financial assistance, which he had long been denied. Nevertheless, his principles demanded that he refuse this offer.[35] The book appeared on 13 February 1841. Within one hour, Paris police had confiscated it and charged both the author and the publisher with impiety and advocacy of insurrection. At his subsequent trial, Lévi sought to define his position before the jury. He declared: "I consider exploitation to be a kind of murder, as wrong as any thievery. My only crime has been a deep love of mankind." The jury was not favorably impressed and found him guilty, fining him $300.00 and sentencing him to eight months in prison. By this time, he was well known, especially in leftist circles. His trial provoked a great deal of debate. Most socialist writers supported him, although some rejected the Christian context of his ideas.[36] During his incarceration at the Prison of Sainte-Pelagie in Paris, he read widely and did a great deal of writing.[37] Eventually, his ideas came to the attention of the Franco-Peruvian socialist and feminist, Flora Tristan, who arranged for him to have better food and a more comfortable cell. This was the beginning of a close relationship which culminated in Lévi's editing of Tristan's posthumously published book *L'Emancipation de a femme*.[38]

Lévi was released from prison in April 1842. His first employment following this incarceration was the painting of murals at Choisy-le-roi. He also began work on a book entitled *La Mère de Dieu* (Paris: C. Gosselin, 1844).[39] At Choisy-le-roi, he sought voluntary self-exile from the political controversies of the capital. There, he received approval of Monsignor Affre, Archbishop of Paris, who urged him to use his mother's maiden name of Bancourt and agreed to find him a suitable ecclesiastical post outside of the diocese of Paris. Thus, he moved to Evreux, where Monsignor Olivier, Bishop of Evreux, became his most intelligent and sympathetic ecclesiastical protector. But even there, Levi was not able to escape controversy. An announcement appeared in *L'Univers*, a Parisian newspaper, regarding the death of "the abbé Constant." Another newspaper, *Le Populaire*, published an article in the 10 June 1843 issue entitled "Resurection de l'abbé Constant," informing its readers that, far from being dead, the abbé was alive and well in

5

Evreux. An article entitled "Le Nouveau Lazare" ("the New Lazarus") appeared in a provincial paper called *L'Echo de la Normandie*, revealing the true identity of the abbé de Bancourt to its readers in Evreux, along with the story of his trial and imprisonment. On 29 June, in its coup de grace, *L'Echo* published excerpts from *La Bible de la liberté*.[40]

As a result of this scandal, Lévi soon found himself unemployed. However, Monsignor Olivier privately provided for his quarters and subsistence. He even offered him a parish in his diocese on the condition that he take the final vows and become a priest. Lévi was not prepared to make such a commitment.[41]

In February 1844, *La Mere de Dieu* was published by Lévi's friend Auguste Le Gallois. The appearance of this book offended Monsignor Olivier, who regarded it as doctrinally unacceptable.[42] In this book, woman is idealized as the Virgin Mary, the Mother of God and the fullest representation of woman's pure and holy life. He saw the orgy of strife, faction, greed, war, and inhumanity to be resolved through the love of Mary as society exchanged the old Adam for the new Christ. He envisioned a new world order arising from the social catharsis of the destructive years, which leveled old values and opened the way for the Holy Spirit, which he saw as feminine.[43] According to one of Lévi's biographers: "Just as Constant's passion is unquestionably real, so are his insights profound. 'Mary and Eve reveal themselves everywhere in human destiny,' he writes, and in his discussion of these revelations he often gets down to the bed rock of man's struggle with history. If <C. G.> Jung's primal archetypes of human experience do in fact exist, then Constant is struggling mightily with them in his book."[44] In this book, Lévi recalled a prophetic vision he had experienced on Easter Eve 1841, in which he was convinced that "the anarchy, strife, and babble of conflicting voices" that characterized his own time was "a prelude to the transfiguration of human society." In this dreamlike state, he saw the apocalyptic downfall of the old order, the death of Satan, and the dawning of a new day. In this vision, a young girl was his guide.[45] In *La Mere de Dieu*, he wrote: "I found nothing vague or uncertain in the dream of life. God's mind came to the aid of my own and explained to me every image and dissipated every shadow."[46] Lévi envisioned a society in which antisocial behavior would be treated as an illness and every branch of learning would be a part of the science of God, with religious understanding seen as "analysis and synthesis of love in all its forms."[47] He spoke of a "Magnificent Synthesis which joins all souls in a single soul, all bodies in a single body, through communion; and which creates a new world."[48]

During this period, Lévi did much research in medieval and Renaissance literature. He was impressed by Guillaume Postel, Raymond Lully, and Heinrich Cornelius Agrippa. He was especially influenced by Francois Rebelais, whose verve, taste for life, and good humor marked his own life to the very end.[49]

In 1843, Lévi published *Le Testament de la liberté*.[50] During the fall of 1844, he joyfully accepted the invitation of his benefactrice, Madame Legrand, to come and live in her house at Guitrancourt, Seineet-Oise, to serve as tutor for her children, Clarisse and Adoiphe. One month later, he formally renounced his holy orders. He remained at Madame Legrand's home for about a year and then returned to Paris for the publication of his pacifist manifesto entitled *La Fête-Dieu, ou le triomphe de la paix religieuse*. This work was published anonymously in 1845 and followed in the same year by two other works: *Le Livre des larmes ou Le Christ consolateur; essai de conciliation entre l'Eglise catholique et la philosophie moderne* (Paris: Paulia, 1845), an essay pleading for conciliation between Roman Catholicism and modem philosophy, and *Les trois harmonies* (Paris: Fellens et du four, 1845), a collection of original songs.[51]

Lévi spent a great deal of the money he earned from his writings on entertaining friends at lavish champagne parties. In attendance at such social events were his old friends, Le Gallois and Esquiros, and a host of journalists and socialist pamphleteers. Other guests may have included Adéle Allenbach, the girl who had first awakened his heart to love; and Charles Fauverty, a visionary who dreamed of establishing a universal religion. In October 1845, Lévi and Fauverty founded a monthly politico-cultural review, *La Vérité sur toures choses*, which lasted only four issues.[52]

In 1846, Lévi published two political pamphlets—"Le Chagrin du Poland" and "La Voix de la famine." The latter publication was seized and condemned, Lévi was charged with "disturbing public order by provoking and inciting hatred between the several classes of society" and with "inciting the people to hatred of His Majesty's government." He went on trial on 3 February 1847. He told the court: "You speak of the abbé Constant. The abbe Constant no longer exists. The abbé Constant is dead. You see before you a layman, Alphonse Constant, a designer, painter, man of letters, a poor man and a friend of the poor." The jury fined him a thousand francs and sentenced him to a year in prison. In August 1847, he was released as a result of special appeal by Noémi Cadiot. a young lady whom he had married, notwithstanding his previous vow of celibacy.[53]

According to one report, Lévi had a number of liaisons with female students over the years.[54] In the mid-1840s, he had become romantically involved with Eugenie C., a teacher in a private school for girls at Choisy-le-roi. One of this teacher's favorite students had been a seventeen-year-old Noémi Cadiot. Frequently, both of these ladies would accompany Lévi on Sunday excursions. Noémi had apparently liked Lévi and soon had exchanged letters with her teacher's "friend."[55] The following summer, Noémi packed all her belongings and traveled to Paris. She presented herself at Lévi's apartment. Apparently, he did not ask her to leave. When her father learned about her living arrangements, he threatened to charge Lévi with contributing to the delinquency of a minor unless the couple became legally married. They agreed to his demands and, on 13 July 1846, the ceremony took place.[56]

Eugénie gave birth to Lévi's son on 29 September 1846. Noémi gave birth to Lévi's daughter, Marie, in 1847.[57] Lévi and Noemi lived a hand to mouth existence in the bohemian and radical circles of Paris during the two years leading to the revolution of 1848.[58] After the fall of the July monarchy, they began to drift further and further apart. Eventually, they became totally estranged. In 1853, she requested a legal separation and this was granted. In *1854*, their seven-year-old daughter died. In 1865, the marriage was annulled on the grounds that Lévi's early ecclesiastical position had made the marriage contract void. He was never able to rid himself of Noemi's memory.[59] No doubt, he was reflecting on personal experience several years later when he wrote: "Make yourself beloved of women, that they be made happier; but never love any woman so much that you cannot be happy without her."[60]

New Directions of Esotericism in Lévi's Religious Interests

In 1846, Lévi's *La dernière incarnation: Légendes evengéliques du XJXe siècle* (Paris: Librairie soci6taire, 1846) appeared.[61] Two years later, an English translation—*The Last Incarnation: Gospel Legends of the Nineteenth Century* (New York: William H. Graham, 1848)—appeared. This work reflected Lévi's religious views, which were, no doubt, greatly influenced by the political conflict of the time. Lévi depicted Jesus as making various appearances during the nineteenth century, with a message to the poor and oppressed of that day. Lévi's desire to be a champion of the poor can be seen in Jesus' words: "It was to holy and austere poverty that was instructed the education of the heirs of God, in order that through privation they might learn the true use of their Father's riches."[62] In this book, the word of Christ is "Liberty, Equality, and Fraternity."[63] Lévi's readers are assured that "everywhere the spirit of the Gospel makes conquests, except in the closed minds and frozen hearts of those who call themselves the depositories of the Gospel."[64] The "Widow's son"—an expression used in Freemasonry—is called a "Brother of Christ." In keeping with this theme, Jesus is made to say "The blind man whom I can guide to prevent him from stumbling over the stones of the road shall be my father, the poor widow who weeps, and whom I can console, shall be my mother, and the deserted orphans who have no one to love them shall be my brothers and my sisters."[65]

The above work, as a whole, is marked by strong socio-human, socio-ethical, and socio-religious overtones. Much concern for the poor and oppressed is repeatedly expressed by Jesus, Who says "You are all brothers, because God is the father of you all: and he loves you all, the poor as well as the rich, but more particularly the poor, because they have more to suffer."[66] Jesus is depicted working with an axe and charging people to be "Intelligent Workmen."[67] Lévi made further references to working people when he depicted Jesus as instructing four rival journeymen that journeymen of all professions need each other. Due to Jesus' influence, the journeymen swear to work unto death for the union of the children of Solomon and Hiram in the great family of the children of Christ.[68] In the legend called "The New Adulterous Woman," Lévi depicted the power of women's tears. Here, Jesus says: "I am the husband of isolated souls; I am the man of the future!" This seems to imply that Lévi believed that the human soul was feminine.[69] Later, Jesus is seen as seeking wisdom in the "House of the Insane" and telling the "Keepers of the Insane": "His madness is only the love of justice carried to extreme, and the more he is tormented, the more dangerous and incurable will his malady become."[70] Those in authority could not have appreciated Lévi's picture of Jesus saying "My Father will require of you an account of all the victims of society. . . . He alone has a right to take away life who can give or restore it. . . . If man wishes to be a judge like unto God, let him therefore be a Saviour like him. . . . He who has made orphans ought to adopt them.[71] The book's utopian spirit is reflected at the end, where Lévi revealed a vision of "fields already green with the first fraternal crops" and sounds of a "mysterious prelude of the chant of union."[72]

La dernière incarnation was followed by a political tract entitled *La Deuil de la Prologue*.[73] In 1847, *Les Trois Malfaiteurs, Legende Orientale* was published. This work was based on imagined earlier associations of Jesus and the two thieves who were later crucified with Him.[74] Also appearing that year was *Rebelais à la Basmette* (Paris: Libraire phalansterienee, 1847). Other works written about this time were later reissued as *Le sorcier de Meudon* (Paris: A Bourdilliat et ce, 1861).[75]

Whereas the crisis years at Saint Sulpice turned a young aspirant to the Roman Catholic priesthood into a man of action, mystic, and herald of the new age that would dawn as soon as men freed themselves from the chains of the old, the crisis of the Revolution of 1848 turned a man of action into a solitary magus, sage, and teacher. Perhaps, by this time, he had concluded that the time was not ripe for the regeneration of humanity as a whole. Nevertheless, it appears, he remained determined to show individuals the way of enlightenment.[76] But how significant were the changes he experienced at this time? According to one writer: "The Revolution of 1848 burned out his radical zeal and gave birth to the Magician."[77] Another writer, however, took a different view when he wrote that "Constant's occultism does not represent a complete break with previous experiences and beliefs. It is simply a new codification of them."[78] From all indications, it appears that, after 1848,

Lévi drifted away from socialism without renouncing it.[79] His major interest shifted from politics to magic and mysticism. The remainder of his life was devoted to teaching and writing.[80]

In 1850, Lévi received a commission from an ecclesiastical publisher to write *Dictionnaire de Litrérature Chrétienne* (Paris: J. P. Migne, 1851).[81] His life at that time has been, thus, described: "Callers at the Constant home would invariably find their host dressed in the garb of a monk, which he adopted whenever possible—a predilection that was to remain with him throughout his life. Indeed with his full beard and towering bald cranium, he looked more than anything like the benevolent abbot that he might have become."[82]

During this period, Lévi met Hoeni Wronski, a Polish mathematician and theosophist who became his mentor. He described Wronski as "learned to the point of becoming unintelligible for everyone else and sometimes even for himself." Wronski may have introduced Lévi to Kabbalah and the traditions of magic. Lévi saw Wronski's real importance in "this century of absolute and universal doubt" as that of trying to establish "the unshakable foundation of a science both human and divine." The two men shared concerns about Messianism, the dawning of a new age, and the apotheosis of human intelligence.[83] If Wronski introduced Lévi to Kabbalah, he made an inestimable contribution to the future of esoteric thought.[84] The following theory of Lévi's thinking after 1848 may be credible:

> To change the world by working revolution in its exoteric political structure might be no longer practicable, but to change the world by transforming one's own consciousness of it was still a viable option and an option that appealed to him more and more strongly. All that was lacking was a conceptual structure that would impose a pattern of meaning on the disparate spiritual, mystical, and rational impulses and insights moving within him. This structure he finally found in the symbolism and doctrines of the Cabala.[85]

In later years, Lévi reflected mixed feelings about Wronski, always recognizing his contributions to his own system of thought but, at times, also noting his shortcomings. He took pride in the fact that, whereas Wronski charged high prices for his teachings of Kabbalah, he offered such to his readers without charge.[86]

By 1853, the transition which began in 1848 was complete. That year, forty-three-year-old Alphonse Louis Constant officially adopted the Hebrew name of Éliphas Lévi Zahed. Three years later, his masterpiece *Dogme et rituel de la haute magie* (Paris: G. Baillière, 1856) was published. Four years after this publication, he amplified his views in the publication *of Histoire de la magie, avec une exposition clair and precise de ses procédés de ses rites et de ses mystères* (Paris: G. Bailhière, 1860). The following year, his third occult work, *La Clef des Grands mystères suivant Hénoch, Abraham, Hermê Trismégiste et Salomon* (Paris: 0. Baillière, 1861), appeared. These three works served as the foundation for all of his later writings.[87]

The Role of Initiation in Lévi's Life and Thought

Lévi joined a number of organizations practicing rites of initiation and promoting the study of magic and mysticism, but the level of his involvement is unclear. It appears, however, that his research and writing on such matters was far more significant than his personal involvement in any initiatory institution.

On 14 March 1861, Lévi was initiated into Freemasonry by a friend named Jean-Marie Lazare Caubet, who was Worshipful Master of *La Loge de la Rose du Parfait Silence*.[88] On 21 August 1861, he received the Master Mason degree. He became a Freemason with the firm conviction that Masonic symbolism was rooted in Kabbalah.[89] As it turned out, however, this association was not a happy one. At that time, the Grand Orient of France — to which this lodge was affiliated — was moving in the direction of secularism and anticlericalism, which Lévi would find quite distasteful.[90] He was quite certain that the real meaning of the complicated and bizarre, but also very rich, Masonic symbolism had been lost to many Masons. One month after his "raising," he was invited to make an address to the lodge. He told the Masons assembled that he had come among them in order to instruct them, so that they might recover the "lost tradition" of Freemasonry and the "exact knowledge" of all its "signs and symbols." He stated that, at a later time, he hoped to teach them why the Masonic order came into existence in the first place. His remarks were not well received by the lodge's established leadership. It seems that the brethren did not desire to receive "more light" from Lévi. As a result, he did not remain active in organized Freemasonry.[91] He wrote: "I ceased being a Freemason, at once, because the Freemasons, excommunicated by the Pope, did not believe in tolerating Catholicism; I thus separated from them to protect my freedom of conscience and to avoid their reprisals, perhaps excusable, if not legitimate, but certainly inconsequential, because the essence of Freemasonry is the tolerance of all beliefs."[92] Interpretations of Masonic philosophy and symbolism, however, are found throughout his writings.[93]

Lévi also became an authority on Rosicrucian symbolism and may have joined one of the Rosicrucian groups that emerged in France. He saw the rose as a type of beauty, life, love, and pleasure, a mystical expression of "the secret thought of all protests manifested at the Renaissance."[94] He understood the union of the rose and the cross as a problem of high initiation.[95] In 1867, in England, the Societas Roscruciana in Anglia was established, with membership limited to Freemasons. Lévi was given honorary membership.[96] American Rosicrucian leader Pascal Beverly Randolph claimed that Lévi installed him in the office of "Supreme Grand Master of the Western World" during a visit to Europe in 1858. Randolph's role in reviving magic and mysticism in America may be seen as comparable to Lévi's in Europe.[97]

Lévi was intrigued with the experiences of initiation and adeptship. He believed that such were, by their very nature, closed to all who were enslaved by passions and prejudices.[98] He understood the end of all ancient initiations as forming men who were prepared to die rather than renounce truth and justice. Such men, he believed, are the most truly living, for they are possessed of immortality.[99] He wrote: "The elect of intelligence are always few on earth and are encompassed by the foolish and the wicked, like Daniel in the den of lions .... absolute science, being an omnipotence, must be the exclusive possession of the most worthy."[100]

Lévi described ancient initiatory societies as "seminaries for priests and kings." He believed that medieval secret societies perpetuated, with diminished power, the initiatory system of the Egyptian Mysteries. He regarded initiation as the essential law of religious life.[101] He wrote: "The intellectual and social chaos in the midst of which we are perishing has been caused by the neglect of initiation. ... Masonry has had its deserters, as Catholicism its apostates. What has been the consequence? The substitution of a cast-iron level for the intellectual and symbolical level.., this work... is an appeal unto all that is yet alive for the reconstitution of life in the very midst of decomposition and death."[102]

To him, the death of Jesus represented "the highest and most sublime of Arcana, the last word of all initiations."[103] He declared that "Christ died as a young man on a cross, and all those whom He has initiated have become martyrs."[104] He interpreted the visit of the Magi from the East to the cradle of Jesus guided by the Star of Solomon symbolic of Jesus' mission to consecrate anew the fires of Zoroaster, to renovate the symbolic treasures of Hiram, and to bind up the mutilated form of Osiris. In the narrative of Jesus' nativity he saw the Magi as honoring the infancy of Christian initiation. In the Magi's return home by another road in order to avoid the wicked schemes of Herod he saw symbolized the road of occultism which is ignored by the world but well known to adepts, whom he regarded as the Magi of his day and beyond.[105] To the latter was Lévi's message directed. Thus, he stated: "Let it be well understood that we are not writing for the profane masses, but for the instructed of a later age than ours and for the pontiffs of the future."[106] He sought to instruct his students in what he understood as the true wisdom of the ages. Such mysteries, he believed, were not fully comprehended by the average initiate in a Masonic or Rosicrucian lodge. In later chapters, it will be demonstrated that his influence in both of these initiatory institutions was far in excess of his personal involvement in either of them.

Éliphas Lévi

Lévi's Literary Contribution to Nineteenth-Century Religion

In addition to the works cited above, Lévi wrote *Doctrines religieuses et sociales* (Paris: A. Le Gallois, 1841); *Fables et symboles avec leur explication, ou sont-révélés les grandes secrets de la direction du magnétisme universel et des principes fondamentaux du grand oeuvre* (Paris: G. Baillière, 1862); *La science des esprits; révélation du dogme secret des kabbalistes esprit occulte des evangiles, appreciation des doctrines et desphénomènes spirites* (Paris: G. Baihière, 1865); *Le carechisme de la paix, suivi de quatrains sur le Bible et de la liberté* (Paris: Chamuel, 1896) *Le grand arcane; ou L'occultisme dévoilé* (Paris: Chamuel, 1898).[107] *La science des esprits* has been described as "a defence of the Christian Gospel against the spirits of table-rapping" and reflects Lévi's horror of spiritism."[108]

Lévi's Last Years

Lévi spent the last twenty years of his life engaged in writing and in giving private instruction to students who visited his apartment in Paris. In 1856, he received a visit from Pascal Beverly Randolph, founder of Fraternitas Rosae Crucis. Reuben Swinburne Clymer, one of Randolph's successors as

13

Supreme Grand Master of this American Rosicrucian body, gave the following account of Randolph's message to Lévi:

> This is the first time you see me, at least in this form, but I know you well. I know everything about your past, present, and future life. It is ruled by the inexorable law of numbers. You are the *man* of the *Pentagram,* and the years marked by the number "5," have always been fatal to you. Look back and recollect. Your mortal life started in 1815, your memory failing to recollect beyond that. In 1825 you entered the Seminary. In 1835 you left the Seminary and entered the *freedom* of *consciousness.* In 1845 you published *The Mother of God,* your first essay on religion, and you broke your connection with the church. In 1855 you were a free man, being deserted by a woman who had absorbed you and forced you to submit to the Law of "Binaire." You then went to England. You were there to dive in the masculine and active principles. It was there you saw *Appolonius (sic),* sad, tired and suffering like yourself, because the Appolonius you saw *was* YOURSELF — a phantom that came out of yourself, again becoming a part of you and still is with you. You will see him in 1865, but then beautiful, radiant and triumphant. The natural end of your life is marked as 1875 <as *is* mine> accidents aside.[109]

On 3 January 1857, Lévi witnessed the assassination of the Archbishop of Paris by Louis Verger, a discontented country priest who shouted, 'Down with the Goddesses." Shortly before this terrible event, Lévi had talked with this priest and warned him against the evils of Black Magic.[110] On another occasion, dairy farmers from the island of Jersey came to him and requested that he remove a curse they believed had been cast on their animals which inhibited the production of milk. Lévi gave them a "sign of the microcosm" and a "magnetized photograph." When the farmers left Paris, they were quite satisfied. Two weeks later, they wrote to Lévi, informing him that Jersey cows were again producing milk and that they were very thankful to their benefactor.[111]

Most of Lévi's last twenty years were spent in Paris. He did, however, visit London in 1854 and again in 1861. He also visited Germany during the summer of 1871. The latter visit occurred at the time of the Franco-Prussian War. That summer, he spent two months in the home of Gustave and Marie Gebhard in Elberfield. Mrs. Gebhard observed that there seemed to be no book on the subject of mysticism which he had not read and that he had a great memory and a way with words.[112] She declared: "I look upon Éliphas Lévi as one of the truest friends I ever had, for he taught me the highest truth which it is in the power of man or woman to grasp."[113] He changed apartments only three times between 1854 and 1875."[114]

Much of Lévi's meager income came from students who sought him out and desired private lessons from him. It appears that he was a very successful teacher, much more interested in opening the minds of students than in indoctrinating them.[115] One of these students, M. Chauliac, described him as follows: "Vested invariably when at home in a long robe, with his long white beard and bald head, he recalled, somewhat confusedly, the astrologers of the Middle Ages."[116]

The humiliating defeat of France in the Franco-Prussian War came as a bitter blow to Lévi, who saw France as the future saviour of civilization. From his book-lined refuge in the Rue de Sèvres, he wrote: "Paris, once the centre of the world, no longer seems part of it. There is silence in the streets and squares, but for the occasional boom of a cannon." He seemed to view the conflict as inevitable and as the result of a more basic conflict between force and right, with Prussia identified with force and France identified with right. He declared: "If everything is but force and matter. . . then Prussia is right. But if force is only the manifestation of the universal intelligence, right exists over and above force, and France is right."[117] Following the siege of Paris, someone thought they saw a shot fired from Lévi's window. An officer from Versailles burst into his apartment and threatened to have him shot. Lévi greeted him calmly, explaining that he was a philosopher and not an assassin and inviting him to search the apartment. The officer found nothing and, impressed by Lévi's sincerity, ordered his troops to withdraw.[118]

During this time, Lévi's health was deteriorating. His periods of illness were becoming increasingly frequent, but in between them he continued to teach and write. In 1873, he completed *L'Evangile de la science*. This was the only book that he ever re-read and corrected. Shortly afterward, he completed *Le Religion de la science*.[119]

Some devoted disciples remained close to Lévi during the last few years of his life. Such included the aforementioned Marie Gebhard and also Jacques Charrot, who would later organize a Rosicrucian society at Lyons. He also received accolades from the literary world.. He received a visit from Judith Mendès, wife of novelist Catulle Mendès and daughter of novelist Theophile Gautier, who wrote novels and poetry under her maiden name of Judith Gautier. Lévi accepted the invitation of Catulle Mendès to visit his home. Mendès was enthused by Lévi's writings and introduced him to the noted author Victor Hugo, who was also familiar with his works. In 1874, Lévi completed the writing of his book *Le livre d'Abraham le Juif* which he composed for Comte Georges de Mniszech in gratitude for the material help given to him. Early in 1875, he finished writing *Le Catechisme de la paix* (Paris: Chamuel, 1896)."[120]

Toward the end of his life, Lévi reflected a great deal of inner peace and a positive attitude toward life and death. He said:

Everyone is good to me.... Everything breathes an atmosphere of deep peace. The earth would be an Eden for me if my brothers were not suffering in it.... Children smile and approach me when I rest in parks and gardens. I have never knowingly or willingly harmed anyone. I still love the things I once loved: knowledge, poetry, religion, liberty, the sun, the world's greenness, and I feel loved by those things in return. Let the dead leaves fall; spring is immortal in her constant return.[121]

As the year 1875 wore on, Lévi's physical condition steadily became worse. He experienced repeated attacks of dropsy and gangrene. His friends constantly attended him. Dr. Wattelet, his personal physician, did everything possible to relieve his condition. Anna Bomet, an old friend, was his nurse until she contracted influenza and, thus, could no longer perform her duties. She was succeeded by Edouard-Adolphe Pascal, son of a benefactor from his time in prison. Lévi faced his last agonizing days with much courage. His mental faculties were preserved to the end. Near his bed was a beautiful image of Jesus, at which he often looked. Pointing to this image, he said to a visitor: "He told me that He would send the Consoler, the Spirit, and now I wait for the Spirit, the Holy Spirit!" He, thus, reflected the radiance of a profound religious faith.[122]

In May 1875, Lévi made his last will and testament. To Comte Georges de Mniszech he left his manuscripts, books, and scientific instruments. Edouath-Adolphe Pascal was given the right to select among his non-scientific books, curios, and works of art. To his sister, Pauline Bousselet, he gave all of his pictures and devotional objects. He gave his clothes and linen to a community of nuns in the Rue Saint-Jacques. He willed that what remained of his belongings should be sold and the proceeds divided between the friends who had cared for him in his final hours.[123]

On 29 May 1875, Lévi was visited by one of his students, Madame Jobert, who could sense that the end was near. She decided to summon a priest. After refusal at one church, she went to a Jesuit chapel in the Rue de Sèvres and talked with Father Lejume, who agreed to visit Lévi. He came the next day but, for some reason, was unable to gain entry. He returned on 31 May. On that day, he had a long talk with Lévi and probably granted absolution. At 2:00 p.m. that day, Lévi died. Pascal arranged for him to be photographed on his death bed.[124] His funeral was held on 2 June at the church of Saint-Francois Xavier, on the Boulevard des Invalides. He was buried at the cemetery of Ivry. A small group of devotees gathered around his grave. His friend Henri Dyrolle delivered the eulogy, praising Lévi for his courage in renouncing the priesthood, his personal charity, his efforts to unite science and religion, and the great writings he had left. His closing words were: "Farewell, Constant! Honest and loyal soul who never knew charity and yet practiced it with dignity, rest in peace and may the sincere grief of your friends be the proof of the void which you have left among them."[125]

Arthur Edward Waite, who edited and translated a number of Lévi's works, was one of his major critics, often charging him with distortions of Kabbalah and other matters. However, in editing a collection of Levi's writings, Waite paid tribute to the French magus in the following manner: "Éliphas Lévi has originated a new departure in Kabbalistic exegesis... his interpretations have fused new life into old symbolism... we need have no hesitation in proclaiming him an initiate of the first order and the prince of the French adepts.... The noble and generous spirit of Éliphas Lévi has passed behind the veil and has doubtless achieved the immortality he aspired to, and the Absolute which he sought in life."[126]

The Primacy of Kabbalah in Lévi's Thought

In his book, *The Holy Kabbalah*, Waite sought to make an assessment of Lévi's importance to Kabbalistic thought:

> It remains to say that Éliphas Lévi represents the invention of a new and gratuitous phase in the study of the Kabbalah ... the standpoint of Lévi is that there is a relationship behind all religions and that it is the veiled mystery of Kabbalism, from which all have issued and into which all return. ... Now it is precisely this standpoint, its derivatives and connections, that created French occultism in the generation which followed Lévi. ... in a very true sense Éliphas Lévi was the magus who opened before his readers the wide field of the imaginary view.[127]

Lévi believed that Kabbalah represented the widest possible synthesis of occult systems and schools. He saw Kabbalah as the origin of the entire esoteric tradition, with every branch leading back to it and included in it.[128] For him, Kabbalah was prior to, superior to, and purer than, every other occult system and, when rightly understood, revealed the unity of all such systems.[129] He saw the major work of Kabbalah—the *Zohar*—as a hidden wisdom unique to his vision. To him, the *Zohar* contained the lost knowledge of the ancient world.[130] He found quite meaningful the teachings of the *Zohar* regarding the spirituality of man, the importance of the human soul, and the manner in which the transcendent God becomes immanent through the emanation of the ten Sephiroth.[131] He saw this secret tradition originating among the children of Seth, the third son of Adam. His theory of transmission was as follows: "Taken from Chaldea by Abraham, communicated by Joseph to the Egyptian priesthood, ingarnered by Moses, concealed by symbols in the Bible, revealed by the Saviour to St. John, and embodied in its fulness in hieratic images, analogous to those of all antiquity, in the Apocalypse of this Apostle."[132]

For Lévi, Kabbalah provided the scientific and religious absolute which was transmitted to the elect of all ancient initiations and handed to the Templars, Rosicrucians, Illuminati, and Freemasons.[133] He insisted that Kabbalah alone consecrates the alliance of universal reason and the divine Word, that it establishes by the counterpoise of two forces an apparent opposition, the eternal balance of being. He declared that Kabbalah alone reconciles reason with faith, power with liberty, and science with mystery. Kabbalah, he said, holds the keys of the past, present, and future.[134] He summarized the Kabbalistic tradition with the following words: "The visible is for us the proportional measure of the invisible." He stated that this symbolical summary of the primitive tradition was attributed by the Hebrews to Enoch, by the Egyptians to Hermes Trismegistus, and by the Greeks to Cadmus, the mysterious builder of the holy city.[135]

Lévi rejected the notion that there was anything pre-scientific about Kabbalah. On the contrary, he regarded it as the world's oldest and truest science; and expressed regret that it was so little known. As a self-proclaimed "Professor of the Highest Science," he felt he had a mission to make Kabbalah and the magical doctrines of the ancient sanctuaries widely known.[136] Thus, he declared: "Let the physicists seek and find out; ever will the Kabalist explain the discoveries of science."[137] In one interesting passage, he contrasted the observations of Kabbalists and shepherds:

> A Kabalist, familiar with mystic hieroglyphics, will perceive signs in the stars, which will not be discerned by a simple shepherd, but the shepherd, on his part, will observe combinations that will escape the Kabalist. Country people substitute a rake for the belt and sword of Orion, while a Kabalist recognizes in the same sign — considered as a whole — all the mysteries of Ezekiel, the Ten SEPHIROTH arranged in a triadic manner, a central triangle formed of four stars, then a line of three stars making the JOD, the two figures taken together expressing the mysteries of BERESHITH, and finally, four stars constituting the wheels of MERCAVAH, and completing the divine chariot.[138]

Lévi saw no contradiction between Christianity and Kabbalah. He called upon Christians to study Kabbalah and recognize that all dogmas were rooted in the secret tradition of Israel.[139] He believed that Kabbalah contained all of the secrets of transcendental theology and that all of the keys to Scripture — from Genesis to the Apocalypse — were Kabbalistic.[140] He called Solomon "the king of Kabalists and Magi."[141] He referred to the Hebrew prophets as "the kings of the Kabalah and the great rabbins of science."[142] He stated that the legend of Nebuchadnezzar's transmutation into a beast was recorded in "the Kabalistic book of Daniel the seer."[143] In one passage, he declared that Jesus Christ was the fulfillment of the teachings of Kabbalah: "That which we expose before the intelligent world, mounted on the cubic chariot and drawn by sphinxes, as a Word of Light, the Divine Fulfiller of the Mosaic Kabalah, the human Son of the Gospel, the man-God who has come as Saviour and will manifest soon as Messiah—that is, as definitive and absolute king of temporal institutions. It is this thought which animates our courage and sustains our hope."[144]

Lévi claimed that the Jews at the time of the Pharisees lost the fundamental cornerstone of the Kabbalistic Temple. He declared that, in the light of the *Zohar* and another Kabbalistic work called *Sepher Yetzirah*, Christianity was revealed as the orthodox tradition of Judaism while the scribes and the Pharisees were exposed as sectarians.[145] He taught that the Apostle Paul suspected Kabbalah, which Jesus revealed through the Apostle John in the Apocalypse. John, he said, borrowed much from the Prophet Ezekiel. Jesus, he insisted, came not to destroy but to fulfill the secret tradition of the Jews.[146] He rejected all notions that God's covenant with Israel had been nullified. Thus, he wrote: 'Do not our apostolic traditions declare that after the decline of faith among the Gentiles salvation shall again come forth out of the house of Jacob, and that when the crucified Jew Who is adored by the Christians will give the empire of the world into the hands of God His Father?"[147] He saw in the Kabbalistic Tree of Sephiroth "an admirable exposition of the mystery of the Trinity."[148]

Despite his negative experience at Saint Sulpice and subsequent renunciation of the priesthood, Lévi was nevertheless strongly attracted to Roman Catholicism throughout his life. In his later years, he came to view it as a great hierarchic system and great sequence of holy pageants of living symbolism. He regarded the church as the heir to Kabbalistic knowledge which deserved respect and "qualified obedience" despite the fact that it had lost the Kabbalistic keys.'[149] He believed that the loss of these keys had resulted in exegetical obscurity related to the sublime imagery of the Book of Ezekiel and the Apocalypse of Saint John—an obscurity that rendered both books completely unintelligible.[150] He saw this loss of the true meaning of the arcana as inseparably linked with the loss of the church's spiritual mission.[151] He observed that, if Saint Thomas Aquinas had followed his logic to its ultimate conclusion, he would have discovered the Philosopher's Stone and, thus, reformed the church.[152] He regarded sovereign priesthood and perpetual sacrifice as "two indisputable marks of a true religion."[153]

Lévi viewed Christianity as the fully realized and vital expression of Kabbalah and the Apocalypse of Saint John as a Kabbalistic book incomprehensible without the Kabbalistic keys.[154] He saw the Apocalypse as inseparably linked with the Book of Ezekiel and called Ezekiel the "most profound Kabbalist of the ancient prophets."[155] One commentator described the significance of Lévi's studies of these two important biblical books:

Both Ezekiel's "Prophecies" and the "Apocalypse" have played a very important role in the speculations and history of esoteric thinking. Still, it was Éliphas Lévi who pointed out the close relationship between the two books. ... Lévi, by explaining the resemblance in meaning of both books of revelation, tries to prove the identity of the ultimate goal of the Old and New Testament, and so established the reconciliation of the western world: Judaism and Christianity.[156]

Lévi believed that Ezekiel wrote his book "in order to preserve, by means of traditional symbols, the great Hebrew doctrines of occult theology, the universal knowledge of the ancient world."[157] In his commentary on Ezekiel, he pointed out, as he did in other writings, the total opposition of Kabbalists to idolatry. He acknowledged, however, the possibility that Kabbalistic hieroglyphs might be perverted into idols.[158] He gave the following interpretation of the wheels which play such a prominent role in Ezekiel 1:

In the prophecy of Ezekiel life is represented by wheels which turn within one another, the elementary forms are symbolized by four beasts, which ascend and descend with the wheel and pursue one another without ever overtaking, like the signs of the Zodiac. The wheels of perpetual movement never return on themselves; forms never go back to the stations which they have quitted; to return whence one has come, entire circle must have been traversed in a progress always the same and yet always new. The conclusion is that whatsoever manifests to us in this life is a phenomenon which belongs to this life and it is not given here below to our thought, to our imagination, or even to our hallucinations and our dreams, to overstep even for an instant the formidable barriers of death.[159]

He drew parallels between the seven curses of Ezekiel and the many uses of the number seven in the Apocalypse.[160] In his discussion of Ezekiel 40-48, he had much to say about the symbolism of King Solomon's Temple:

All of these figures symbolizing the great mysteries of science had been executed and fixed in their places under the direction of Hiram.
Modern Freemasons still mourn the death of that architect, giving us to understand that the sublime theology of Solomon has fallen into oblivion and that the spirit of anarchy among the subordinate workers killed the genius that was Hiram's.

The hieroglyphic sign of the cross, a symbol of the name which contains all names, image of the four cardinal points of the squaring of the circle ... embodies and represents all the philosophy and theology of the Qabalah. And so Ezekiel sees an angel who traces this sign on the forehead of the elector in the understanding of priests and of doctrines. And all those who do not bear the mark of *Thau* must die, as must perish all doctrines which are not established on the bases of eternal truth.[161]

According to Lévi, Ezekiel desired that the rebuilt temple would be the prototype of a universe governed by a theocracy reigning on holy ground. Thus, he said, Ezekiel was seeking to announce the coming of a hierarchy of intelligence and truth, which would unite all the kingdoms of the earth into one.[162] He interpreted the new temple to be born from the ruins of King Solomon's Temple as symbolic of the Kabbalistic theology of the Hebrews.[163] He believed that Ezekiel served as a bridge by which the latter theology could be attached to Christianity. He saw Ezekiel as a model for the Apocalypse, in which Saint John, behind the emblems of Kabbalah, hid the most profound secrets of Christian theology.[164]

Lévi insisted that John the Revelator was greatly influenced by Ezekiel's teaching about heaven, which was Kabbalistic in nature, and that John's vision of the New Jerusalem was analogous to Ezekiel's vision of the restored temple. Both, he said, embodied absolute and universal truth.[165] He wrote:

> In the Apocalypse of Saint John there is a reference to the two witnesses or martyrs on whom prophetic tradition confers the names of Elias and Enoch--Elias, man of faith, enthusiasm, miracle; Enoch, one with him who is called Hermes by the Egyptians, honoured by the Phoenicians as Cadmus, author of the sacred alphabet and the universal key to the initiations of the Logos, father of the Kabalah, he who, according to sacred allegories, did not die like other men, but was translated to heaven, and will return at the end of time. Much the same parable is told of Saint John himself, who recovered and explained in his Apocalypse the symbolism of the word of Enoch. This resurrection of Saint John and Enoch, expected at the close of the ages of ignorance, will be the renovation of their doctrine by the comprehension of the Kabalistic keys which unlock the temple of unity and of universal philosophy, too long occult and reserved for the elect, who perish at the hands of the world.[166]

Lévi interpreted the symbolism of the book closed with seven seals as implying that the secrets of the Holy Kabbalah were lost and that the mysterious meaning of the Scripture was hidden from the priesthood as well as from the people.'[167] He saw the sealing of the 144,000 in Revelation 7 as symbolic of the baptism of initiation and the anointing with truth.[168] He interpreted the seven thunderclaps of Revelation 10 as symbolic of "all truths scattered and separated in analysis and reunited in synthesis."[169] Regarding the seventh trumpet of Revelation 12, which features a woman covered with sunlight and with the moon under her feet, he wrote:

> Religion or the church symbolizes eternal wisdom.... She was above that which changes.... Her thought was at the centre of heavenly movement in the middle of the zodiac.... All religion gives birth to new knowledge and a new world. This is the reason for sacrifice, for penitence and its rigours, for preaching and its eloquent clamour.... Evil attacks woman because of her weakness and yet she is holy because she is to become a mother.... Woman is the mother of God in humanity. She is the queen mother of the world. What is said of her may also be said of the society and church she typifies.[170]

In his commentary on the number 666, as found in Revelation 13:11-18, he wrote:

> Six represents equilibrium in the finite, three balanced by three, that is, the soul in conflict with matter.
>
> Ancient qabalists admitted three spiritual elements in the human soul, Psyche, Nephesch and Neschemah: that is, sensitive soul, reasonable soul and pure spirit. The three forms of the soul corresponded to three worlds: the material, the spiritual and the divine, and in matter they had their correspondence in the three elementary forms called: salt, sulphur, and mercury.
>
> The number six is represented in the Qabalah by two triangles which form the seal of Solomon when they are brought together and given a common centre representing Seven.[171]

Lévi predicted that humanity's blood, like the blood of Christ, would one day become the communion wine for peoples of the future.[172] He compared the second angel, who emptied his cup with one foot on the land and the other on the sea, to the Egyptian goddess Isis.[173] In regard to Revelation 14, he compared the spilling of Jesus' blood to the spilling of the blood of Israel, declaring that "the martyrdom of the God-man is expiated by the martyrdom of God's people."[174] In regard to the "Marriage Supper of the Lamb" of Revelation 19, he presented the Saviour not as a solitary crucified man but as a young, triumphant husband. He interpreted the marriage between Christ and His Church as the union of genius with beauty.[175] In regard to the "Mark of the Beast" in Revelation 20, he stated that those who do not have this mark are those who have not acted according to the views of the materialistic world as slaves of money and falsehood, insisting that "those who did not love justice cannot take part in the reign of the just."[176]

Lévi gave a symbolical interpretation of the doctrine of the Millennium, as seen in Revelation 20:4. Thus, he wrote: "The just are priests and kings and are to reign with Jesus Christ. The thousand years, as we have said, are symbolic and ought not to be understood literally according to the heresy of the milenarists."[177] He interpreted the high mountain of Revelation 21:10 as representing "lofty religion of superior initiation."[178] He interpreted the "New Jerusalem" mentioned in the same verse as a "City where Liberty, Equality and Fraternity might reign, a city of the elect, of the just."[179] He interpreted the great high wall as symbolic of the fact that "it is not given to everyone to enter the centre of mysteries."[180] He interpreted the measuring rod of Revelation 21:15, as symbolic of balance and proportion and of the fact that the laws of nature are based on eternal mathematics.[181] He commented on the streets of pure gold of Revelation 21:21, as follows: "Gold is the symbol for truth and light. The Lamb is the sun of understanding, its sacrifice ardent.... It is the Shechinah of the Qabalah, which modern Masons still call the Shekenna.... It is the sun of mind and the warmth of soul, the temple of the universal cult, for it changes the whole world into a temple where one worships inaccessible reason and perfect justice."[182] Regarding the command, recorded in Revelation 22:10, not to seal up the words of prophecy, he insisted that a key existed and that such was possessed by the initiates at the time these words were written by Saint John.[183] He understood the Apocalypse as a whole as a resume of initiatory knowledge and the key to the high Kabbalah. He declared that any New Testament interpreter who was ignorant of the mysteries of Kabbalah was absolutely incapable of understanding the Apocalypse, since the latter was a Kabbalistic book.[184]

Lévi predicted that the rebirth of Christianity would be the result of the prophetic spirit and the manifestation of Kabbalistic truth.[185] He saw the church of his day as much an obstacle to the reign of the Holy Spirit as the first century synagogue had been to the reign of Jesus Christ.[186] Yet he still held out hope for the church — a hope inseparably linked to recovery of the Kabbalistic keys. Thus, he foresaw the placing of the triple crown of the mystical Trimurti on the wounded head of Jesus, Whom he called "the new and eternal Solomon." He predicted the rebuilding of the temple on the model prophesied by Ezekiel.[187] In 1856, he observed that "Once again does the whole world await its Messiah, and he will not delay his advent... We have materialized spirit, and we must now spiritualize matter."[188] Five years later, he predicted that the day would come when "religion will have conquered the world, and the Jews, our fathers and brothers, will join us in greeting the spiritual reign of the Messiah. This is the future prospect for our earth, which is now so desolate and unhappy: the second coming of the Saviour, the manifestation of grand Catholicism and the triumph of Messianism, our hope and our faith!"[189] Thus, he predicted that science and religion will be reconciled and, as a result, "the letter will give place to the spirit" and "the great universal religion" will be ushered in.[190]

Lévi's Views of Kabbalah and Tarot

One of Lévi's major contributions to esoteric thought was his claim of correspondences between Kabbalah and Tarot.'[191] He was the first writer to "discover" a connection between the twenty-two Tarot trumps and the twenty-two paths of the Kabbalistic Tree of Life, symbolized by the twenty-two Hebrew letters.[192] As a result, critics such a Gershom Scholem have charged him with "supreme charlatanism" in mistaking a matter of coincidence for an organic and historical connection.[193] A totally different view, however, is held by Stephan Hoeller, Bishop of Ecciesia Gnostica (Gnostic Church), who argued that, from the perspective of Jungian psychology, the Kabbalah-Tarot connection is quite reasonable. Thus, Hoeller wrote:

> In the theory of synchronicity enunciated by Jung, we find the proposition that being coincidental does not negate the innate value of a fact.... Applying this principle to our dilemma we may state that whether the Tarot Arcana were ever applied to symbolize the twenty-two paths on the Tree of Life before Éliphas Lévi or not makes no difference whatsoever. The coincidence of the two systems, if such it is, is not a mere haphazard concurrence of unrelated circumstances, but it is a meaningful coincidence of great psychological, or if you prefer, mystical power and purpose. Thus, from both the pragmatic and the psychological-theoretical point of view, the combined use of Kabalah and Tarot appears fully justified.[194]

Lévi, who always seemed concerned about origins, claimed that Tarot was written in Egypt by a priest of Thoth and that it later contributed to the development of Kabbalah, Zoroastrianism, the Mystery Religions, and early Christianity. He believed that the esoteric understanding of Tarot was lost to the church at the time of the confrontation with Gnosticism and Manicheanism. Thus, he said, the church lost the inner meaning of the Scriptures, especially that of the Apocalypse. By the restoration of Tarot, he sought to demonstrate the full esoteric sense of Christian symbolism, showing its harmony with other religious traditions.[195] He regarded Tarot as the miraculous work which inspired all sacred books of antiquity and the most perfect instrument of divination due to the analogical precision of its figures and numbers.[196] He declared: "When the sovereign priesthood ceased in Israel; when all oracles were silenced in the presence of the Word made man.., the mysteries were drawn by some learned Kabalists... on simple cards... Hence came those Tarots."[197] He believed that only by the mastery of the insights of Kabbalah, Tarot, the Rosetta Stone, and occult symbolism could religion be restored to its ancient integrity and unity.[198]

Lévi declared that, if there exists a key to the symbolism of the ages, this key might be Tarot. He drew parallels between the twenty-two Tarot trumps and the twenty-two chapters of the Apocalypse.[199] He wrote: "There exists a principle and a rigorous formula, which is the Great Arcanum. Let the wise man seek it not, since he has already found it; let the profane seek for ever: they will never find.... This Universal Arcanum, the final and eternal secret of transcendent initiation, is represented in the Tarot by a naked girl.., analogous to the cherub of... Ezekiel. The comprehension of this figure is the key of all occult sciences.[200] In accord with the popular theory that Tarot spread by the Gypsies, he claimed that the Gypsies originated in India and learned Tarot from "the infidelity and imprudence of some Kabalistic Jews."[201]

In his book, *The Magical Ritual of the Sanctum Regnum Interpreted by the Tarot Trumps,* Lévi gave his personal interpretation of each of the twenty-two trumps and concluded with a "Kabalistic Prayer," which ended with the following words:

> Without obedience no society can continue to exist. This is why the Magi worshipped the Christ in the stable at Bethlehem. Christ, that son of God, greatest of initiates, and the last initiator.
>
> But Christ had, as all great teachers have had, one teaching for the people and also an esoteric doctrine. To John, the beloved disciple, he confided the deepest mysteries of the Holy Kabalah; and John in after years revealed or revelled them in his Apocalypse, which is indeed a synthesis of all earlier magical, prophetic, or Kabalistic works. The Apocalypse requires as its key of Clavicula the Wheel of Ezekiel, which is itself explained by the hieroglyphs of the Tarot.[202]

An important contemporary study of Tarot gave the following assessment of Lévi's approach: "The Tarot is so exceptionally full of symbolism that it has elements in common with practically every other symbol system that has ever existed — and so it may easily seem to be a fragment of some great, coherent, lost *supersystem* of esoteric knowledge. Levi [and] other nineteenth century commentators jumped to this conclusion and, recognizing the superb symbolic facility of the Tarot, believed it to be a key relic of some ancient golden age."[203]

Other Concepts Significant to Lévi's Thought

One of Lévi's most important concepts was that of the Astral Light, which he equated with the Great Magical Agent in which are preserved all impressions of things, all images formed by rays or reflections. He understood this as the source of dreams and hallucinations.[204] He described the Astral Light as the common mirror for every imagination.[205] He considered it the essence of the book of consciences which will be opened at the last day.[206]

An important symbol found throughout Lévi's writings was the five-pointed star called the Pentagram. Lévi called the Pentagram the Kabbalistic sign of the Microcosm[207] and regarded it as an absolute sign of human intelligence[208] and the symbol of human sovereignty acquired by intellectual initiative.[209] He believed that it was best to draw this symbol on unblemished lambskin, which is emblematical of integrity and light.[210] He quoted the Renaissance physician Paracelsus, who called the Pentagram the "greatest and most potent of all signs."[211] He wrote:

> The ancient Magi were priests and kings and the Saviour's advent was proclaimed to them by a star. This star was the magical Pentagram, having a sacred letter at each point. It is the symbol of intelligence which rules by unity of force over the four elementary Potencies; it is the Pentagram of the Magic, the Burning Star of the children of Hiram, the prototype of the equilibriated light. . . . The Pentagram, profaned by men, burns over unclouded on the right hand of the Word of Truth, and the inspired voice guarantees to him that overcometh the possession of the Morning Star.[212]

Another concept important to Lévi was the Great Work, the goal of the alchemical process.[213] He understood the Great Work as inclusive of the Universal Medicine, the transmutations of metals, the quadrature of the circle, and the secret of perpetual motion.[214] He saw the beginning of the Great Work as found in self-knowledge.[215] Thus, he rejected the notion that such could be explained in terms of a physical process of transforming base metals into gold. Rather, he saw such in terms of "directing the natural fire as a gardener directs water to nourish his plants." The end and perfection of the Great Work, he believed, was most appropriately represented by a triangle surmounted by a cross.[216] He described this as a "Priestly and Royal Secret"[217] and as "an actual creation of the human Word initiated into the power of the Word of God Himself."[218] He charged his readers to "silence every desire which is foreign to the fulfilment of the Great Work."[219]

For Lévi, closely related to the Great Work was the discovery of the Philosopher's Stone, which he understood as the foundation of absolute philosophy, supreme and immovable reason, and the true certitude which human prudence assures to conscientious researches and modest doubt.[220] He interpreted the sun and moon of the alchemists as corresponding to the perfection and stability of the Philosopher's Stone. He insisted that this stone was not promised to fanatics and inquisitors but only to genuine initiates.[221]

The theology of numbers was very important to Lévi. In his book *The Key of the Mysteries,* he devoted a great deal of attention to this. For him, "I" (unity) symbolized the alliance of God and man, reason and faith.[222] "II" (binary) was the number of woman, whose archetype was found in the Blessed Virgin Mary.[223] "III" (ternary) symbolized creation.[224] "IV" (quaternary) was the number of force, indicating rebellious unity reconciled to sovereign trinity.[225] Regarding "V," he wrote:

> In rescuing the children of liberty from the tyranny of the Pharaohs, Moses inaugurated the reign of the Father.
>
> In breaking the insupportable yoke of Mosaic Pharisaism, Jesus welcomed all men to the brotherhood of the only Son of God.
>
> When the last ideals fall, when the last material chains of conscience break, when the last of them that killed the prophets and the last of them that stifled the Word are confounded, then will be the reign of the Holy Ghost.[226]

He regarded this Quinary as symbolic of religion, as the number of God united to the number of woman.[227] "VI" (Senary) was the number of initiation by ordeal and of equilibrium.[228] "VII" (Septenary) was the key of creation and symbolic of all religion.[229] "VIII" (Ogdoad) was the number of reaction and equilibrating justice.[230] "IX" was the number of initiates and prophets. He charged his readers to "rebuild all the altars, purify all the temples and hold yourselves in readiness for the visit of the Spirit."[231] "X" was the absolute number of Kabbalah.[232] "XI" was the number of force, strife, and martyrdom."[233] "XII" was the cyclic number of the universal creed.[234] "XIII" was the number of death, birth, property, inheritance, society, family, war, and treaties.[235] "XIV" was the number of fusion, association and universal unity.[236] "XV" was the number of antagonism and catholicity.[237] "XVI" was the number of the temple.[238] "XVII" was the number of the star, intelligence, and love.[239] "XVIII" was the number of religious dogma, poetry, and mystery.[240] "XIX" was the number of light.[241] He stated that the first nineteen letters of the sacred alphabet were the keys of occult theology, while the other letters were the keys of nature.[242]

The concept of equilibrium was also important to Lévi, who insisted that absolute liberty cannot exist apart from perfect equilibrium.[243] To him, harmony consisted in equilibrium and equilibrium subsisted by the analogy of contraries.[244] He called for equilibrium rather than antagonism between body and spirit.[245]

Summation

The focus of this book is to ascertain the influence of Lévi's teachings regarding Kabbalah, Tarot, and related concepts as they are perceived in various religious circles in America. In this chapter, an attempt has been made to provide an evaluative and descriptive account of his life and thought within his French context. It now becomes necessary in this next chapter to determine the extent of his influence in France and Great Britain. This will serve as the prelude to determining the impact of his thought on esoteric religious institutions in America.

End Notes

1. "Éliphas Lévi Zahed" is the Hebrew equivalent of 'Alphonse Louis Constant. Robert A. Gilbert, "Foreword,' in Éliphas Lévi, *The Book of Splendours: the Inner Mysteries of Qabalism: Its Relationship to Freemasonry, Numerology and Tarot* (York Beach, Maine: Samuel Wiser, Inc., 1973), 13. Some sources mention "Zahed" but it appears that Lévi rarely employed his third Hebrew name.

2. Thomas A. Williams, *Éliphas Lévi: Master of Occultism* (University, Alabama: University of Alabama Press, 1975), 2.

3. W. B. Butler, *Practical Magic and the Western Occult Tradition*, ed. Delores Ashcroft-Nowicki (Wellingborough, U. K.: Aquarian Press, 1986), 15. Another writer gave Lévi credit for coining the word 'occultism"; see Cynthia Giles, *The Tarot: History, Mystery and Lore* (New York: Paragon House, 1992), 28.

4. Éliphas Lévi, *The History of Magic, including a Clear and Precise Exposition of Its Procedures, Its Rites and Its Mysteries*, ed. and trans. Arthur Edward Waite (York Beach, Mn.: Samuel Weiser, Inc., 1970), 98.

5. Arthur Edward Waite, *The Holy Kabbalah: A Study of the Secret Tradition in Israel as Unfolded by Sons of the Doctrine for the Benefit and Consolation of the Elect Dispersed Through the Lands and Ages of the Greater Exile* (New Hyde Park, New York: University Books, 1960), 478-79.

6. Gershom Scholem, *Kabbalah* (New York: New American Library, 1974), 203. Scholem was also critical of Waite, categorizing his book *The Holy Kabbalah* among "essentially rather confused compilations made from secondhand sources."

7. Presentation par Paul Redonnel; preface de Victor Emile Michilet (Paris: Cacornac frères, 1926).
8. (London: Rider and Company, 1972).
9. See footnote 2.
10. Williams, *Éliphas Lévi: Master of Occultism*, 7.
11. Mcintosh, *Éliphas Lévi and the French Occult Revival*, 73. Their street of residence is now called Rue de l'Ancienne Comedic and is located in Paris between Boulevard Saint Germain and the Seine, not far from Café Perocope, Paris' oldest cafe.
12. Éliphas Lévi, *L'Assomption de la femme; ou Le livre de l'amour* (Paris: A. Le Gallois, 1841), i. The English title of this book is *The Assumption of the Woman; or the Book of Love*.
13. Williams, *Éliphas Lévi: Master of Occultism*, 8.
14. Éliphas Lévi, *The Mysteries of Magic: A Digest of the Writings of Éliphas Lévi*, ed. and trans. Arthur Edward Waite (New Hyde Park, N. Y.: University Books, 1974), 2.
15. Williams, *Éliphas Lévi: Master of Occultism*, 8-9. In his lectures, the abbé also denounced Mesmerism as inspired by the devil. In doing so, he only succeeded in awakening Lévi's curiosity about forbidden matters; see Colin Wilson, *The Mammoth Book of the Supernatural*, ed. Damon Wilson (New York: Carroll and Graf Publishers, Inc., 1991), 385.
16. Mcintosh, *Éliphas Lévi and the French Occult* Revival, 76.
17. Gilbert, "Forword," in Lévi, *The Book of Splendours*, 10-11.
18. R. I. Clegg, "More Leaves from a Freemason's Note-Book," *American Freemason* (May 1913): 314.
19. Williams, *Éliphas Lévi: Master of Occultism*, 10.
20. Ibid., 11.
21. Ibid., 11-12. In later years, he defined Heaven as "the harmony of generous thoughts" and Hell as "the conflict of cowardly instincts"; see Éliphas Lévi, *The Key of the Mysteries*, ed. and trans. Aleister Crowley (London: Rider and Company, 1959), 29.
22. McIntosh, *Éliphas Lévi and the French Occult Revival*, 79-80. Lévi included a chapter entitled "Mathematical Magic of Pythagoras" in his *History of Magic*.
23. Ibid., 82.
24. Arthur Edward Waite, "Biographical Preface,': in Éliphas Lévi, *Transcendental Magic: Its Doctrine and Ritual*, cci. and trans. Arthur Edward Waite (York Beach, Mn.: Samuel Weiser, Inc., 1968), xix.
25. McIntosh, *Éliphas Lévi and the French Occult Revival, 82.*
26. Williams, *Éliphas Lévi: Master of Occultism*, 84.
27. Ibid., 13.
28. Ibid., 14. However, in later years, Allenbach visited him at various times and always looked to him as her spiritual guide. In *1875,* then bent with age, she moved among the mourners at his funeral; ibid., 13.

29. McIntosh, *Éliphas Lévi and the French Occult Revival*, 84.

30. Waite, "Biographical Preface," in Lévi, *Transcendental Magic*, xx. A woman who traveled with Ganneau claimed to be a reincarnation of Marie Antoninette.

31. The English title is *The Bible of Liberty*.

32. Williams, *Éliphas Lévi: Master of Occultism*, 14-15.

33. McIntosh, *Éliphas Lévi and the French Occult Revival*, 87; the English title is *The Rosebud of May*.

34. Williams, *Éliphas Lévi: Master of Occultism*, 16.

35. Ibid., 16-17.

36. Ibid., 17-19.

37. Ibid., 20.

38. Ibid., 20. Flora Tristan, in the 1830s, dramatized the feminist cause by invading the all-male House of Lords in London disguised as a male Turk; see James H. Billington, *Fire in the Minds of Men: Origins of the Revolutionary Faith* (New York: Basic Books, Inc., 1980), 11. In the 1840s, she drew up the first plan for an all-Europe proletarian alliance called *Union ouvrière*; ibid., 182. Her book *Peregrinations de'une paria (Prereginations of a Pariah)* was a recitation of her physical and spiritual wanderings. She was horrified by the poverty and inhumanity of London and acquired a sense of messianic calling while visiting the lunatic asylum at Bedlam. She desired to save society from economic, social, and sexual divisions. She predicted that, in His Second Coming, Christ would no longer be single but would be accompanied by a female guide. She envisioned a coming socialist age ruled by a Holy Trinity of Father, Mother, and Embryo. She died in 1844. Two years later, *L'Emanciopation de la femme ou, le testament de la paria* (Paris: Au Bureau de la Direction de la Verité, 1846) was published. The English title is *The Emancipation of the Woman or, the Testament of the Pariah*; see ibid., 487-88. Lévi edited this work, which was greatly influenced by his book *L'Assomption de la femme*.

39. Williams, *Éliphas Lévi: Master of Occultism*, 20-21. The English title is *The Mother of God*.

40. Ibid., 21.

41. Ibid., 22.

42. McIntosh, *Éliphas Lévi and the French Occult Revival*, 89-90.

43. Williams, *Éliphas Lévi: Master of Occultism*, 22-25.

44. Ibid., 26. Swiss psychologist Carl Gustav Jung, who continues to have great influence in esoteric circles, was born in 1875 — the year of Lévi's death.

45. Ibid., 27-28. Jung would describe the young girl as Lévi's anima (feminine image in the masculine psyche).

46. Éliphas Lévi, *La Mère de Dieu, epopee religieuse et humanitaire* (Paris: C. Gosselin, 1844), 63. The full English title is *The Mother of God, Religious and Humanitarian Epic*.

47. Williams, *Éliphas Lévi: Master of Occutlism*, 31.

48. Ibid., 31-32. In 1861, Lévi wrote: "Soon one more century will be judged by history, and one will write upon a mighty tomb of ruins: 'Here ends the parricide century! The century which murdered its God and its Christ!" see Lévi, *The Key of the Mysteries*, 47. Seven years later, he expressed the following conviction: "I believe we have yet to see the realization of the Messianic hope which will regenerate a long succession of centuries. I trust the last word on the human species will not be that on the civilizations of Nineveh, Tyre, Babylon, Athens, Rome and Paris"; see Éliphas Lévi, *The Great Secret or Occultism Unveiled* (York Beach, Mn.: Samuel Wiser, Inc., 1975), 163.

49. Ibid., 32.

50. Ibid., 33; the English title is *The Testament of Liberty*.

51. McIntosh, *Éliphas Lévi and the French Occult Revival*, 90. The English titles of these works are: *Corpus Christi, or the Triumph of Religious Peace*; *The Book of Tears*; *The Christ Consoler: Essay on Conciliation between the Catholic Church and Modern Philosophy*; and *Three Harmonies*.

52. Ibid. The English title is *The Truth in All Things*.

53. Williams, *Éliphas Lévi: Master of Occultism*, 33-35. The English titles are "Poland's Grief" and "The Voice of Famine."

54. Gilbert, "Foreword," in Lévi, *The Book of Splendours*, 11.

55. Williams, *Éliphas Lévi: Master of Occultism*, 62-63.

56. Ibid., 64-65.

57. McIntosh, *Éliphas Lévi and the French Occult Revival*, 92. Reportedly, Lévi's son did not see his father until after the latter's death but was among the people who accompanied the body to its place of burial. Paul Chacornac referred to Levi's son as "M.A.C." and provided the following information about him: "We were especially acquainted with M.A.C. It was in the spring of 1914 that we had this pleasure. M.A.C. lived in the Rue Chanoinesse, near Notre Dame. He was a fine old man of medium height with white hair; we were immediately struck by his resemblance to Éliphas Lévi. . . . M.A.C. smiled happily on hearing the name of his father, whom he told us, held in great veneration. He then showed us numerous manuscripts which he had himself patiently drawn up according to the works of Éliphas Levi. Then, opening a bookcase, he showed us the entire works of his father, in the sumptuous bindings of the period. . . . Unfortunately, our relationship stopped there, due to the dreadful calamity which shook the entire world at that moment; and in 1916 we learned with sorrow of the death of M.A.C. . . . In 1919 we met the son of M.A.C. We are indebted to him for much precious information about the life of his grandfather"; see Chacornac, *Èliphas Lévi, renovateur de loccultisme en France, 1810-1875*, 290-91.

58. Williams, *Éliphas Lévi. Master of Occultism*, 65. The year 1848 has been described as "one of the most troubled years of the century for France."

Lévi had vivid memories of the beginnings of the revolution. He recalled that, before the Hôtel des Capucines a pistol shot was fired upon the people. He stated: "This shot started the revolution, and it was fired by a fool"; see McIntosh, *Éliphas Lévi and the French Occult Revival*, 92-93.

59. Williams, *Éliphas Lévi. Master of Occultism*, 65.

60. Éliphas Lévi, *The Magical Ritual of the Sanctum Regnum*, ed. and trans. W. Wynn Westcott (Edmonds, Washington: Holmes Publishing Group, 1922), 35.

61. McIntosh, *Éliphas Lévi and the French Occult Revival*, 92.

62. Éliphas Lévi, *The Last Incarnation: Gospel Legends of the Nineteenth Century*, trans. Francis George Shaw (New York: William H. Graham, 1848), 5.

63. Ibid., 6.

64. Ibid., 8.

65. Ibid., 16.

66. Ibid., 20.

67. Ibid., 23.

68. Ibid., 34-35. This reflects Lévi's concerns about reconciliation between Roman Catholicism and Freemasonry. As in many of Lévi's writings, there are a number of references here to King Solomon's Temple — the edifice so important in Freemasonry. Lévi depicted Jesus as saying: "The cross is the square, multiplied and rendered universal. It is the symbol of equality before God, and of the fraternity of all.... Humanity will construct the great universal temple, of which Solomon's was formerly the first figure.... Build up the new society, the great universal association, the communion of all with all, and of all with each"; see ibid., 31-33.

69. Ibid., 46.

70. Ibid., 52.

71. Ibid., 55.

72. Ibid., 88.

73. McIntosh, *Éliphas Lévi and the French Occult Revival*, 92; the English title is *The Mourning of the Prologue*.

74. Williams, *Éliphas Lévi: Master of Occultism*, 33; the English title is *The Three Malefactors, an Oriental Legend*.

75. Waite, "Biographical and Critical Essay," in Lévi, *The Mysteries of Magic*, 9; the English titles are *Reblais at Basmette* and *The Sorcerer of Meudon*.

76. Williams *Éliphas Lévi: Master of Occultism*, 6 1-62.

77. Gilbert, "Foreword," in Lévi, *The Book of Splendours*, 11.

78. Williams, *Éliphas Lévi: Master of Occultism*, 145.

79. Peter Partner, *The Murdered Magicians: The Templars and Their Myth* (Rochester, Vermont: Inner Traditions, International, 1987), 14.

80. Lévi's disillusionment with politics may have resulted, at least in part, from his unsuccessful efforts to be elected to the National Assembly in 1848; see Williams, *Éliphas Lévi: Master of Occultism*, 93-94.

81. McIntosh, *Éliphas Lévi and the French Occult Revival*, 93. The English title is *Dictionary of Christian Literature*.

82. Ibid., *94-95*.

83. Ibid., 66-69.

84. It is unknown whether Wronski introduced Lévi to Kabbalah or inspired his greater interest in it. It appears that Lévi had been attracted to mysticism from an early age and may have been familiar with Christian Knorr von Rosenroth's *Kabbala Denudata (Kabbalah Unveiled)* before he met Wronski; see McIntosh, *Éliphas Lévi and the French Occult Revival*, 96.

85. Williams, *Éliphas Lévi: Master of Occultism*, 70; in various sources, Kabbalah spelled "Kabbala," "Kabalah," "Cabala," and "Qabalah."

86. Lévi, *The History of Magic*, 331. No doubt Lévi received royalties from the sale of his books. He also gave private lessons to students who visited his apartment. He charged no fees but accepted freewill offerings; see Williams, *Éliphas Lévi: Master of Occultism*, 55.

87. Williams, *Éliphas Lévi: Master of Occultism*, 2-3. These three works have been translated into English. Arthur Edward Waite translated the first two as, respectively, *Transcendental Magic: Its Doctrine and Ritual* and *The History of Magic, Including a Clear and Precise Exposition of Its Procedures, Its Rites and Its Mysteries*. The third work was translated by Aleister Crowley as *The Key of the Mysteries*. Crowley was born in 1875 – a few months after Lévi's death. He claimed to be Lévi reincarnated.

88. McIntosh, *Éliphas Lévi and the French Occult Revival*, 115. Lévi had been invited by Caubet and another friend, Ch. Fauvety, who was Worshipful Master of Lodge Renaissance par les Emules d'Hiram; see "Éliphas Lévi was a Freemason—Briefly," www.freemasonry.bcy.ca/biography/esoterica/levi_e/levi_notes.html, 1. Caubert also served as representative of the Prince Hall Grand Lodge of Missouri to the Grand Orient of France; see Joseph A. Walkes, Jr., E-mail to writer, 10 December 2004.

89. W. N. Schors, "Foreword" in *Éliphas Lévi, The Mysteries of the Qabalah, or the Occult Agreement of the Two Testaments, as Contained in the Prophecy of Ezekiel and the Apocalypse of Saint John* (Wellingborough, U. K.: Aquarian Press, 1974), 16.

90. Williams, *Éliphas Lévi: Master of Occultism*, 154. Eventually, the Grand Orient of France removed the Bible from its altars and the name of the Grand Architect of the Universe from its rituals. As a result, few Masonic bodies in any nation recognize the Grand Orient. There are, however, more "orthodox" Masonic bodies in France today.

91. "Éliphas Lévi was a Freemason—Briefly," 1. In *Le Livre des sages (The Book of the Sages)*, Lévi explained his reasons for leaving Masonry.

92. "Éliphas Lévi was a Freemason—Briefly," 2.

93. For example, Lévi wrote: "Freemasonry is the first attempt at universal synthesis and truly catholic association..., the so-called Catholics are the most

exclusive of men and the Freemasons who, under the guise of the profane, seem to exist at the fringes of human majority, are in reality the only serious partisans of universal alliance. To reconcile Freemasonry and Catholicism what would be necessary? Bringing mutual distrust to a halt and the cultivation of mutual understanding. For these two contrary but not contradictory doctrines are at bottom of reason and faith. . . . harmony results from the analogy of opposites; see Lévi, *The Book of Splendours*, 96.

94. Lévi, *The History of Magic*, 263.

95. Ibid., 264.

96. Christopher McIntosh, *The Rosicrucians: The History, Mythology and Rituals of an Occult Order* (Wellingborogh, U. K.: Aquarian Press, 1987), 104.

97. J. Gordon Melton, *Encyclopedic Handbook of Cults in America*, rev. ed. (New York: Garland Publishing, Inc., 1992), 99. For more on Randolph's life and work, see chapter four.

98. Lévi, *Transcendental Magic* , 27.

99. Ibid., 31-32. He also declared that those whose presence extinguishes all faith and enthusiasm are "dead people whom we mistake for living beings" and described such individuals as "vampires whom we regard as friends"; see Lévi, *Transcendental Magic* , 127.

100. Ibid., 183.

101. Ibid., 269-70

102. Ibid., 271. He compared the Masonic oath of secrecy to Jesus' charge to not cast pearls before swine; see Éliphas Lévi, *The Paradoxes of the Highest Science* (Boise, Id.:Kessinger Publishing Company, 1992), 65. He also observed that Masonic symbolism constitutes a religious synthesis which is missed by the Roman Catholic priesthood; see Lévi, *The Great Secret,* 91.

103. Lévi, *The Key of the Mysteries*, 57-58.

104. Lévi, *The Great Secret,* 71. On the theme of martyrdom, he also wrote: "Every man who dies for an idea is a martyr... There is one man stronger than the man that slays; it is he who dies to save others... every head that falls upon the scaffold may be honoured and praised as the head of a martyr"; see Lévi, *The Key of the Mysteries,* 42-43.

105. Lévi, *The Paradoxes of the Highest* Science, 48.

106. Lévi, *The Great Secret, 105*. In keeping with his belief that occultism was only for the instructed, he warned that there was nothing more dangerous than making magic a pastime or part of an evening's entertainment; see Lévi, *Transcendental Magic*, 264.

107. Waite, "Biographical and Critical Essay," in Lévi, *The Mysteries of Magic*, 11.

108. Ibid. Throughout most of his career, Lévi spoke out strongly against efforts to communicate with the dead. However, on one occasion, during a visit to London, he made three attempts to evoke the ancient Greek magician Apollonius of Tyana. During this ceremony, a ghostly figure appeared

in the smoke from the altar. Lévi pointed at the figure with his ritual sword and commanded it to obey him. His arm became numb to the elbow. He became physically exhausted and fainted. It took him several days to recover from this experience. As a result, he never attempted another evocation; see Louis Stewart, *Life Forces: A Contemporary Guide to the Cult and Occult* (Kansas City, Mo.:Andrews and McMeel, Inc., 1980), 220

109. Reuben Swinburne Clymer, *Book of Rosicruciae* (Quakertown, Pa.: Philosophical Publishing Co., 1948), 2:62. Clymer claimed that, as a result of this visit, Lévi adopted the Pentagram as his seal. He also reported that, in 1861, Randolph accompanied Lévi to London to visit novelist Edward Bulwer-Lytton, Grand Master of the English Rosicrucians. Both Lévi and Randolph died in 1875.

110. Williams, *Éliphas Lévi: Master of Occultism*, 151.

111. Ibid., 151.

112. Ibid., 157.

113. Waite, "Biographical and Critical Essay," Lévi, *The Mysteries of Magic*, 11. Gustave Gebhard was a wealthy banker and silk manufacturer who had served as German Consul to Iran. On his first business trip to New York, he met his future wife Marie, the daughter of a British major and his Irish wife. Marie Gebhard studied Hebrew with an Elberfield clergyman in order to facilitate her research into Kabbalah. After Lévi's death, the Gebhards were among his many European followers who became Theosophists; see Sylvia Cranston, *HPB: The Extraordinary Life and Influence of Helena Blavatsky, Founder of the Modern Theosophical Movement* (New York:

G. P. Putnam's Sons, 1993), 262.

114. Williams, *Éliphas Lévi: Master of Occultism*, 153.

115. Ibid., 155.

116. Waite, "Biographical and Critical Essay," in Lévi, *The Mysteries of Magic*, 11.

117. McIntosh, *Éliphas Lévi and the French Occult Revival*, 136.

118. Ibid., 137.

119. Ibid. The English titles are, respectively, *The Gospel of Science* and *The Religion of Science*.

120. Ibid., 138. The English titles are, respectively, *The Book of Abraham the Jew* and *The Catechism of Peace*.

121. Chacornac, *Éliphas Lévi, renovateur de l'occultisme en France*, 273-74.

122. McIntosh, *Éliphas Lévi and the French Occult Revival*, 138-39.

123. Ibid., 139.

124. Ibid. In this picture, Lévi holds a large crucifix. At the time of his death, on his desk lay his unfinished manuscript of the Vision of Ezekiel, his last mortal work; see Williams, *Éliphas Lévi: Master of Occultism*, 159.

125. McIntosh, *Éliphas Lévi and the French Occult Revival*, 139-40.

126. Waite, "Biographical and Critical Essay," in Lévi, *The Mysteries of Magic*,

45-46.
127. Waite, *The Holy Kabbalah*, 493-94.
128. Williams, *Éliphas Lévi: Master of Occultism*, 78.
129. Ibid., 87.
130. Gilbert, "Foreward," in Lévi, *The Book of Splendours*, 9. The *Zohar* (*Book of Splendours*) was probably written at Grenada, Spain by Rabbi Moses de Leon (1250-1305) but is attributed to Rabbi Simeon ben Yohai, who lived at the time of the destruction of the second temple in 70 A.D.
131. Gilbert, "Foreword," in Lévi, *The Book of Splendours*, 10. "Sephiroth" is the Kabbalistic word for divine emanations.
132. Lévi, *The History of Magic*, 138.
133. Ibid., 32.
134. Lévi, *Transcendental Magic*, 19.
135. Ibid., 95.
136. Lévi, *The Paradoxes of the Highest Science*, 100.
137. Lévi, *Transcendental Magic*, 214.
138. Ibid., 335.
139. Waite, *The Holy Kaballah*, 459-60; Lévi called the Jews "our fathers in religion"; see Lévi, *The Key of the Mysteries*, 69.
140. Lévi, *Transcendental Magic*, 268-69.
141. Ibid., 370.
142. Ibid., 272.
143. Ibid., 302.
144. Lévi, *The History of Magic*, 52-53.
145. Ibid., 148. He also wrote that the true Kabbalist is a truer Catholic, Protestant, Jew, or Muslim than the so-called "orthodox" of any religion because the Kabbalist is "above systems and the passions which darken truth"; see ibid., 48.
146. Lévi, *The Book of Splendours*, 15.
147. Lévi, *Transcendental Magic*, 18.
148. Lévi, *The Great Secret*, 119.
149. Waite, "Preface to the English Translation," in Lévi, *The History of Magic*, 175. Lévi seems always to have viewed Catholicism in ambivalent terms. He contrasted the cruelty of the Inquisition with the charity of Saint Vincent de Paul and attributed this contrast to radically different understandings of the Incarnation; see Lévi, *The Paradoxes of the Highest Science*, 6. He expressed the willingness to be "more catholic than the Pope and more protestant than Luther when occasion demands"; see Lévi, *The Great Secret*, 36.
150. Lévi, *The History of Magic*, 175.
151. Williams, *Éliphas Lévi: Master of Occultism*, 95.
152. Ibid., 101.
153. Lévi, *The History of Magic*, 148.

154. Ibid., 148-49.
155. Ibid., 147.
156. W. N. Schors, "Foreword," in Éliphas Lévi, *The Mysteries of the Qabalah*, 14-15. Lévi regarded the Jews as his brothers and was also sympathetic to Muslims. He declared that the laws of Moses, the Apostles, and the Popes were transitory but the Law of Charity was eternal; see Lévi, *The Book of Splendours*, 125-26.
157. Lévi, *The Mysteries of the Qabalah*, 21.
158. Ibid, 72.
159. Lévi, *The History of Magic*, 282.
160. Lévi, *The Mysteries of the Qabalah*, 83.
161. Ibid., 98-99.
162. Ibid., 108.
163. Ibid., 86.
164. Ibid., 119.
165. Ibid., 120-21.
166. Lévi, *Transcendental Magic*, 43.
167. Lévi, *The Mysteries of the Qabalah*, 142.
168. Ibid., 156.
169. Ibid., 187.
170. Ibid., 190-94. Elsewhere, he described this woman as the celestial Isis or Gnosis. In the same passage, he called upon Jewish Kabbalists to recognize the truth of the Apocalypse, which connects "the Highest Mysteries of Christianity with the secret but invariable doctrine of all the masters in Israel"; see Lévi, *Transcendental Magic*, 275
171. Lévi, *The Mysteries of the Qabalah*, 206. Lévi strongly disliked many of the popular interpretations of the beast which appeared on the scene in his day. Thus, he wrote: "To discover Napoleon in the angel Apollyon, Luther in the star, which falls from heaven, Voltaire or Rousseau in the grasshopper armed like warriors, is merely high fantasy. It is the same with the violence done to the names of celebrated persons so as to make them numerically equivalent to the fatal number 666"; see Lévi, *Transcendental Magic*, 275-76.
172. Ibid., 209.
173. Ibid., 212.
174. Ibid., 216.
175. Ibid., 235. His vision of the Marriage Supper of the Lamb included both Christian and non-Christian elements. He summoned Muslims to this feast as he saw "the dark legends of the North brightened by the Qur'an" and said "Let the East adore Jesus Christ in its mosques and on the minarets of a new Santa Sophia let the Cross rise in the midst of the Crescent"; see Lévi, *The Key of the Mysteries*, 55-56. He expressed the belief that the Hebrew Bible, the Gospel, and the Qur'an are "three different translations of the

same book," and called upon Jews, Christians, and Muslims to recognize that "Mohammed is the shadow of Moses. Moses is the forerunner of Jesus"; see ibid., 50.

176. Ibid., 241.
177. Ibid., 242.
178. Ibid., 251.
179. Lévi, *The Paradoxes of the Highest Science*, 122.
180. Lévi, *The Mysteries of the Qabalah*, 253.
181. Ibid., 254.
182. Ibid., 260-62.
183. Ibid., 265.
184. Ibid., 271. For information on Shechinah, see Robert L. Uzzel, "The Divine Feminine and the Demonic Feminine: A Message for all Good Men and Masons," *Hautes Grades: The Transactions of the Scottish Rite Research Institute (PHA)* III (2003): 5-54.
185. Ibid., 280.
186. Ibid., 283.
187. Lévi, *The Key of the Mysteries*, 55.
188. Lévi, *Transcendental Magic*, 109.
189. Lévi, *The Great Secret*, 93.
190. Ibid., 99. Elsewhere, he wrote that this universal religion would be a blend of Roman Catholicism, Greek Orthodoxy, and Buddhism; see Lévi, *Transcendental Magic*, 211.
191. Tarot appeared in Renaissance Italy and its origin remains a mystery. In 1781, in *Le Monde Primitif*, Court de Gebelin asserted that Tarot was one book of the ancient Egyptians which escaped the burning of the Alexandrian library and contained "the purest knowledge of profound matters possessed by the wise men of Egypt." Lévi accepted this theory of Egyptian origin; see Stephan A. Hoeller, *The Royal Road: A Manual of Kabalistic Meditations on the Tarot* (Wheaton, Ill.: Theosophical Publishing House, 1975), 1. Excavations in Egypt do not support such a claim.
192. Ibid., 26.
193. Scholem, *Kabbalah*, 203.
194. Hoeller, *The Royal Road*, 227. Bishop Hoeller, who is a member of the Theosophical Society in America and a Master Mason of the Grand Orient of France, was quite helpful to me in my research for this dissertation. Consecrated as a bishop in 1967, he teaches classes, delivers lectures, and conducts weekly worship at his headquarters in Hollywood, California. In 1992, Ecciesia Gnostica reported approximately 250 affiliated lay members, eight priests, and three congregations. Hoeller's books include *The Enchanted Life* (Hollywood, Ca.: Gnostic Society, n.d), *The Gnostic Jung and the Seven Sermons to the Dead* (Wheaton, Ill.: Theosophical Publishing House, 1975), and *The Tao of Freedom: Jung, Gnosis and a Voluntary Society* (Rolling Hills Estates,

Ca.: Wayfarer Press, 1984).
195. Williams, *Éliphas Lévi: Master of Occultism*, 132.
196. Lévi, *Transcendental Magic*, 40-41.
197. Ibid., 381.
198. Williams, *Éliphas Lévi: Master of Occultism*, 14.
199. Lévi, *The Mysteries of Magic*, 40-41.
200. Lévi, *Transcendental Magic*, 181-82. The naked girl is found on the seventeenth page of Tarot. She symbolizes truth, nature, and wisdom; and is depicted pouring out fire and water upon the earth. There is a glittering star above her which, according to Lévi, symbolizes the blazing star of Freemasonry and expresses the mysteries of Rosicrucianism; see Lévi, *Transcendental Magic*, 154.
201. Ibid., 240.
202. Lévi, *The Magical Ritual of the Sanctum Regnum Interpreted by the Tarot Trumps*, 101-02.
203. Giles, *The Tarot*, 65.
204. Lévi, *Transcendental Magic*, 121. He defined an hallucination as "an illusion produced by an irregular movement of the Astral Light"; see Lévi, *The Key of the Mysteries*, 98. He understood the Astral Light as the auxiliary of both good and evil; see Lévi, *Transcendental Magic, 85.*
205. Lévi, *The Great Secret*, 16.
206. Lévi, *Transcendental Magic,* 77.
205. Lévi, *The Great Secret*, 16.
206. Lévi, *Transcendental Magic,* 77.
207. Ibid., 68-69.
208. Ibid., 115.
209. Lévi, *The Key of the Mysteries*, 256.
210. Lévi, *Transcendental Magic, 238.*
211. Lévi, *The Key of the Mysteries*, 241.
212. Lévi, *Transcendental Magic,* 200, 239-40.
213. There are many references to alchemy in Lévi's works. He referred to alchemy as "the Daughter of the Qabalah"; see Lévi, *The Key of the Myteries*, 141. He called electricity "the secret fire of the masters of alchemy"; see ibid., 157.
214. Lévi, *Transcendental Magic*, 11-12.
215. Ibid., 30.
216. Ibid., 115-16.
217. Ibid., 277.
218. Ibid., 283.
219.Ibid., 207.
220.Ibid., 164.
221. Ibid., 166-67.
222. Lévi, *The Key of the Mysteries*, 22.

223. Ibid., 25-26.
224. Ibid., 26.
225. Ibid., 27.
226. Ibid., 27-28. 227. Ibid., 30.
228. Ibid., 33.
229. Ibid., 34.
230. Ibid., 38.
231. Ibid., 40-41. 232. Ibid., 42.
233. Ibid., 42-43. 234. Ibid., 43.
235. Ibid., 45.
236. Ibid., 49.
237. Ibid., 53.
238. Ibid., 54.
239. Ibid., 56.
240. Ibid., 57.
241. Ibid., 58.
242. Ibid., 59.
243. Lévi, *Transcendental Magic*, 79.
244. Ibid., 179. He considered such analogy of contraries to be the final word of science and the first word of faith. 245. Lévi, The Great Secret, 120-21.

CHAPTER II

The Influence of Éliphas Lévi in France and Great Britain as a Prelude to the American Scene

A contextual understanding of Éliphas Lévi's influence in France and Great Britain is essential to the understanding of his impact on religious circles in America. Many individuals and organizations in America, past and present, have had direct and indirect links with counterparts in both France and Britain. The nineteenth and twentieth centuries were marked by much religious and cultural interchange between these countries and this continues into the twenty-first century. Thus, a brief treatment of Lévi's influence in France and Britain is necessary in order to elucidate what is crucial to this book.

Éliphas Lévi's Influence in France

Some of Éliphas Lévi's most influential writings concerned the medieval crusading order of Knights Templar, the majority of whom were from his native France. He did much to popularize the idea that the Templars were a secret elite who were custodians of secret knowledge. He probably obtained some of his information on the Templars from the records of their suppression by the Council of Vienne in 1312. Such records were part of the Vatican archives which were brought to Paris in 1810 by Napoleon Bonaparte. While some of these documents were eventually returned to Rome, some remained in Paris. These included many occult books and manuscripts and were sifted, catalogued, and explored by Charles Nodier, chief librarian at the Arsenal Library, the major depository of medieval and specifically occult manuscripts. Lévi was among those who assisted Nodier in this endeavor.[1] No doubt, Lévi utilized much of this material in his writings.[2]

Lévi insisted that the Knights Templar had inherited the mystic gospel of the Egyptian priesthood which passed through Jesus and the Apostle John. He viewed this Johannite doctrine as a Gnostic Kabbalah which had been transmitted to the Templars and later extended to a wider audience in the establishment of Masonic lodges by Jacques de Molay, the last Grand Master of the Templars.[3] He wrote that the concealed end of this Gnostic Kabbalah was the rebuilding of King Solomon's Temple as foreseen by the prophet Ezekiel. Lévi envisioned such a temple as consecrated to Catholic worship and as becoming "the metropolis of the universe." He wrote that the Templars took for their scriptural models the military Masons of Zerubbabel, who worked with a sword in one hand and a trowel in the other.[4] He described the Templars as "Jesuits who failed," and claimed that they had an orthodox Catholic doctrine for the public and a Johannite doctrine for the select few. He also claimed that, under the Templars, the original Johannite doctrine had degenerated into a pantheistic nature worship. This degeneration, he said, had influenced the Templars to give divine honors to a demon called Baphomet, "the better to isolate themselves from obedience to a religion by which they were condemned beforehand."[5] He identified Baphomet with the Egyptian goat-god Mendes and regarded Baphomet as a symbol of ultimate wisdom and of the Philosopher's Stone.[6]

Baphomet

Lévi gave to the Templars a central place in his magical explanation of the world. He claimed that the Templars' real crime was betrayal of the great secret to the profane through Masonic lodges.[7] Legends arose that de Molay, who was burned at the stake on 18 March 1314, had organized four such secret societies in prison awaiting execution. These lodges, he said, were located "at Naples for the East, Edinburgh for the West, Stockholm for the North, and Paris for the South."[8] De Molay's charge to these "Templar Masons" was to carry out the revenge of the Templars, regardless of how long this might take and "to exterminate all kings and the Bourbon line, to destroy the power of the pope, to preach liberty to all peoples, and found a universal republic." According to these legends, these Masons eventually infiltrated other lodges whose members did not know their secret design and, over the centuries, infiltrated many organizations, including the Jesuits. The Templars were charged with supplying the assassin of Henri IV and the attempted assassin of Louis XV. The claim was made that they launched the French Revolution with an attack on the Bastille because it stood on the site of the place where de Molay was confined.[9] Lévi regarded the Revolution as "the revenge of Jacques de Molay, which stemmed from a secret and irresistible impulse to destroy a decadent civilization, "as a liberation from dead institutions and ideas."[10]

Lévi's claim that the Templars were custodians of secret knowledge influenced French political movements, both on the left and on the right. According to one historian of the Templars:

> The radicals had maintained the Templars to have been an early form of enlightened opposition to Church and State.... The conservatives... condemned as diabolical what their opponents hailed as inspired by secret truth. But the nature of the Templars and of the secret society myths was so amorphous that it was quite easy to adapt their message and to turn it from the radical Left to the radical Right. When a new, anti-clerical, and romantic Right emerged in the 1890s, some of its members could adopt the Templars as a secret elite who were the custodians of superior knowledge. Later, this was destined to confer on its adepts the supreme power in modern society. When... Lévi... acquired readers and disciples in the France of the Third Republic, these post-1870 followers incorporated much of this magical doctrine, including Templarism, into the new theory of aristocratic politics.[11]

Arthur Edward Waite gave the following assessment of the importance of Lévi to French occultism as a whole:

> The standpoint of Lévi is that there is a religion behind all religions and that it is the veiled mystery of Kabbalism, from which all have issued and into which all return.... Now it is precisely this standpoint, its derivatives and connections, that created French occultism in the generation which followed Lévi. In the past the magician was content to evoke spirits, the alchemist to produce gold when he could, the astrologer to spell the dubious messages of the stars, the Kabbalist of sorts to be wise in anagrams and word-puzzles, but these things were regarded henceforth as parts of a greater mystery, and in a very true sense Éliphas Lévi was the magus who opened before his readers the wide field of this imaginary view.[12]

From all indications, Lévi was the most widely read of all French occult writers. After the appearance of his books, the number of French writings on occult themes increased dramatically. While Lévi was not alone responsible for this increase, he did more than any other author to contribute to it.[13] Toward the end of the nineteenth century, occult themes became quite prominent in French literature. Thus, Anatole France observed: "A certain knowledge of the occult sciences became necessary for the understanding of a great number of literary works of this period. Magic occupied a large place in the imagination of our poets and novelists. The vertigo of the invisible seized them, the idea of the unknown haunted them."[14]

In 1888, the Cabalistic Order of the Rosy Cross was established at Paris, with three grades of initiation. Each of these grades included an examination. The names of the grades were baccalaureat, licentiate, and doctorat of Cabala.[15] This order was founded by a Frenchman, the Marquis Stanislaus de Guaïta, along with a Spanish-born physician, Dr. Gerard Encausse (better known by his pen name of "Papus"). During the same year, de Guaïta joined forces with amateur artist Oswald Wirth to produce a revised Tarot deck, as envisioned by Lévi.[16]

Stanislaus de Guaïta was of an old Lombardy family. He was born on 6 April 1861 at Alteville in Lorraine, on an estate inherited by his great-great-grandfather when he married the daughter of a French baron. He was educated by the Jesuits at Dijon and, in 1878, he entered the Lyceé at Nancy. He was intrigued by chemistry and developed a passion for poetry and a great admiration for the poet Baudelaire. At Paris, he studied law and developed friendships with the poets of the Latin Quarter. He published the following works *Oisseaux de passage* (1881), *La Muse noire* (1883), and *Rosa Mystica* (1885). One of his poetic mentors, Catulle Mendès, urged him to read Éliphas Lévi. De Guaïta found Lévi to be a "revelation."[17] As a result, he took up occultism with passionate enthusiasm. Like other occultists of his day, he believed in the existence of a concealed tradition by means of which a secret knowledge had been handed down through the centuries. This knowledge, he believed, was transmitted through a long chain of initiates. He sought to demonstrate the existence of such a mystery tradition, beginning with the "sanctuaries of the ancient world" and the "occult Christianity of the early Fathers."[18] He assigned to Lévi a prominent place in this chain and regarded Lévi's works as constituting "the most cohesive, absolute and unimpeachable synthesis that can be dreamed by an occultist."[19] Papus described him as "the most direct continuator of Éliphas Lévi."[20] De Guaïta's later works included *On the Threshold of Mystery and The Serpent of Genesis*.[21]

De Guaïta praised the Theosophical Society but never joined it, preferring the Western Mystery Tradition to the Hindu-inspired works of Madame Helena P. Blavatsky.[22] He lived in rooms hung in scarlet and was accused of constantly dressing up like a cardinal on account of his favorite red gown. He was known for his experiments with morphine, cocaine, and hashish.[23] Perhaps his drug use contributed to his death in 1897 at the age of thirty-six. His demise caused great sorrow in Paris occult circles, where his works were widely read.[24]

De Guaïta's associate, Joséphin Péladin (1858-1918), has been described as "a character who would have been quite at home in one of the more bohemian enclaves of twentieth-century California."[25] He was probably influenced by Lévi in his understanding of the andrygone as the perfect fusion of voluptuousness and intelligence of the active and contemplative faculties.[26] His 1884 book *Le Vice Supreme* contained references to Lévi's concept of the Astral Light.[27] In a letter to Péladin, de Guaïta wrote: "It is your *Vice supreme* that revealed to me (me, a sceptic, though respectful to all things holy) that the Cabala and High Magic can be more than just a mystification. I knew Éliphas Lévi by name; I immediately obtained his complete works and have been meditating on them—too superficially—during my rustic exile with my mother (at the château of Alteville)."[28] However, Péladin combined his occultism with a strong adherence to Roman Catholicism. In 1890, he broke with de Guaïta's Cabalistic Order of the Rosy Cross and established his own rival Order of the Catholic Rosy Cross, the Temple, and the Grail. He explained that there were many aspects of occultism which he could not take with him to Mass and that he was uncomfortable with the associations of de Guaïta's order with spiritualism, Freemasonry, and Buddhism.[29] He hoped to bring occultism back under the wing of Catholicism and, thus, prepare for the reign of the Paraclete.[30]

Dr. Gerard Encausse, the co-founder of the Cabalistic Order of the Rosy Cross, wrote under the pen name of "Papus," a name he derived from the works of Apollonius of Tyana.[31] Papus was initiated into the Isis Lodge of the Theosophical Society in Paris on the approval of Col. Henry Steele Olcott, co-founder of the society. Early in his career he concluded that the Law of Sacrifice was as significant as the Law of Struggle for Life.[32] To him, the findings of the alchemists were as significant as those of modern chemists. While deeply involved in occult studies, he wrote a brilliant thesis for his Doctor of Medicine degree, which he received in 1894.[33] After graduation from medical school, he traveled throughout Europe and studied homeopathy and other unorthodox methods of healing.[34] He was the author of a large number of medical works. At the outbreak of World War I, he entered the Army Medical Corps. In 1916, he died of tuberculosis and a brain seizure.[35]

Papus spent much time in Russia—the home of the legendary magus Grigory Rasputin. Thus, it was no accident that Papus' death would result in the rise of a number of Russian legends about him. A disciple of Rasputin interpreted the death of Papus as a sign of the "immanent return of Tsarism."[36]

Papus was a Freemason, Rosicrucian, Theosophist, and Martinist.[37] He affirmed Christian spirituality but refused to submit to any ecclesiastical authority.[38] He was best known for his book *The Tarot of the Bohemains* (1889), which did more than any previous work to perpetuate Lévi's idea of connections between Kabbalah and Tarot.[39] According to an important contemporary study of Tarot:

> The several streams of esoteric thought which flowed through Papus's mind enabled him to weave a strong fabric of occult associations into his interpretation of the Tarot. He contended that, in ancient times, all knowledge had been condensed into a few simple principles. The fundamental laws, Papus believed, could be glimpsed in the Bible, Homer, the Koran, and all the important documents of early civilization; they had been handed down through a chain that included the classical mystery religions and Gnosticism. After being lost to the West in the Dark Ages, these ideas had been passed back to the Renaissance through the discovery of Arabic texts. They were perpetuated by the alchemists, the Knights Templar, Raymond Lull, and the Rosicrucians, and finally preserved by the Masons and the Martinists.[40]

When Lévi's work on the Zohar, *Livre des Splenduers (The Book of Splendours)*, appeared in 1894, Papus wrote the Appendix, seeking to explore Lévi's concerns with "the three great subjects whose essence man seeks, namely: himself, the universe and God."[41] He gave Lévi credit for solving the most obscure problems of Kabbalah based on the law that "harmony results from the analogy of opposites."[42] He observed that a proper understanding of Kabbalah required extensive study of Hebrew but that, nevertheless, Jewish mysticism "found in Éliphas Lévi an admirable revelator."[43] He expressed the belief that moral regeneration required study, understanding, and practice of the higher Kabbalistic teachings.[44] He defined the art of performing miracles as the art of illuminating other beings in accordance with the laws of the Astral Light.[45] He well reflected the sentiments of Lévi when he declared that "never will the stupid and vulgar comprehend the high wisdom of the Magi!" He described esoteric Kabbalah as "the soul of the Western world" and was convinced that "Eliphas Lévi was chosen by the Invisible to reveal the principles."[47] He drew parallels between the preservation of Gnostic symbols by Freemasons and the preservation of Kabbalistic hieroglyphs by Israel.[48]

Lévi's influence can also be seen in the works of Victor-Emile Michilet. The latter occultist wrote about Baphomet as "the Kheroub of Assyria and Israel, the Arabic Kharouff, the Egyptian and Greek Sphinx, the pentacle which combines the four animals of the Apocalypse."[49] His works included Of Esoteric Philosophy in Art, a series of esoteric lectures to the "Independent Group for Esoteric Studies"; and a series of lectures on "Magic and Love," delivered at La Salle des Capucines.[50]

According to Papus, M. Alber Jhouney, the founder of the mystic re-

view *Star*, was a Kabbalist most deeply influenced by Lévi.[51] Papus wrote:
Living a life of retirement in the country, far from quarrels and rival sects, M. Jhouney spends his time writing very interesting commentaries on the classics of the Qabalah; at the present time he is working on an important study of the *Siphra Dzeniuta*, the book of mysteries which occupied Éliphas himself at the beginning of this volume. Especially interesting is the noble form which M. Jhouney has given to his thought, and the poetical works of this young Qabalist deserve a special place in the library of any occultist devoted to the cult of beauty.[52]

Lévi's teachings were propagated by René Callié, the founder of *The Anti-Materialist* and *The Review of High Studies*. Callié was the first Frenchman to direct and maintain a magazine defending contemporary occultism. He later served as editor of *Star*. Papus observed: "All those acquainted with the sincere faith and generous heart of René Callié cannot help but admire the Master who produced such a disciple."[53]

Lévi's theory of analogy was the intellectual foundation of symbolist doctrine adopted by a number of French poets, writers, and artists.[54] The symbolist writer Philippe Valliers de l'Isle-Adam contested the reality of the phenomenal world and sought to confirm his belief in the presence of a purely spiritual universe. In his novel *Claire Lenoir*, he presented a character named Césaire Lenoir as an expert on spiritualist doctrine and a fervent reader of Emanuel Swedenborg, Raymond Lull, and Éliphas Lévi. This writer was greatly influenced by Lévi's *Dogme et rituel de la haute magie*, which he first encountered in 1866.[55] Lévi's influence on the symbolist movement can also be seen in such writers as Charles Baudelaire, Arthur Rimbaud, and Paul Verlaine.[56]

Another symbolist writer influenced by Lévi was Joris Karl Huysmans, who once lived on Rue de Sèvres in Paris—Lévi's last earthly residence.[57] Huysmans' most famous work was a novel called *Là-Bas*, which was completed in 1890 and had great public impact.[58] This work, which became pre-eminent in occult fiction, was centered around a man Durtal, a novelist who had adhered to natural subjects and found them sterile. Thus, Durtal sought supernatural subjects. Throughout his life, he was periodically attracted to and repelled by religion. This character probably reflects the problems confronting not only Huysmans himself but also a large section of French intelligentsia in the late nineteenth century. Huysmans projected himself into the character of both Durtal and his confidant, des Hermines. The latter individual regularly associated himself with astrologers, Kabbalists, and alchemists. Des Hermines supplied Durtal with a number of occult books, including an alchemical manuscript supposedly translated and with a commentary by Éliphas Lévi. However, Durtal did not find Lévi's commentary helpful at all.[59] His reaction to this manuscript was as follows:

Éliphas Lévi explained the symbolism of these bottled volatiles as fully as he cared to, but abstained from giving the famous recipe for the grand magisterium. He was keeping up the pleasantry of his other books, in which, beginning with an air of solemnity, he affirmed his intention of unveiling the old arcana, and, when the time came to fulfil his promise, begged the question, alleging the excuse that he would perish if he betrayed such burning secrets. The same excuse, which had done duty through the ages, served in masking the perfect ignorance of the cheap occultists of the present day.[60]

In *Là-Bas*, the theme of the reign of the Paraclete again appeared. One character is Geringery, an astrologer who smoked a pipe and expressed the following belief:

There are three kingdoms. Of the Old Testament, that of the Father, the kingdom of fear. Of the New Testament, that of the Son, the kingdom of expiation. Of the Johannite Gospel, that of the Holy Ghost, the kingdom of redemption and love. They are the past, present, and future; winter, spring, and summer. The first, says Joachim of Floris, gives us the blade, the second, the leaf, and the third, the ear. Two of the Persons of the Trinity have shown themselves. Logically the Third must appear.[61]

Huysmans ended his days as an oblate attached to a Benedictine monastery. His conversion to Catholicism was indebted to his interest in occultism, which was his first real glimpse of the spiritual world.[62]

One of Lévi's biographers believed that the influence of occultism in twentieth-century France was much more limited than in the previous century. Thus, he wrote:

Most of the groups that were active in the early years of the twentieth century were in some sense continuations of the occult movement of the previous century whose antecedents I have traced in this study back to the period preceding the Revolution. The momentum which had carried de Guaïta, Papus, and Péladan was now slowing down. Though there was a continuation of occult activity which connects with the present day it is impossible to discern the setting up of a new momentum after the First World War. If occultism tends to flourish in a period of impending crises, when the crisis actually arrives the opiates of occultism cease to be effective and men must turn their minds to the preservation of their lives or the defence of their country. The era that forms the subject of this book can be said to have ended with the holocaust of the First World War. By the time that the smoke had cleared all of the most important figures from the occult movement of the nineteenth century were dead.... Only the visions they had nurtured remained. The Kingdom of the Paraclete had yet to arrive.[63]

The influence of Lévi, however, extended far beyond World War I. It can be seen in surrealism, a movement created by poet and author André Breton. For Breton, who lived until 1966, surrealism was the crystallization of the notion of life, a new experience firmly rooted in the realities of life. He sought to develop surrealism as an attack against a society that nourished an outmoded literary and artistic style. Breton's concerns were rooted in personal experience. In 1915, he became a medical assistant at an army mental hospital. At that time, one of the most important influences on his life was the poet Guillaume Apollinaire, who died of wounds two days before the armistice on 11 November 1918. Apollinaire coined the term "surrealism" and inspired Breton with the image of poetry as magic, directing his attention to some of the magicians of the past. For Breton, Éliphas Lévi was the most influential magician of all.[64] In his work *Manifeste du surréalism* (Paris: Simon Kra, 1924, Breton wrote that "Perhaps the imagination is on the verge of recovering its rights. If the depths of our minds conceal strange forces capable of augmenting or conquering those on the surface, it is in our greatest interest to capture them." These words reveal the influence of Lévi, Pierre Janet, and Sigmund Freud.[65]

Éliphas Lévi's Influence in Great Britain

Éliphas Lévi twice visited England and had contact with a number of British occultists.[66] He also had a number of British disciples. For example, Louise Hutchinson, an English woman who studied with him in Paris, wrote about him in the August 1890 issue of *Initiation*:

> He used to wear a black velvet robe which set off his fine white beard. He was short, too stout for his height, with irregular features. But his light blue eyes sparkled with joyous and witty life; a world of speculation was revealed in his broad, high brow.... Strength of will and joy of living were dominant features of his physiognomy.... He initiated me into the Holy Science by revealing to me what was within my reach.... As soon as he saw me become enthusiastic for one idea, he led me to consider its opposition, thus producing equilibrium.[67]

It appears that Lévi's most influential British disciple was Edward Bulwer--Lytton (1803-1873), the author of The Last Days of Pompeii.[68] Bulwer-Lytton had contact with Lévi and was inspired not only to borrow some of his ideas but also to undertake the formation of a short-lived British society for the study of ceremonial magic.[69] He may have been present when Lévi performed his evocation of Apollonius of Tyana[70] Lévi's influence is evident in Buiwer-Lytton's novel *Zanoni* (New York: P. F. Collier and Son, 1842). This work was a portrayal of Mejirour, a mysterious, highly initiated member of the Rosicrucian fraternity, and his disciple Zanoni.[71]

The Societas Rocicruciana in Anglia (S.R.I.A.) was founded in 1866 by Robert Wentworth Little (1840-1878), a clerk at Freemasons' Hall in London. Reportedly, Little was a student of Lévi's works.[72] This organization limited its membership to Freemasons. One of its prominent members was Rev. A. F. A. Woodford. On 5 July 1894, he delivered a lecture in which he stated that Lévi's "Kabbalistic Exhortation of Solomon to his Son Rehoboam" was the key to "a vast mass of information still studied by large colleges of Rosicrucians, both on the Continent and in England."[73] Another article on "Occult Science" appeared in *The Rosicrucian* in January 1870 and indicated familiarity with Lévi's books.[74]

In 1872, Kenneth Robert Henderson Mackenzie (1833-1886) was initiated into the S.R.I.A. A prolific writer and magazine editor, Mackenzie already held membership in the Society of Antiquaries and the Royal Asiatic Society.[75] He wrote several articles for *The Rosicrucian*. One of the first described his visit with Lévi in Paris in 1861. In this article, Mackenzie called himself "Baphometus," either as a result of his Masonic interest in the Templars or as a tribute to the best known of Lévi's illustrations.[76] He reported that Lévi expressed high regard for Bulwer-Lytton and an interest in the state of magical and occult studies in England. However, he seemed somewhat disappointed that Lévi totally rejected his belief that it was possible for the dead to return and communicate with the living.[77] According to some of Lévi's unpublished correspondence, the French magus found Mackenzie very intelligent but excessively involved with magic and spiritism.[78] Mackenzie had been introduced to Tarot by Lévi.[79] Lévi showed him his own hand-drawn pack of Tarot cards—the work of twenty years—and encouraged him to publish a set in England. Reportedly, Mackenzie prepared a book-length manuscript on Tarot but it was never published.[80] In a letter to his fellow Rosicrucian F. O. Irwin, dated 23 October 1874, Mackenzie described Lévi as "one of my preceptors." In another letter to the same individual dated 6 November 1877 (two years after Lévi's death), Mackenzie asked if Lévi had left exact instructions for the working Tarot. In this letter, he acknowledged that his method of working Tarot involved the aid of astrology, which was quite foreign to Lévi.[81] After Lévi's death in 1875, Mackenzie hoped to contact him through a medium.[82]

Lévi influenced a number of Christian esotericists such as Rev. Edward Burton Penny, rector at Devon, who was a student of theosophy and mysticism and had read the works of Lévi and other French writers.[83] He visited with Lévi in Paris during the spring of 1867.[84] In a letter dated 9 June 1867, he gave the following description of this visit:

> You will find a wonderful analogy between what he claims for the Kabbala and we claim for Theosophy!
>
> Lévi's great aim is to bring his science into practical, positive form — he is eminently synthetical... I hope you will see this remarkable man when you go to Paris.... A man in his position, himself so much higher than all others of the school — or any other school he knows of — must necessarily feel strongly fortified in his own conclusions and dogmas; — but he professes not to be above being taught.
>
> His studies and experiments in Magic I conceive to have gone much further than those of any man I know of... I have still to read his *Histoire de la Magie* and his *Clef des Grands Mystéres* — perhaps they may tell me more about the man and his attainments.[85]

Penny's visit with Lévi occurred six years after Mackenzie's visit. Contrary to Mackenzie, Penny approached Lévi in a condescending manner. As a result, Lévi did not respond to Penny's subsequent letters, while he maintained contact with Mackenzie and his circle.[86]

Lévi's works were read and often recommended by Lady Caithness (1830-1895), a Christian spiritualist who wrote *Old Truths in a New Light*.[87] While many spiritualists were hostile to Roman Catholicism, she believed that Catholic myths, symbols, and rituals preserved a valid and living stream of universal Gnosis.[88] Seeking to be a social and spiritual bridge builder, she fraternized with French socialists and British peers and entertained Theosophists, cardinals, and mediums. Her favorite authors included Lévi, Jacob Boehme, and Emanuel Swedenborg.[89]

Lévi's influence can be seen in the Hermetic Brotherhood of Luxor, which first became public in 1884. This order offered a course in practical occultism to disenchanted Theosophists.[90] The founder was Max Theon (1850-1927), who was born in Poland of Hasidic Jewish background.[91] He lived for a time in Saint John's Wood in the North of London and later settled in Algeria. His Cosmic Philosophy combined Kabbalistic and Vedic elements.[92] Another important leader was Peter Davidson (1842-19 16), a Scottish violin maker who praised India as the cradle of music as of all of the arts and sciences. In his writings, he often spoke of Lévi's Astral Light.[93] Among the order's secret documents was one related to Lévi's "invocation of the spirits of the four elements." Davidson included Lévi's works among the recommended reading in his instructions to members.[94] After the demise of the order, many members with Eastern interests constituted the Esoteric Section of the Theosophical Society. Others, whose interests lay in the

Western Mystery Tradition, became members of the Hermetic Order of the Golden Dawn.[95]

On 1 March 1888, the Hermetic Order of the Golden Dawn was organized. Members included would-be magicians, serious scholars, and poets and artists interested in symbolism.[96] The founders of this order put forth a legend that Lévi was one of their members, despite the fact that he died thirteen years before their establishment.[97] The order was inspired by a bound manuscript composed in ciphers and reportedly found in a London bookstall by Rev. Adolphus A. F. Woodford.[98]

One of the organizers of the Golden Dawn was Dr. William Wynn Westcott, a coroner with much interest in Freemasonry and occultism.[99] He claimed that an address found on the manuscripts led him to contact a lady in Nuremberg, Germany, named Anna Sprengel. This lady, he said, revealed to him the existence of the order, initiated him, and authorized him to initiate others. Reportedly, before anyone else could contact Ms. Sprengel, she had died. No scholar of this movement takes Westcott's account seriously.[100] He apparently was eager to form an esoteric group which, contrary to Freemasonry and Rosicrucianism, would admit women as well as men. He may also have been motivated by the desire to offer a Westernized alternative to the Theosophical Society.[101] Evidence indicates that the cipher manuscripts were written in the handwriting of Kenneth R. H. Mackenzie. After the latter individual's death in 1886, his widow gave his Masonic papers to Westcott. These included the cipher manuscripts which Westcott used as foundation for the order. Mrs. Mackenzie was one of the first initiates. There were rumors that these manuscripts had passed through the hands of Lévi.[102]

Like Lévi, Westcott saw the necessity of guarding secret wisdom from the profane. Thus, he wrote: "The whole Kabalistic theories are of a nature similar to the secrets of Freemasonry ... the great Kabalists of old did not cast pearls of wisdom before the ignorant or the vicious, or suffer the unclean to enter the Temple of Wisdom."[103] He prepared a document called "The Historic Lecture for Neophytes," which included the following words:

> The Order of the G.D. in the Outer is an Hermetic Society whose members are taught the principles of Occult Science and the Magic of Hermes. During the early part of the second half of the century, several eminent Adepti and Chiefs of the Order in France and England died, and their deaths caused a temporary dormant condition of the Temple work. Prominent among the Adepti of our Order, and of public renown were Éliphas Lévi, the greatest of the modern French Magi; Ragon, the author of several classical books of occult lore; Kenneth Mackenzie, the author of the famous and learned *Masonic Encyclopedia* and Frederick Hockley possessed of finer vision in the crystal, and whose MSS were highly esteemed. These and other contemporary Adepti of this Order

received their knowledge and power from predecessors of equal and even Greater eminence. . . . an attentive study of the High Grades will reveal the sources of much of the culture and illustrate the language of the late Éliphas Lévi, through whose adeptship and advocacy the study of occultism has been popularized.[104]

Westcott regarded the following individuals as Christian Kabbalists: Saint Jerome, Raymond Lull, Pope Sixtus IV, Pico de Mirandola, Johannes Reuchlin, H. Cornelius Agrippa, Jerome Cardan, Guielmus Postellus, John Pistorius, Jacob Boehme, Robert Fludd, Henry More, Athanasius Kircher, Christian Knorr von Rosenroth, Edoard Schuré, Éliphas Lévi, Anna Kingsford, and Edward Maitland.[105] He once wrote to Albert Pike, Grand Commander of the Southern Jurisdiction of the Scottish Rite of Freemasonry in America, inviting him to join the Golden Dawn. Pike declined.[106]

In 1896, Westcott translated *The Magical Ritual of the Sanctum Regnum* from one of Lévi's manuscripts.'[107] The illustrations for Lévi's *Transcendental Magic* may have been drawn by Mina Bergson, the future wife of S. L. M. Mathers, a leader of the Golden Dawn.[108]

Prominent Golden Dawn members included Anniue Horminan (founder of Abbey Theatre in Dublin, Ireland, painter Gerald Kelly (who later served as president of the Royal Academy), and Noble poet laureate William Butler Yeats.[109] The latter poet studied Theosophy, Hermeticism, Kabbalah, Celtic legends, and fairy tales. He sought to employ an eclectic and synthetic approach to bring about a spiritual renovation of human affairs. He recognized Lévi's inspiration in the establishment of the Golden Dawn and sought to use the order as a laboratory for experimentation in ritual magic, including rites of purification and rebirth in the style of the ancient mysteries.[110] Golden Dawn members Frederick Hockley and Francis Irvin were reported to have visited Lévi in Paris.[111]

The Golden Dawn answered the need for instruction in practical occultism which the Theosophical Society failed to provide. However, after 1892, elaboration of the simple rituals of the order resulted in the transformation of a society of practical occultism into a vehicle for magical inititations.[112] The order sought to draw together the best of Hermeticism, Kabbalah, alchemy, and Enochian magic (based on the Book of Enoch, which tells of the fall of angels and their magical practices).[113] Their understanding of archetypes—the idea that certain symbols can strike a chord in the unconscious mind of every human being—antedated the analytical psychology of Carl Gustav Jung.[114]

Arthur Edward Waite was a Freemason and Rosicrucian who had much influence on various aspects of British esotericism. His introduction to Éliphas Lévi came when he read *Isis Unveiled* by Helena P. Blavatsky and noted the references to Levi's writings.[115] He became very interested in Lévi and, as a result, studied all of Lévi's works in the British Museum. However, he soon became quite disillusioned by the French magus.[116] He observed that Lévi had taken a seat on a particular "intellectual throne" but expressed the view that he was "neither Hierophant nor Adept."[117] He edited a digest of Lévi's writings called *The Mysteries of Magic*, which was published in 1885. In his autobiography, Waite described the following reaction to this work:

> Theosophical reviews were conscious, I think, of an unbeliever come to birth among them; but the volume appeared under the auspices of a publisher who was dealing in their own wares, and policy dictated caution, while Spiritist Journals, which of course knew nothing of Lévi, were naturally puzzled enough and yet seemed vaguely aware that the things classed under the problematical name of Magia were not very far apart from the things called psychic. They steered their course accordingly.[118]

Arthur Edward Waite

Waite joined the Golden Dawn in January 1891. He dropped out shortly after receiving the seventh degree of the order in April 1892. His recollections of his experiences during this time were negative. This may have been due to the fact that the organization emphasized magic, while his personal interest was in mysticism. He recalled that Westcott and Mathers did not regard him as an occultist and, as a result, objected to his "codification of

Éliphas Lévi."[119] He later wrote:

> Looking back at the days of my work on Lévi and on that meticulous *Digest*—which I should have liked to annotate throughout—it seems probable enough that Westcott and Mathers were right; that I was not an occultist after their manner; that I knew them sufficiently well to loathe their false pretences, their buskined struttings and their abysmal ignorance of the suppositious arcana which they claimed to guard. It happened, however, that I was nourishing still a forlorn hope that there might be something behind the occult pseudo-Temple.[120]

Waite's translation of a number of Lévi's works into English caused Lévi's influence to extend into the mainstream of modern Western literature.[121]

The influence of Lévi in England can be seen in a unique way by examining the life and work of Edward Alexander ("Aleister") Crowley, who claimed to be Lévi reincarnated. Crowley was born on 12 October 1875—four and a half months after the death of Lévi.[122] He believed that it took a few months for the disembodied spirit of Levi to descend into the womb of his mother.[123]

Crowley was the son of a wealthy and puritanical brewer and grew up in Leamington near Stratford-upon-Avon. From an early age, he developed an intense dislike of the Plymouth Brethren, the strict religious sect to which his father belonged. He also developed a strong obsession with sex. Reportedly, his first of numerous seductions occurred at the age of fourteen and involved a young family servant. In his later teens, he discovered S. L. M. Mathers' translation of Christian Knorr von Rosenroth's book *Kabbala Denudata* (*Kabbalah Unveiled*). As a result, he established contact with the Golden Dawn.[124]

In 1898, Crowley became a member of the Golden Dawn. In August 1899, he rented a house in Boleskine, Scotland on the shores of Loch Ness, conferred on himself the title "Laird of Bolesldne," donned a kilt, and began the practice of what he called "the magic of Abrahamelin the Mage." In December of that year, he went to London and demanded initiation into a higher grade of the order. This demand was refused.[125] As a result, he went to Paris, where he found Mathers and persuaded him to perform the necessary rituals.[126] The following year, he went to Mexico, where he studied Kabbalah and practiced yoga and magic. In 1902, he returned to Paris and again had contact with Mathers. However, this contact was not good. Eventually, the two men became estranged and finally began to place magical curses on each other.[127]

Crowley traveled to Ceylon and Egypt. While in Cairo, he heard a disembodied voice ordering him to write. The result of this experience was a manuscript called *The Book of the Law*, upon which much of his later teaching was based. He claimed that it was dictated by Aiwass, one of the "Secret Chiefs" with whom he had contact. It basic teaching was summed up in the expression "Do What You Will."[128] This book included the following observation of conditions during the year 1904:

> Above us today hangs a danger never yet paralleled in history. We suppress the individual in more and more ways. We think in terms of the herd. War no longer kills soldiers; it kills all indiscriminately. Every new measure of the most democratic and autocratic governments is Communistic in essence. It is always restriction. We are all treated as imbecile children. Dora, the Shops Act, the Motoring Laws, Sunday suffocation, the Censorship—they won't trust us to cross the roads at will.
>
> Fascism is like Communism, and dishonest into the bargain. The dictators suppress all art, literature, theatre, music, news, that does not meet their requirements; yet the world only moves by the light of genius. The herd will be destroyed in mass.
>
> The establishment of the Law of Thelema is the only way to preserve the individual liberty and to assure the future of the race.[129]

In 1912, Crowley received a communication from Theodor Reuss, Head of the Order of the Temple of the Orient (O.T.O.) who accused him of publishing its secrets.[130] Crowley met with Reuss regarding the secret in question, which related to sex magic, a practice directed at using the power of sexual energy to fuel the drive toward higher consciousness. Reuss granted permission for Crowley to set up an English branch of the O.T.O.[131] Reuss, prior to his death in 1923, designated Crowley as his successor. Crowley served as Head of O.T.O. from that time until his own death in 1947. During this period, he rewrote the rituals, giving them a sexual and anti-Christian cast.'[132] He insisted on alignment of the predominately religious expression of O.T.O. to Thelema, a religion based on his discovery of The Book of the Law. The latter work forms the primary religious focus of O.T.O. today. He did much to expand the membership.[133]

Crowley lived in America during World War I. During this time, he had an endless series of mistresses, each of whom he liked to call the "Scarlet Woman." According to one writer: "He undoubtedly had an exceptional sexual appetite, but it must also be said that he genuinely believed that sex magic heightened his self-awareness, and enabled him to tap increasing profound levels of consciousness."[134]

By the early 1920s, Crowley was suffering from asthma and was continuously in debt. A legacy of $12,000 enabled him to move to a small farmhouse in Cefalu, Italy. He called it the Abbey of Thelema. There he practiced magic with devoted disciples. Reportedly, he provided limitless quantities of drugs for anyone wishing to use them.[135] Attractive female disciples were expected to help him practice sex magic. He wrote a novel called *Diary of a Drug Fiend* and began work on his *Confessions*, which he called his hagiography (the biography of a saint). He announced that the earth had passed beyond Christianity and had entered the new epoch of Crowleyanity. However, he was forced to leave Italy as a result of a media scandal. The latter erupted after one of his disciples died after sacrificing a cat and drinking its blood.[136]

Edward Alexander ("Aleister") Crowley

The British press denounced Crowley as "the wickedest man in the world." One of his disciples committed suicide. Crowley remarried. His second wife, like his first, went insane. In need of money, he sued the English sculptress Nina Hamnett for calling him a black magician. But when witnesses described his magic, the judge stopped the case, declaring he had never heard such "dreadful, horrible, blasphemous, and abominable stuff." By the time of World War II, Crowley was addicted to alcohol as well as heroin and cocaine. Yet, he still was able to generate financial support from wealthy contributors. Inevitably, however, these supporters would lose patience with him. He retired to a rooming house near Hastings in southern England, where he died in December 1947. Few people respected him at that time. It was not until the beginning of the magical revival of the mid-1960s that his reputation began to rise again.[137]

Crowley used every thread of evidence at his disposal to support his claim of being Lévi reincarnated. While visiting a certain district in Paris, he said he experienced a sense of "being at home again." Later, to his delight, he discovered that Lévi had once lived there. He drew parallels in their lives, including the intention of each set of parents that their son follow a religious career; inexplicable ostracism experienced by each; and events related to marriage. In Crowley's copy of Paul Chacornac's *Éliphas Lévi, renovateur de loccultisme en France, 1810-1875*, there were a number of penciled notes. On page 108, there was a quotation from letters of Lévi to Baron Spedalieri in which Lévi described his experience of reviving his daughter who seemed near death. Crowley noted "Cf. saving Lola Zaza." He believed that he used the same means to save his daughter's life. On page 213 is a passage describing how Lévi wrote under involuntary impulse and later read the words with "a sort of delight mingled with terror." Crowley's *The Book of the Law* was written in this way and his reactions to it were the same. On page 242, Chacornac reported: "One evening he found himself at a dinner party where a lawyer who prided himself as a word-spinner was telling a story as though it were his own. While the raconteur was searching for a telling phrase Éliphas Lévi suddenly broke in and continued the story by reciting an old fifteenth-century narrative poem which the lawyer had plagiarized." Crowley noted, "As I did with Frank Harris."[138]

Crowley translated and edited Lévi's *The Key of the Mysteries*, which he called "the high-water mark of the thought of Éliphas Lévi" in which "he reaches an exaltation of both thought and language which is equal to that of any other writer known to us." He complained of the "pedantry and stupidity of such commentators as Waite."[139] He gave the following interpretation of Lévi's defense of the Roman Catholic Hierarchy:

> When Lévi says that all that he asserts as an initiate is subordinate to his humble submissiveness as a Christian, and then not only remarks that the Bible and the Qur'an are different translations of the same book, but treats the Incarnation as an allegory, it is evident that a good deal of submission will be required.... His very defense of the Catholic Hierarchy is a masterpiece of that peculiar form of conscious sophistry which justifies itself by reducing its conclusion to zero. One must begin with one and that one has no particular qualities. Therefore, so long as you have an authority properly centralized it does not really matter what the authority is. In the Pope we have such an authority ready made, and it is the gravest tactical blunder to endeavor to set up an authority opposed to him. Success in doing so means war, and failure anarchy. This, however, does not prevent Lévi from ceremonially casting a pa-

pal crown to the ground and crying "Death to the tyranny and superstition!" in the bosom of a certain secret Areopagus of which he was the most famous member.[140]

The International Order of Kabbalists was founded in London in 1966 as a small study group. As a result of letters of interest from various countries, the order grew rapidly with a number of lodges organized and many corresponding members added to the rolls. The order's Principal, D. L. Sturzaker, was quite interested in Tarot. Sturzaker read Lévi and called the Paths of the Kabbalistic Tree of Life by the Tarot attributes. Sturzaker died on 8 October 1993 and was succeeded by D. M. Dalton, who expressed the opinion that there is no link whatsoever between Kabbalah and Tarot. Dalton recognized that the Golden Dawn picked up many of Lévi's ideas and acknowledged that "some of these may have filtered down to us." His order does not follow the Golden Dawn system yet, as he stated in a letter, "there are inevitably some. similarities."[141]

Summation

Research indicates that many individuals and organizations in France and England have been influenced by Éliphas Lévi. His influence took a variety of forms. Various French religious and political movements took note of his writings about the Knights Templar. The use of his works depended on the agenda of the organization involved. French Rosicrucianism developed as a part of the occult revival inspired by Lévi's writings. Some individuals and organizations were influenced mainly by his general subject matter while others adopted some of his specific ideas. Some claimed him as an actual or honorary member. Some individuals—such as Arthur Edward Waite—were highly critical of him. Others—such as Aleister Crowley---tried to reshape him in their own mold. At any rate, many in both France and Britain took note of him. Many of these same individuals and organizations have direct and indirect links with individuals and organizations in America. Chapters three and four will be devoted to exploration of the latter, in efforts to determine Lévi's influence on the American tradition.

End Notes

1. Michael Baigent, Richard Leigh, and Henry Lincoln, *Holy Blood, Holy Grail* (NewYork Dell Publishing Company, 1983), 150-51.
2. Lévi wrote: "Owing to the profanation and impieties of Gnostics the Church proscribed Magic. The condemnation of the Knights Templar completed the rupture"; see Lévi, *The History of Magic*, 223.

3. Peter Partner, *The Murdered Magicians: The Templars and Their Myth* (Rochester, Vt.: Inner Traditions, International, 1987), 165.

4. Lévi, The History of Magic, 207-08. Elsewhere, Lévi described Count Cagliostro as an agent of the Templars who believed the time had come to build the "Temple of the Eternal" and introduce new rite under the name of Egyptian Masonry, seeking to restore devotion to the Egyptian goddess Isis; see ibid., 301.

5. Ibid., 211. One possible source Lévi may have used for his information on Baphomet was Joseph von Hammer-Purgstall's *Mystery of Baphomet Revealed*, which was published in 1818. In the latter book, this Austrian scholar presented theories concerning the relationship of the Templars to Freemasonry, revolutionism, and satanism; see Carl A. Raschke, *Painted Black: From Drug Killings to Heavy Metal, the Alarming True Story of How Satanism is Terrorizing Our Convnunities* (San Francisco, Ca.: Harper and Row, 1990), 91.

6. Ibid. In the opinion of many scholars, the goat is derived from Pan, a fertility deity of ancient Greece. In medieval Christian art, the goat-like image was often associated with Satan. "Baphomet" is a corrupted form of the name "Muhammad" and alludes to the claim that the Templars had embraced Islam and demonstrated their renunciation of Christianity by the symbolic gesture of spitting on the cross. Lévi's well-known engraving of Baphomet has become a classic article of iconography in contemporary Black Magic and has been described as "a sort of satanist Mona Lisa"; see Raschke, *Painted Black*, 91. This does not imply that it was ever Lévi's desire that his art should be used in such a manner.

7. Partner, *The Murdered Magicians*, 165.

8. Lévi, *The History of Magic*, 212. The legend of the Templar lodge in Scotland later influenced the adoption of the name "Scottish Rite" for a major branch of Freemasonry.

9. Ibid.

10. Partner, *The Murdered Magicians*, 165-66. Jacques de Molay was sentenced to death by order of King Philip IV of France and with the cooperation of Pope Clement V. Reportedly, as he was dying, he summoned both Philip and Clement to meet him before the throne of God. When both the king and pope died within a year of de Molay's death, the Grand Master was hailed as a prophet. According to another legend, at the time of the beheading of King Louis XVI in 1789, an unnamed individual ascended the platform and, plunging his hands into the dead king's blood and throwing the blood over the crowd, shouted, "Jacques de Molay, thou art avenged!"; see John J. Robinson, *Dungeon, Fire and Sword: The Knights Templar in the Crusades* (New York: M. Evans and Company, Inc., 1991), 473.

11. Ibid., 66.

12. Waite, *The Holy Kabbalah*, 493-94.

13. McIntosh, *Éliphas Lévi and the French Occult Revival*, 170.

14. Anatole France, *Revue illustrée*, 15 February 1890; quoted in Maria Carlson, *"No Religion Higher than Truth": A History of the Theosophical Movement in Russia, 1875-1922* (Princeton, N. J.: Princeton University Press, 1993), 19.

15. Ibid.

16. Giles, *The Tarot*, 34. Oswald Wirth was a hypnotic healer who became de Guaïta's most devoted disciple. He had previously been involved in Theosophy and was initiated into Freemasonry in 1884. De Guaïta introduced him to Tarot as a magical system. In 1927, Wirth wrote *Le Tarot des Imagiers du Moyen Age* (*The Tarot of Medieval Images*); see McIntosh, *Éliphas Lévi and the French Occult Revival*, 169-70.

17. McIntosh, *Éliphas Lévi and the French Occult Revival*, 164. The English titles of de Guaïta's

18. Jean Pierrot, *The Decadent Imagination, 1880-1900* (Chicago, Ill.: University of Chicago Press), 116.

19. Waite, *The Holy Kabbalah*, 503.

20. Papus, "The Doctrine of Éliphas Lévi," in Lévi, *The Book of Splendours*, 188.

21. Ibid.

22. Ibid., 168-69. For more detailed information on Blavatsky and Theosophy, see chapter four.

23. Giles, *The Tarot*, 36.

24. Waite, The Holy Kabbalah, 503.

25. McIntosh, *Éliphas Lévi and the French Occult Revival*, 165.

26. Ibid. In *Templiers et Rose-Croix* (1955), Robert Ambelain stated that Lévi was initiated into Rosicrucianism in London in 1853 and, on his return to Paris, initiated Abbé Lacuna who, in turn, initiated Dr. Adrien Péladan, a distinguished homeopath and hermetic scholar, who initiated his brother Josephin; see ibid., 163-64.

27. Pierrot, *The Decadent Imagination*, 102. The English title is *The Supreme Vice*.

28. Ibid

29. McIntosh, *Éliphas Lévi and the French Occult Revival*, 171.

30. Ibid., 172. The reign of the Paraclete (Holy Spirit) is a major theme of occult literature and demonstrates the close link between utopianism and occultism.

31. Pierrot, *The Decadent Imagination*, 103.

32. McIntosh, *Éliphas Lévi and the French Occult Revival*, 157.

33. Ibid., 158-59.

34. Ibid., 160.

35. Ibid., 162-63.

36. Ibid., 161.

37. Ibid., 163.

38. Pierrot, *The Decadent Imagination*, 113.

39. McIntosh, *Éliphas Lévi and the French Occult Revival*, 163.

40. Giles, *The Tarot*, 37-38. This work, which appeared in 1889, was the first book devoted exclusively to Tarot; see ibid. 34.

41. Papus, "The Doctrine of Éliphas Lévi," in Lévi, *The Book of Splendours*, 143. Papus identified himself as "President of the Independent Group for Esoteric Studies, President of the Supreme Council of the Martinist Order, <and> General Delegate of the Qabalistic Order of the Rosicrucians"; see ibid., 191.

42. Ibid., 146.

43. Ibid., 147.

44. Ibid., 153.

45. Ibid., 158-59.

46. Ibid., 166.

47. Ibid., 184.

48. Ibid., 186.

49. Partner, *The Murdered Magicians*, 169.

50. Papus, "The Doctrine of Éliphas Lévi," in Lévi, *The Book of Splendours*, 189.

51. Ibid., 190.

52. Ibid.

58. Ibid.., 186. The English title is *Down There*. When this work appeared, de Guaïta and Papus accused Huysmans of being a profane dabbler in-occultism who distorted the meaning of the movement. Such reaction tended to reinforce public curiosity about occult matters; see Pierrot, *The Decadent Imagination*, 110.

59. Joris Karl Huysmans, *Down There*, trans. Keene Wallis (New York: Albert and Charles Boni, 1924), 81.

60. Ibid., 82.

61. Ibid., 287.

62. Ibid., 191.

63. Ibid., 224. Guaïta, Papus, and Huysmans sought to demonstrate in the fulfillment of prophecies the rational proofs of a counter history set against "science without God." They were determined to apply cyclical and Kabbalistic exegeses to modern times. Thus. they sought to bridge the gulf between science and faith. Unfortunately, by the early twentieth century, they were viewed as part of the problem rather than part of the solution; see Jean Pierre Laurant, "Primitive Characteristics of Nineteenth-Century Esotericism," in *Modern Esoteric Spirituality*, ed. Faivre and Needleman, 283-86.

65. Ibid., 218. This work was later published in English as *The First Surrealist Manifesto*.

66. Ellic Howe, *The Magicians of the Golden Dawn: A Documentary History of*

a Magical Order 1887-1923 (York Beach, Me.: Samuel Wiser, Inc., 1987), 9.

67. Williams, *Éliphas Lévi. Master of Occultism*, 155-56. On one occasion, Lévi reportedly cured Ms. Hutchinson of "uncontrolled bleeding" by the laying on of hands.

68. Stewart, *Life Forces*, 473. Some writers have contend that the word "disciple" is inappropriate here. Jocelyn Godwin called Bulwer-Lytton "the pivotal figure of nineteenth-century occultism" and expressed the opinion that it is more likely that Bulwer-Lytton led Lévi into magic, rather than vice versa; see Godwin, *The Theosophical Enlightenment*, 195-96.

69. David Farren, *Living with Magic* (New York: Simon and Schuster, 1974), 167.

70. Godwin, *The Theosophical Enlightenment*, 198. Later, Anna Kingsford, the co-founder of the Hermetic Society who spent much time in trance, claimed to have received a number of visitors from the spirit world, including Apollonius of Tyana. Her colleague Edward Maitland insisted that, whereas Lévi had seen only Apollonius' astral phantom, Kingsford had met his true self; see ibid., 339.

71. Howard Kerr and Charles L. Crow, *The Occult in America: New Historical Perspectives* (Urbana, Ill.: University of Illinois Press, 1983), 128.

72. Howe, *The Magicians of the Golden Dawn*, 26.

73. Arthur Edward Waite, *The Brotherhood of the Rosy Cross, Being Records of the House of the Holy Spirit in Its Inward and Outward History* (New Hyde Park, N. Y.: University Books, 1961), 58 1-82.

74. Ibid., 32.

75. Godwin, *The Theosophical Enlightenment*, 212.

76. Ibid., 218. One of Mackenzie's major interests was Freemasonry. His major work was his *Royal Masonic Encyclopedia*, whose long articles on Count Cagliostro and Kabbalah reflect his determination not to separate Freemasonry from occultism. Its major importance appears to lie in its coverage of fringe Masonic orders such as Sat B'hai and the Rite of Swedenborg; see ibid., 219.

77. Ibid., 216.

78. Howe, *The Magicians of the Golden Dawn*, 27-28.

79. Giles, *The Tarot*, 41.

80. Godwin, *The Theosophical Enlightenment*, 216.

81. Howe, *The Magicians of the Golden Dawn*, 29.

82. Godwin, *The Theosophical Enlightenment*, 219.

83. Ibid., 240. Christian esotericists of this period protested the fact that the thirst for direct spiritual experience was lacking in the men of the Enlightenment. They tended to be more tolerant of other religions than most of their fellow Christians. They also tended to interpret the Bible allegorically rather than literally, in a manner analogous to Jewish Kabbalists' interpretation of the Torah and Sufis' interpretation of the Qur'an; see ibid., 227.

84. Ibid., 241.
85. Ibid., 242-43.
86. Ibid., 243.
87. Ibid., 338.
88. Ibid., 368.
89. Ibid., 338.
90. Ibid., 347. A contrast can be seen in the Brotherhood's concern with sexual matters and the puritanical approach of the Theosophical Society; see ibid., 348.
91. Ibid., 349. Hasidic Judaism began in Poland during the early eighteenth century. The founder was Israel ben Eliezer (1700-1760), who was better known as "Baal Shem Tov" ("Master of the Holy Name"). As a young man, this charismatic rabbi studied Kabbalah and reported receiving visits from heavenly messengers who revealed to him the deep mysteries of the Torah. He received inspiration for his movement in seven years of solitude, poverty, prayer, meditation and study of the medicinal properties of herbs and grasses; see Jacob S. Minkin, "Baa! Shem, The," in *The Universal Jewish Encyclopedia*, ed. Isaac Landman (New York: Universal Jewish Encyclopedia, Inc., 1940), 2:3-4. He declared his heart's desire was "making myself a vessel for God" and taught that the ideal means of communion with God is prayer recited with exalted joy and ecstatic fervor. To establish such ecstasy, he prescribed bodily movements, chanting, and dancing; see Isidor Epstein, *Judaism: A Historical Perspective* (New York: Penguin Books, 1959), 272-73. He has often been pictured by artists telling stories to listeners, always with his pipe in his hand or mouth; see "Israel ben Eliezer Ba'al Shem Tov," Encyclopedia Judaica (Jerusalem: Keter Publishing House, Ltd., 1971), 9:1050. During the nineteenth century, Hasidism experienced some decline but managed to survive. Driven from the Soviet Union, Hasidic Jews reconstructed their movement and survived the Nazi Holocaust, although greatly reduced in size. Their teachings consist of Jewish mystical ethics based on Kabbalistic symbolism, combined with interpretation of verses from the Torah, sayings from the Talmud, and elements from every aspect of Jewish life; see Joseph Dan, *Jewish Mysticism and Jewish Ethics* (Seattle, Wa.: University of Washington Press, 1986), 117. It is possible that Max Theon's introduction to Kabbalah occurred in the context of his Hasidic upbringing.
92. Ibid., 349-50.
93. Ibid., 35 1-52.
94. Ibid., 357.
95. Ibid., 361-62.
96. Giles, The Tarot, 39. It is possible that the roots of this organization can be traced to the "Orphic Circle" or "Orphic Society" which began in England in the 1830s. Various organizations of this type may have existed from time to time, but not necessarily in any unbroken succession. According to

Jocelyn Godwin: "Probably a secret magical group did exist in London between the crystal-gazing craze of the 1830s and the Dialectical Society's investigation of the late 1860s, and Bulwer-Lytton took part in it. Éliphas Lévi's evocation of Apollonius of Tyana. . . .might have taken place under its auspices"; see Godwin, *The Theosophical Enlightenment*, 212.

97. Howe, *The Magicians of the Golden Dawn*, 26.

98. Godwin, *The Theosophical Enlightenment*, 223-24.

99. Ibid., 224. Waite once observed that Westcott "is a man whom you may ask by chance concerning some almost nameless Rite and it will prove very shortly that he is either its British custodian or the holder of some high office therein"; see Ellic Howe and Helmut Möller, "Theodor Reuss: Irregular Freemasonry in Germany, 1900-23," *Transactions of Quaruor Coronari Lodge* 91(16 February 1978): 30.

100. Ibid., 224.

101. Giles, *The Tarot*, 40. In 1888, Westcott delivered lectures on Kabbalah before the Society of Hermetic Students. He believed that his knowledge of Kabbalah was enlarged due to his position as Supreme Magus of the Rosicrucian Society; see William Wynn Westcott, *An Introduction to the Study of the Kabalah, with Eight Diagrams* (London: John M. Watkins, 1926), i-iii.

102. Godwin, *The Theosophical Enlightenment*, 224.

103. Westcott, *An Introduction to the Study of the Kabalah*, 67.

104. Howe, *The Magicians of the Golden Dawn*, 22-24.

105. Westcott, *An Introduction to the Study of the Kabalah*, 20.

106. Robert A. Gilbert, letter to the author, 28 May 1994. Gilbert, who lives in London, is a noted Masonic writer and the editor of the *Transactions of Quatuor Coronati Lodge*, the publication of Freemasonry's premier research lodge. For more information on Albert Pike, see chapter three.

107. Ibid., 37. Westcott obtained this manuscript from Edward Maitland, co-founder of the Hermetic Society (an organization unrelated to the Hermetic Society of the Golden Dawn). Maitland obtained it from Baron Giussepe Spedalieri, Lévi's disciple and literary executor, during an 1887 visit to France; see Godwin, *The Theosophical Enlightenment*, 345.

108. Ibid., 393.

109. Giles, *The Tarot*, 39.

110. Carl A. Raschke, *The Interruption of Eternity: Modern Gnosticism and the Origins of the New Religious Consciousness* (Chicago., Ill.: Nelson-Hall, 1989), 115-16.

111. Godwin, *The Theosophical Enlightenment*, 223-24.

112. Ibid., 224.

113. Wilson, *The Mammoth Book of the Supernatural*, 394.

114. Ibid., 393.

115. Arthur Edward Waite, *Shadows of Life and Thought: A Retrospective Review in the Form of Memoirs* (London: Selwyn and Blount, 1938), 73. Waite

reported that he hated the anti-Christian bias found in *Isis Unveiled*. Nevertheless, he found this work helpful in his study of esoteric claims and pretenses; see ibid., 66-68.

116. Ibid., 75.
117. Ibid., 95.
118. Ibid., 100.
119. Howe, *The Magicians of the Golden Dawn*, 71.
120. Waite, *Shadows of Life and Thought*, 99.
121. Williams, *Éliphas Lévi: Master of Occultism*, 1.
122. CollinWilson, *The Occult: A History* (New York: .Random House, 1971), 348. Crowley was a very prolific writer. He translated into English Lévi's *The Key of the Mysteries*.
123. John Symonds, *The Magic of Aleister Crowley* (London: Frederick Muller, Ltd., 1980), 68. Symonds insisted that Crowley's "Magical memory" revealed nothing about Lévi's life that could not be obtained by reading Waite's biographical preface to *Transcendental Magic*.
124. Colin Wilson, *The Mammoth Book of the Supernatural*, ed. Damon Wilson (NewYork: Carroll and Graf Publishers, Inc., 1991), 394-95.
125. Ibid., 395. According to Wilson, William Butler Yeats and other senior members regarded Crowley as "an overgrown juvenile delinquent."
126. Ibid.
127. Ibid., 396. When Mathers died during an influenza epidemic in 1918, Crowley claimed that his curses were responsible for Mathers' death.
128. Ibid., 396-97. Crowley received the writing instructions from his first wife, Rose Kelly, who spoke while in a trance-like state. Later, in India, Crowley deserted her and their baby. The baby died of typhoid. Rose later became an alcoholic and died insane.
129. Aleister Crowley, *The Book of the Law* (York Beach, Mn.: Samuel Weiser, Inc., 1976), 14-15. The "Law of Thelema," Crowley claimed, was derived from ancient Egyptian religion.
130. Ibid., 397. For more detailed information on Theodor Reuss and the O.T.O., see chapter four.
131. Ibid. Sex magic remained a major preoccupation of Crowley throughout his life. However, in his later years, his sex drive was impaired by his addiction to heroin and cocaine. It should be noted that Crowley's views of sex magic were quite different than those of Peter Davidson and the American Rosicrucian leader Pascal Beverly Randolph. According to Jocelyn Godwin: "Randolph had a typical nineteenth-century horror of masturbation, and neither he nor Davidson had the slightest tolerance for homosexuality — both integral parts of Crowley's practice"; see Godwin, *The Theosophical Enlightenment*, 361.
132. Antoine Faivre, *Access to Western Esotericism* (New York: State University of New York Press, 1994), 91.

133. Bill Heidrick, letter to the author, 31 December 1994. Heidrick currently serves as Grand Treasurer General of O.T.O.
134. Wilson, *The Mammoth Book of the Supernatural*, 397-98.
135. Ibid., 398. Crowley's advocacy of the use of drugs to expand consciousness antedated the work of "LSD Guru" Timothy Leary by forty years.
136. Ibid., 398.
137. Ibid., 398-99.
138. McIntosh, *Éliphas Lévi and the French Occult Revival*, 226-27.
139. Crowley, "Introduction," in Lévi, *The Key of the Mysteries*, 7-8.
140. Ibid, 7.
141. D. M. Dalton, letter to the author, 9 November 1994.

CHAPTER III

Lévi in America: Albert Pike

One of the first Americans to come under the influence of Éliphas Lévi was the noted Masonic writer Albert Pike. Pike's experiences as a lawyer, poet, journalist, and Confederate general have been the subject of a large amount of scholarly attention, especially in his adopted state of Arkansas. However, there can be no doubt that his main "claim to fame" was Masonic in view of his thirty-two years of service as Grand Commander for the Southern Jurisdiction of the Scottish Rite of Freemasonry and his voluminous writings on Masonic subjects. The fact is well established that Pike borrowed extensively from the writings of Éliphas Lévi in the preparation of his best known book, *Morals and Dogma*. Through the latter work, Lévi's ideas reached a wide audience of Scottish Rite Masons and other interested persons. Carl A. Raschke described Pike as Lévi's most notable apostle in America."[1] Literary research indicates that such a claim overstates the case considerably. Lévi was not the only influence on Pike, but he was certainly one of the major ones. Pike was the primary agent for transmission of Lévi's ideas in nineteenth-century America. Thus, an adequate understanding of Pike is essential to an understanding of Lévi's influence on the American mystery tradition. Masonic apologist John J. Robinson gave the following assessment of Pike's career:

> Albert Pike (1809-91) was a lawyer, a poet, a prolific writer, general in the army of the Confederate States of America, and a Freemason. He was a voracious reader, especially interested in the religious and philosophical systems of ancient cultures, which he saw as having shaped the thinking and codes of morality of people around the world. As a general, he commanded neither white nor black troops but American Indians. He studied and respected their religious beliefs. But no matter how deeply he probed into other religions, nothing Pike learned ever shook his own faith as a Trinitarian Christian. Politically, he did not favor stronger central control, as is evidenced by his willingness to risk life and fortune in a war that started not over the issue of slavery, but over the political concept of states' rights. In hindsight Pike may be judged to have been wrong politically, but at least he was willing to die for what he believed.[2]

Life and Work of Albert Pike

Albert Pike was born on 29 December 1809 in Boston, Massachusetts, the son of Benjamin and Sarah Andrews Pike. His father was a Boston cobbler described as the "black sheep" of his family "who laughed too easily, drank too much, and refused to take life seriously." His mother, on the other hand, had the reputation of being "sober, intensely religious, staunchly Puritan, with a clear view of this troublesome world as a brief and necessary prelude to the happier vale of heaven." One of Albert Pike's biographers contended that the son of these very different personalities was "destined to be forever torn between the two extremes, between the penchant for moral order which would eventually lead him into the bizarre religions of the ancient world, and the ungovernable appetites of the flesh which he would satisfy in unusual ways."[3] As a child, Pike moved with his family to Newburyport, Massachusetts, the place of his father's birth. He made excellent grades in the Newburyport schools. After graduation, he went to live with his uncle, Alfred W. Pike, a professor at Framingham Academy, who became his tutor.[4]

Albert Pike in Scottish Rite Regalia

It did not take long for his uncle to realize that young Albert was more than an average student, that he possessed a prodigious memory, capable of absolute retention and complete recall. Professor Pike tutored his nephew in Latin, Greek, philosophy, and mathematics. Albert's mind absorbed these subjects in a sponge-like manner. After eight months, his uncle was convinced that he was ready to take the entrance examinations for Harvard University.[5] The promising student found the examinations very easy, but lack of finance became a major obstacle preventing his acceptance at Harvard. His family was poor. His uncle tried unsuccessfully to find someone to finance his higher education. Even an interview with the president of Harvard yielded no results. Pike decided to teach school in order to finance his tuition, while educating himself at night in the freshman and sophomore subjects. He made plans to take the junior entrance examinations and enter as an advanced student. His self-imposed curriculum included English grammar, Roman history, Italian, and Spanish. He took a position in a common school at Gloucester. He saved money to pay for his junior year at Harvard and succeeded in teaching himself in one year all of the knowledge that Harvard would teach in two. He easily passed the junior entrance examinations. Lack of finance, however, persisted as a problem. Harvard's officials told him they would be delighted to have him as a junior but he would still be required to pay the tuition for the two preceding years. He was quite embittered by this demand. Despite his protests, Harvard was not prepared to make any concessions.[6] He was, thus, deprived of the opportunity to earn a formal college degree and he had no more contact with Harvard until 1859. At that time, when his fame as a poet and as a champion of the American Indian was well established, the prestigious New England school conferred upon him an honorary Master of Arts degree.[7]

Embittered by his treatment at Harvard, Pike decided to devote his life to poetry, returning to school teaching as a temporary livelihood until he could support himself as a writer. He obtained a position at a school in Newburyport and devoted much of his spare time to writing. His poetry and essays were published in Boston newspapers and magazines. This brought him local prestige but no financial rewards. His efforts to publish a magazine called *The Scrap Book* were short-lived.[8]

In Newburyport, Pike had regular contact with his mother, although she strongly disapproved of his poetry and his other activities. The Newburyport school board had strict rules, expecting teachers to live chaste lives. He did not seek to hide the fact that he enjoyed drinking wine and indulging in intimacies with members of the opposite sex. Despite his reputation, he was promoted to principal but, shortly afterward, was fired on grounds of "impiety."[9]

Pike had saved money from his teaching. With the loss of his position, he decided to spend it on a western journey instead of pursuing further higher education. On 10 March 1831, accompanied by two friends, he set out for New Mexico.[10] His journey South has been called the beginning of the "literary discovery of the Southwest."[11] A year later, in the autumn of 1832, he was a member of one of the first Anglo-American groups to cross the Llano Estacado of eastern New Mexico.[12] His party then journeyed in a northeastern direction, arriving at Fort Smith, Arkansas on 10 December 1832.[13] He taught school in Fort Smith until October 1833, after which he set out for the Arkansas capital of Little Rock.[14] His first year in Little Rock was spent in the newspaper business. He also became involved in the study of law, memorizing legal concepts with the same ease that he had mastered other subjects while in Massachusetts. In August 1834, he was granted a license by Judge Thomas Lacy of the Superior Court of Arkansas.[15] On 18 November 1834, he married Mary Ann Hamilton.[16] In April 1837, he decided to abandon journalism to devote his full time to the legal profession.[17]

With the outbreak of the Mexican War, Pike served as a captain in the Arkansas Home Guard; in 1842, he participated in the Battle of Buena Vista.[18] In the years immediately following the war, he reached the zenith of his popularity as a poet and orator.[19] With his shoulder-length hair and full beard, he exhibited an impressive public image. Biographer Robert Lipscomb Duncan described him as follows:

> His broad expansive forehead, his serene countenance, and his powerful frame awoke thoughts of some far-off time. The conventional dress of an American citizen did not seem suited to such a splendid personality. The costume of an ancient Greek would have been more in keeping with such a face and figure—such a habit as Plato wore when he discoursed upon divine philosophy to his students among the groves of the Academy at Athens, beneath the brilliant sun of Greece.[20]

During this period Pike became involved in an organization that was destined to play a major role in his life, and on which he was destined to leave his permanent imprint, viz. Freemasonry. In July 1850, he became a Master Mason in Western Star Lodge No. 2 in Little Rock.[21] Later that year, he entered the York Rite of Freemasonry by becoming a Royal Arch Mason on 29 November. In February 1853, he continued his work in the York Rite as a Knight Templar. The following month, he received the degrees of Scottish Rite Masonry, climaxing with the 32nd degree on 20 March.[22] In 1854, he became Worshipful Master of Magnolia Lodge No. 60 in Little Rock. In 1857, he received the 33rd degree of the Scottish Rite. In following year, he became an active member of the Supreme Council, Southern Jurisdiction. In 1859, he was elected to the highest office in Scottish Rite Masonry—Most Puissant Sovereign Grand Commander. He held this office until his death in 1891.[23]

When the Civil War broke out in 1861, Boston-born Pike had been a resident of Little Rock for twenty-eight years. He was faced with a dilemma but soon made the decision to cast his lot with the Confederacy.[24] His knowledge of Indian languages and customs made him invaluable to the South in negotiating treaties with Native Americans. He had earned a position of trust in representing the Creeks, one of the Five Civilized Tribes, in a victorious lawsuit before the war. He was able to use large cash, subsidies and gifts to persuade portions of the Creeks, Chickasaws, Choctaws, Cherokees, and Seminoles to the Confederate cause. He was appointed brigadier general in the Confederate Army on 15 August 1861 and, on 22 November 1861, he was given command of the newly created Department of Indian Territory. Despite his insistence that treaties prohibited the use of Indian troops in offensive warfare, he led a brigade of Indians at the Battle of Pea Ridge in northern Arkansas in early March 1862. Things did not go well for the Confederacy there.[25] Rumors spread about various atrocities committed by the "red men in gray." Much was said about this battle in northern newspapers, with Pike depicted as the perfect villain and Union General Samuel Curtis as the ideal hero. One pamphlet charged that Pike had maddened the Indian troops with liquor and, thus, "led them in a carnage of savagery, scalping wounded and helpless soldiers."[26]

As a result of this battle, Pike's troops were ordered to other commands. Claiming that his command was independent from the others, Pike ignored or circumvented the orders. On 31 July 1862, he resigned his command and published an open letter to the Indians indicting his superiors for ignoring treaty obligations. Confederate President Jefferson Davis refused to accept the resignation and hinted that Pike might be charged with treason. In October, Davis sent two hundred soldiers to arrest him. However, the following month, as the Confederate position in the West collapsed, Pike was released.[27] Worried that he would be arrested and possibly executed by fleeing Confederate forces or killed by Union soldiers determined to avenge the Pea Ridge atrocities, he fled to the hills of Arkansas, spending the rest of the war years in seclusion in the community of Greasy Cove. There, he spent long hours "losing himself once again in ancient mysteries that had no connection with the hostile outside world."[28] When Union troops occupied Little Rock, Col. Thomas H. Benton, Jr. , Grand Master of Masons in Iowa, served as occupation commander. During this time, he placed a guard about Pike's home and, thus, saved Pike's valuable Masonic library from destruction.[29]

At the end of the war, Pike knew he could not expect to be treated like an ordinary Confederate soldier. His vilification in the northern press made this impossible. He had friends in Washington, D. C., however, and they petitioned Attorney General James Speed to arrange a pardon for him.[30] Following the assassination of President Abraham Lincoln, support for Pike's pardon accelerated, with many letters addressed to President Andrew Johnson, asking for executive clemency. Meanwhile, his enemies had sworn an indictment against him in the Circuit Court for the Eastern District of Arkansas, resurrecting an old and previously forgotten statute which read: "Every person who sends any talk, message or letter to any Indian nation, tribe, chief or individual, with an intent to produce a contravention or infraction of any treaty or law of the United States, or to disturb the peace or tranquillity of the United States is liable to a penalty of $2,000."[31]

Pike angrily responded that, at the time he had negotiated with the Indians, the South had already seceded to form a separate republic. As a representative of that republic, he argued, he was outside the jurisdiction of the United States. By this time, a large part of his property had been sold and he seemed liable to lose the rest of it.[32] He wrote to President Johnson, requesting that his books be exempt from confiscation, stating "I need not tell him how dear the books of a scholar are to him, nor why."[33] He swore an oath of allegiance before a district judge in Little Rock. He was allowed to retain most of his books, as it was reasoned that they would bring little money on the open market. In April 1866 he received his pardon; he was summoned to the White House and, in a ceremony attended by high-ranking Scottish Rite Masons, President Johnson pardoned him for his part in the war and restored all of his civil rights.[34]

In December 1865, Pike established a law practice in Memphis, Tennessee. From 1867 to 1868, he served as editor of the *Memphis Appeal*.[35] Late in 1868, unable to earn a living in Memphis, he moved to Washington, D. C., where he practiced law and devoted more time to his work as Grand Commander of Scottish Rite Masons. Gradually, his interest in the practice of law waned and, finally, he abandoned it altogether, devoting all of his time to Masonic work and to research and writing. He rewrote the Scottish Rite degrees, from the 4th to the 33rd, giving a mystical and arcane interpretation to simple Masonic teachings.[36] In 1871, his most famous work, *Morals and Dogma,* was published. In Robinson's evaluation of this book, he expressed the view that Pike had asserted a more complex, esoteric interpretation of the precepts of Freemasonry:

> Some of the critics of Masonry cite the degree work, but more find their raw material for Masonic condemnation in Pike's writings, especially his ponderous *Morals and Dogma,* an 861-page volume that many Masons own, but few have read. It is not only tedious reading, but is full of Pike's own perceptions of Masonry. Many Masons will agree with some statements, but there are others that no Mason will ever believe. Pike was so wrapped up in his knowledge of ancient faiths and philosophic systems that he tended to make the background of Masonry far more complex and esoteric than it was ever meant to be.[37]

In the mid-1870s, unable to afford the expenses of a house, Pike moved into the House of the Temple, the headquarters of the Scottish Rite, Southern Jurisdiction.[38] For the remainder of his life, he devoted much of his time to the "unraveling of the mysteries that so fascinated him." In his large office he spent long hours, producing manuscripts on diverse and obscure subjects which amounted to thousands of pages. Such works included *Translations of the Rig-Veda, the Maruts; Translations of the Rig-Veda, Friends of Indra:*

Svadha: the Purusha Sukta: Savitri: Names of Rishis; Translations of the Rig-Veda, the Devas Generally and of Passages Which Mention the Arya and Dasya; Indo-Aryan Deities and Worship as Contained in the Rig-Veda; Irano-Aryan Faith and Doctrine as Contained in the Zend-Avesta; Lectures of the Arya; and *Vocabularies of Sanskrit Languages.* By 1887, he had become a recluse, walking each day from his quarters to his office and back to his quarters, always with his meerschaum pipe in his mouth.[39]

In the fall of 1889, his health began to deteriorate. He experienced headaches, fevers, gout, boils, rheumatism, neuralgia, and dyspepsia. Only with the utmost agony could he hold a pen to write. His condition worsened during 1890. Finally, he took to his bed and never left it again. Despite visits from numerous physicians, his condition further deteriorated. In February 1891, recognizing that death was near, he called for writing materials and gave instructions as to the handling of his remains. He died at 8:00 p.m. on 2 April 1891. His body lay in state at the House of the Temple, where thousands of people came to view in death a man whose legend was larger than life. His body was moved to the Congregational Church, where the mysterious Rites of Kadosh were conducted at midnight in a room lighted with candles and with the walls draped in black. The next day, a second funeral service was held in the Church of the Ascension according to the liturgy of the Episcopal Church. On 10 April, he was buried in Washington's Oak Hill Cemetery.[40]

Shortly after Pike's death, the Supreme Council commissioned the noted Italian sculptor Gilbert de Trentanove to create an appropriate memorial. The result was a life-size standing statue of the late Grand Commander with a book in his left hand and his right hand extended in token of friendship and brotherly love. At the base of the granite pedestal is a mourning female figure, symbolic of peace. On 4 April 1898, the Congress of the United States authorized the use of government land for its site at Third and D Streets, Northwest. The statue was dedicated by Grand Commander James D. Richardson on 23 October 1901. Later, the construction of a new building for the United States Department of Labor forced its removal and storage. Eventually, however, it was placed in a new location at Judiciary Square on Indiana Avenue, Northwest. On 3 October 1977, the statue was rededicated by Grand Commander Henry C. Clausen.[41] Since 1992, followers of anti-Masonic politician Lyndon LaRouche have demanded removal of the statue on grounds that Pike was a Satanist and leader of the Ku Klux Klan.[42]

Lévi's Influence on Pike's Understanding of Kabbalah in Freemasonry

Albert Pike believed that virtually all Masonic symbolism was derived from Kabbalah — or, at least, that the more profound interpretations of Masonic symbols were those given by Kabbalistic writers. Literary research indicates that his primary sources for his understanding of Kabbalah were the writings of Éliphas Lévi and *Kabbala Denudata* by Christian Knorr von Rosenroth.[43] Pike was convinced that all of the ideas embodied in the Kabbalah originated among the ancient Aryans and were learned by the Jews during the period of Persian rule over Palestine.[44] He argued that the Kabbalah contains only what the Jewish rabbis learned from the Median Magi, including the belief that the Deity, before Creation, was the universally diffused Light.[45] He further insisted that such Kabbalistic doctrines as the sephiroth (emanations) were a reproduction of such Persian concepts as *Amesha Spentas* "transplanted from the Aryan into the Hebrew mind."[46] He saw the Kabbalistic concept of the Ancient of Days as adapted from the Persian Archetype of Light and the Hindu Brahman.[47] Arthur Edward Waite, translator and critic of Éliphas Lévi, contended that Pike's consuming goal was the transformation of the Scottish Rite of Freemasonry into a "seminary of occult study." He charged that, whereas Pike was a well-read person, he quite uncritically accepted *en bloc* Lévi's ideas on Kabbalah.[48] Notwithstanding his reliance on Lévi's ideas, Pike made no mention of Lévi by name in any of his writings. In his "Preface" *Morals and Dogma*, he did, however, make the following acknowledgment:

> In preparing this work, the Grand Commander has been about equally Author and Compiler; since he has extracted quite half of its contents from the works of the best writers and most philosophic or eloquent thinkers. Perhaps it would have been better and more acceptable if he had extracted more and written less.
>
> Still, perhaps half of it is his own; and, in incorporating here the thoughts of others, he has continually changed and added to the language, often intermingling, in the same sentences, his own words and theirs.[49]

Pike's first established borrowing from Lévi appeared early in *Morals and Dogma,* where he spoke of the ornament in the lodge called the Blazing Star, "an emblem of Divine Providence, and commemorative of the star which appeared to guide the wise men of the East to the place of our Saviour's nativity."[50] Pike, furthermore, wrote of four rivers flowing out of the symbolic Garden of Eden, including "Pison, which flows around the land of gold, or light; Gihon, which flows around the land of Ethiopia, or Darkness." This is clearly a statement of Lévi.[51]

Pike expanded his research into the field of ancient classical writers, including Pythagoras, whom Lévi described as "the great divulger of the philosophy of numbers." Pike accepted Lévi's claim that Pythagoras visited Judea, where he was circumcised and, thus became qualified for initiation into Kabbalah by the prophets Ezekiel and Daniel, and was later initiated into the Egyptian Mysteries. Lévi and Pike attributed to Pythagoras the precept that "there is no evil that is not preferable to Anarchy."[52]

Pike also affirmed Lévi's theory of the origin of Kabbalah in the following passage: "The Holy Kabalah, or tradition of the children of Seth, was carried from Chaldaea by Abraham, taught to the Egyptian priesthood by Joseph, recovered and purified by Moses, concealed under symbols in the Bible, revealed by the Saviour to Saint John, and contained, entire, under hieratic figures analogous to those of all antiquity, in the Apocalypse of that Apostle."[53]

The passage which follows, written by Pike, needs to be recorded in full, in that it has been the source of much controversy among anti-Masons for decades. For this reason these passages are important in my evaluation of Pike's dependence on Lévi's writings. Pike wrote:

> The true name of Satan, the Kabalists say, is that of Yahveh reversed; for Satan is not a black god, but the negation of God. The Devil is the personification of Atheism or Idolatry.
>
> For the Initiates, this is not a *Person,* but a Force, created for good, but which *may* serve for evil. *It is the instrument of Liberty or Free Will.* They represent this force which presides over the physical generation, under the mythologic and horned form of the God PAN; thence came the he-goat of the Sabbat, brother of the Ancient Serpent, and the Light — heaven or *Phosphor,* of which the poets have made the false Lucifer of the legend.[54]

There is every indication that Pike also adopted Lévi's approach to animal symbolism.

Thus, he wrote:

> Gold, to the eyes of the Initiates, is Light condensed. They style the sacred numbers of the Kabalah "golden numbers," and the moral teachings of Pythagoras his "golden verses." For the same reason, a mysterious book of Apuleius, in which an ass figures largely, was called "The Golden Ass."
>
> The Pagans accused the Christians of worshiping an ass, and they did not invent this reproach, but it came from the Samaritan Jews, who, figuring the data of the Kabalah in regard to the Divinity by Egyptian symbols, also represented the Intelligence by the figure of the Magical Star adored under the name *of Rempham,* Science under the emblem of Anubis, whose name they changed to *Nibbas,* and the vulgar faith or

credulity under the figure of Thartac, a god represented with a book, a cloak, and the head of an ass. According to the Samaritan Doctors, Christianity was the reign of Thartac, blind faith or credulity erected into a universal oracle, and preferred to Intelligence and Science.[55]

On the same and the following page, Pike affirmed another statement of Lévi:

> The first Druids were the true children of the Magi, and their initiation came from Egypt and Chaldaea, that is to say, from the pure sources of the primitive Kabalah. They adored the Trinity under the name of Isis or *Hesus*, the Supreme Harmony, of *Belen* or *Bel*, which in Assyrian means Lord, a name corresponding to that of ADONAI; and *of Camul* or *Camael*, a name that in the Kabalah personifies the Divine Justice. Below this triangle of Light they supposed a divine reflection, also composed of three personified rays: first, *Tentates* or *Teuth*, the same as the *Thoth* of the Egyptians, the Word, or the Intelligence formulated; then Force and Beauty, whose names varied like their emblems. Finally, they completed the sacred Septenary by a mysterious image that represented the progress of the dogma and its future realizations. This was a young girl veiled, holding a child in her arms; and they dedicated this image to "the Virgin who will become a mother."[56]

On the same page, there is evidence that Pike was influenced by Lévi's understanding of names of God. Thus, he spoke of "one of the mysterious pantacles of the Kabalah" which represents an equilateral triangle reversed, inscribed in a double circle. According to Lévi and Pike, this symbolized the equilibrium of the forces of guiding spirits, the equilibrium of the forces of nature, and the harmony of numbers. He ascribed creation to the Father, redemption or reformation to the Son, and sanctification or transformation to the Holy Spirit. He related these to the mathematic laws of action, reaction, and equilibrium. This was followed by a discussion of the letters of the Tetragrammaton, leading to the conclusion that the divine name "expresses the synthesis of the whole dogma and the totality of the Kabalistic science, clearly indicating by the hieroglyphics of which this admirable name is formed the Triple Secret of the Great Work."[57]

Pike, like Lévi, had much to say about contraries. Thus, he repeated Lévi's words about Kabbalistic symbolism of light (or the sun) as representing the active or masculine principle and darkness (or the moon) as representing the passive or feminine principle. Pike shared Lévi's belief that the two are interdependent "because it is from the bosom of darkness itself that we see the Light born again."[58] After a brief interlude, Pike continued his repetition of Lévi's discussion of the analogy of contraries. Lévi believed such analogy provided "the solution of the most interesting and most difficult problems of modern philosophy." The philosophical problems listed included the relationship between reason and faith, authority and liberty of examination, science and belief, and God's perfection and man's imperfection. The two columns of King Solomon's Temple were seen as symbolic of these contraries. Stress was placed on the importance of these remaining separate and parallel. Pike affirmed Lévi's conviction that "as soon as it is attempted by violence to bring them together, as Samson did, they are overturned, and the whole edifice falls upon the head of the rash blind man or the revolutionist whom personal or national resentments have in advance devoted to death."[59]

In view of the recent resurgence of unfounded claims that Pike was a Satanist, it is interesting to note that Pike borrowed the following passage from Lévi: "Lucifer—*Light-bearer!* Strange and mysterious name to give to the Spirit of Darkness! Lucifer, the Son of the Morning! It is *he* who bears the *Light*, and with its splendors intolerable blinds feeble, sensual, or selfish Souls? Doubt it not! for traditions are full of Divine Revelations and Inspirations."[60]

After a brief comment on the nature of "Divine Inspiration,"[61] Pike returned to Lévi's ideas in a discussion of the Apocalypse as a Kabbalistic book as obscure as the *Zohar*. Pike upheld Levi's position that the Apostle John—"the Depository of all the Secrets of the Saviour"—wrote to appeal not to the multitude but "to the intelligence of the Initiated." He declared, with Levi that the fullness of occultism was embodied in the *Sepher Yetzirah*, the *Zohar*, and the Apocalypse.[62] Later, he made further comments on the Apocalypse when he discussed the closure of the book with seven seals and declared: "In it we find the seven genii of the Ancient Mythologies; and the doctrine concealed under its emblems is the pure Kabala; already lost by the Pharisees at the advent of the Saviour. The pictures that follow in this wondrous epic are so many pantacles, of which the numbers 3, 4, 7, and 12 are the keys." This reference was followed by a discussion of the symbolic meaning of the cherub, or symbolic bull, which Lévi and Pike associated with the sphinx.[63]

In further elaboration on Lévi's view that the church had lost the Kabbalistic keys, Pike wrote: "Among the sacred books of the Christians are two works which the infallible church does not pretend to understand, and never attempts to explain,—the prophecy of Ezekiel and the Apocalypse, two cabalistic clavicules, reserved, no doubt, in Heaven, for the exposition of the Magian Kings; closed with the Seven seals for all faithful believers; and perfectly clear to the unbeliever initiated in the occult sciences.[64] Pike then skipped two paragraphs in Lévi's text and continued as follows: "For Christians, in their opinion, the scientific and magical clavicles of Solomon are lost. Only those things which men cease to understand no longer exist for them, at least as WORD; then they enter into the domain of enigma and mystery."[65] Pike then described the Magi who visited Jesus in His cradle as "the hieratic ambassadors from the three analogical worlds of the occult philosophy." He presented magic and Christianity as "almost taking each other by the hand" in the school of Alexandria and described Emperor Julian the Apostate as "no Pagan, but a Gnostic, infected with the allegories of Grecian polytheism, and whose misfortune it was to find the name of Jesus Christ less sonorous than that of Orpheus."[66] Pike began another quote from Lévi on the same page when he wrote about the "Christianization" of science in Alexandria under Pseudo-Dionysius the Aeropogite. Pike concurred with Lévi that the aspirants to knowledge of that period "sought for the Philosophical Stone, or the squaring of the circle, or the universal medicine." All of these were presented as expressions of "the grand magical secret" found in the High Kabbalah.[67]

In his discussion of Hermetic Philosophy, Pike copied nearly the entire chapter called "The Mastery of the Sun," from Lévi's *Transcendental Magic*. He wrote:

> To find the Absolute in the Infinite, the Indefinite, and in the Finite, this is the Magnum Opus, the Great Work of the Sages, which Hermes called the Work of the Sun. ... . He who desires to attain to the understanding of the Grand Word and the possession of the Great Secret, ought carefully to read the Hermetic philosophers, and will undoubtedly attain initiation, as others have done; but he must take, for the key of their allegories, the single dogma of Hermes, contained in his tablet of Emerald, and follow, to class his acquisitions of knowledge and direct the operation, the order indicated in the Kabalistic alphabet of the Tarot.[68]

This chapter contains a detailed discussion of the alchemical process, whose goal is the creation of "the living gold, the living sulphurs, or the true fire of the philosophers," which can be found only in "the house of Mercury." According to Lévi and Pike, mercury was personified by Hermanubis, with the head of a dog; while sulphur was personified by "the Baphomet of the Temple," with the head of a goat.[69]

In further discussion of alchemy, Pike wrote:

> The double triangle of Solomon is explained by Saint John in a remarkable manner: there are, he says, three witnesses in Heaven, — the Father, the Word, and the Holy Spirit; and three witnesses on earth, — the breath, water, and blood. He thus agrees with the Masters of the Hermetic Philosophy, who give to their Sulphur the name of Ether, to their

Mercury the name of philosophical water, to their Salt that of blood of the dragon, or menstruum of the earth. The blood, or Salt, corresponds by opposition with the Father, the Azothic, or Mercurial water, with the Word, or Logos; and the breath, with the Holy Spirit. But the things of High Symbolism can be well understood only by the true children of Science.[70]

In his discussion of the Knights Templar (also known as the Templars), Pike utilized a great deal of Lévi's chapter "Some Famous Persecutions." This chapter includes an evaluation of different types of government, along with the claim that republics tend to become tyrannies "in the absence of all duty hierarchically sanctioned and enforced." The focus is on the idea of an initiatory society which would be the sole depository of all religious and social secrets and would, thus, have the power to create religious and secular rulers. According to Lévi and Pike, this idea was prominent among "the great religious orders so often at war with the secular authorities" and among the Gnostics and Illuminati. Such a claim was preparatory to a discussion of the Templars as an order of monks initiated into the mysteries of Kabbalah who became a menace to both church and state. Openly, the Templars claimed to protect pilgrims en route to Christian holy places; secretly, their aim was to re-build the Temple of Solomon, as prophesied by Ezekiel. Despite his strong anti-Catholicism, Pike apparently was not bothered by Lévi's vision of "the Temple of Solomon rebuilt and consecrated to Catholic worship." Perhaps Pike longed for the loss of power by Rome when, according to Lévi, "the East would prevail over the West, and the Patriarchs of Constantinople would possess themselves of the Papal power."[71]

After skipping one paragraph, Pike returned to Lévi's text, as follows: "The Templars, or *Poor Fellow-Soldiers of the Holy House of the Temple*, intended to be re-built, took as their models in the Bible, the Warrior-Masons of Zorobabel, who worked, holding the sword in one hand and the trowel in the other. Therefore it was that the Sword and the Trowel were the insignia of the Templars, who subsequently, as will be seen, concealed themselves under the name of *Brethren Masons*."[72] Pike deviated from the text to explain the derivation of "Freemasons" and related terms and then returned to his quote from Lévi: "The trowel of the Templars is quadruple, and the triangular plates of it are arranged in the form of a cross, making the Kabalistic pantacle known by the name of the Cross of the East."[73] After skipping a paragraph, Pike moved to the next page of Lévi's book and wrote:

> The Johannites ascribed to Saint John the foundation of their Secret Church, and the Grand Pontiffs of the Sect assumed the title of *Christos, Anointed,* or *Consecrated,* and claimed to have succeeded one another from Saint John by an uninterrupted succession of pontifical powers.

He who, at the period of the foundation of the Order of the Temple, claimed these imaginary prerogatives, was named THEOCLETE; he knew HUGUES DE PAYENS, he initiated him into the Mysteries and hopes of his pretended church, he seduced him by the notions of Sovereign Priesthood and Supreme royalty, and finally designated him as his successor.[74]

Albert Pike

At this point, Pike sought to amplify Lévi's statements when he declared that the Templars were, from their beginning, opposed to both king and pope. He described the Templars as a Gnostic Order and the Apostle John as the "Father of the Gnostics." He insisted that they presented an orthodox doctrine to the public while concealing their true, esoteric teachings from all but their highest officials.[75] Pike then returned to a direct quote from Lévi in regard to the aim of the Templars to use wealth and influence in order "to establish the Johannite or Gnostic and Kabalistic dogma" and, thus, to "constitute the equilibrium of the Universe" and rule the world.[76] This is one example of how Pike not only quoted extensively from Lévi but also engaged in elaboration of Lévi's ideas.

Pike adopted Lévi's interpretation of Rosicrucian symbolism and extracted a lengthy passage related to the Italian poet Alighieri Dante. Lévi and Pike described Dante's *Divine Comedy* as "Johannite and Gnostic, an audacious application, like that of the Apocalypse, of the figures of the Kabalah to the Christian dogmas, and a secret negation of every thing absolute in these dogmas." Dante's reversal of head and feet is interpreted as acceptance of "the direct opposite of the Catholic dogma." Dante's ascent to the light with the devil as his ladder is compared to a similar ascent by Faust. Lévi and Pike conclude that human beings are freed from the bondage of hell by their audacity. Dante's hell is called "but a negative Purgatory." Dante's heaven is compared to the Pentacle of Ezekiel. The blooming of the rose amid the cross is interpreted as public exposure of Rosicrucian symbolism. Dante's *Divine Comedy* and Guillame de Lorris' *Romance of the Rose* are described as "two opposite forms of one and the same work." Mutual themes cited include independence of spirit, satirical treatment of contemporary institutions, and the allegorical formula of Rosicrucian secrets. Lévi impressed Pike by the emphasis he placed on the fact that both works coincided with the period of the fall of the Templars.[77]

Pike then moved thirty pages forward in Lévi's text when he declared that "Swedenborg's system was nothing else than the Kabalah minus the principle of the Hierarchy. It is the Temple, without the keystone and the foundation."[78] He continued his forward move with his very next statement: "Cagliosto was the Agent of the Templars, and therefore wrote to the Free-Masons of London that the time had come to begin the work of re-building the Temple of the Eternal. He had introduced into Masonry a new Rite called the *Egyptian,* and endeavored to resuscitate the mysterious worship of Isis."[79] Pike then turned to the following page of Lévi's text and continued: "The three letters L.. . P.. . D.. . on his seal, were the initials of the words '*Lilia pedibus desture,*' read underfoot the Lilies <of France>, and a Masonic medal of the sixteenth or seventeenth century has upon it a sword cutting off the stalk of a lily, and the words '*talem dalir ultio messem,*' such harvest revenge will give."[80] "The remainder of this chapter of *Morals and Dogma*[81] was extracted from Lévi's chapter "The French Revolution" in *The History of Magic.* Although Pike did not use the entire chapter, he used much of it in these last two paragraphs, stating:

> A Lodge inaugurated under the auspices of Rousseau, the fanatic of Geneva, became the centre of the revolutionaiy movement in France, and a Prince of the blood-royal went thither to swear the destruction of the successors of Philippe le Bel on the tomb of Jacques de Molai. The registers of the Order of Templars attest that the Regent the Duc d'Orleans was Grand Master of that formidable Secret Society, and that his successors were Duc de Maine, the Prince of Bourbon-Condé, and the Due de Cossé-Brissac.

The Templars compromised the King; they saved him from the rage of the People, to exasperate that rage and bring on the catastrophe prepared for centuries; it was a scaffold that the vengeance of the Templars demanded.[82]

Pike concluded this chapter with further excerpts from Lévi:

> The secret movers of the French Revolution had sworn to overturn the Throne and the Altar upon the Tomb of Jacques de Molai. When Louis XVI was executed, half the work was done and thenceforward the Army of the Temple was to direct all its efforts against the Pope.
>
> Jacques de Molai and his companions were perhaps martyrs, but their avengers dishonored their memory. Royalty was regenerated on the scaffold of Louis XVI. The Church triumphed in the captivity of Pius VI, carried a prisoner to Valence, and dying of fatigue and sorrow, but the successors of the Ancient Knights perished, overwhelmed in their fatal victory.[83]

Pike's next excerpt from Lévi came from the "Introduction" to *The History of Magic*. Here, Pike echoed Lévi's words: "Magic is the science of the Ancient Magi: and the Christian religion, which has imposed silence on the lying oracles, and put an end to the prestiges of the false Gods, itself reveres those Magi who came from the East, guided by a Star, to adore the Saviour of the world in His cradle."[84]

Pike's last excerpt from Lévi appeared in the final chapter.[85] Here, Pike wrote:

> The orthodox traditions were carried from Chaldea by Abraham. They reigned in Egypt in the time of Joseph, together with the knowledge of the True God. Moses carried Orthodoxy out of Egypt and in the Secret Traditions of that Kabalah we find a Theology entire, perfect, unique, like that which in Christianity is most grand and best explained by the Fathers and the Doctors, the whole with a consistency and a harmoniousness which it is not as yet given to the world to comprehend. The Sohar, which is the key of the Holy Books, opens also all the depths and lights, all the obscurities of the Ancient Mythologies and of the Sciences originally concealed in the Sanctuaries. It is true that the Secret of this Key must be known, to enable one to make use of it, and that for even the most penetrating intellects, not initiated in this Secret, the Sohar is absolutely incomprehensible and almost illegible.[86]

Research indicates that there is ample evidence that Albert Pike, in writing *Morals and Dogma*, made extensive use of materials from the original French editions of Éliphas Lévi's *History of Magic* and *Transcendental Magic*. There is no evidence that Pike ever met Lévi or that he had his permission to utilize these texts. Pike never mentioned Lévi by name. Such an action today would be called plagiarism. However, there was less opposition to such during the nineteenth century. Evidence indicates that Albert Pike was the primary agent for the transmission of Éliphas Lévi's ideas in nineteenth-century America.

Pike's Importance to the Contemporary Scene

Albert Pike left a permanent imprint on American history in general and on American Masonic history in particular. To a large extent, perceptions of Freemasonry, for good or ill, have been shaped by what he said or was accused of saying. Through his *Morals and Dogma*, the ideas of Éliphas Lévi reached a wider audience in America than the French magus ever envisioned. To many Caucasian Freemasons, especially those of the Scottish Rite, Southern Jurisdiction, Albert Pike was a saint. Since his death in 1891, numerous articles in Masonic books and journals have been full of his accolades. Until recent years, it was unusual to find any word of criticism of him in white Masonic publications. However, the current generation of Masonic scholars seems to take a more critical and evaluative approach, in which limitations in Pike's thought are acknowledged. Research leads to the conclusion that Pike brought together much of the best of eighteenth and nineteenth-century scholarship in his writings on Freemasonry. Much of this has now been supplanted by developments in twentieth-century scholarship. Dr. Rex Hutchens, a great admirer of Pike, is candid about this fact. Hutchens' writings are highly praiseworthy of Pike's wisdom but are accompanied by his words of critical analysis of what he considered to be error. For example, Hutchens pointed out deficiencies in Pike's understanding of the life of Buddha:

> Pike's assertion that he wandered across the Asian steppes, became identified by the Scandanavians as Odin, and then founded the Druids is probably the most ridiculous claim made in *Morals and Dogma*. In fairness to Pike, however, we should note that he did not invent this nonsense, it having a more or less general circulation in the eighteenth century; see especially the writings of William Stukely, Godfrey Higgins, and Thomas Maurice.. For example, the phrase"... for Buddha or Bodh was represented to have been crucified" (p. 505) betrays the influence of Godfrey Higgins' *Anacalypsis* on *Morals and Dogma*. In the original we find: "Buddha is said <by whom?> to have been crucified

for robbing a garden of a flower" (vol. 2, p. 244). Higgins later explains "robbing" as a metaphor for the acquisition of knowledge, as in the *Garden of Eden* (vol. 2, p. 249). Pike's claim that Buddha lived "about a thousand years before the Christian era" is an obvious error.[87]

Today, most Masons who have studied Pike acknowledge that, while he was an intellectual giant, he was far from perfect. Whereas this may now be acknowledged by white Masons, this has for long been the understanding of Pike by members of the predominately black Prince Hall Masonic fraternity.[88] In 1875, Pike reportedly acknowledged the legitimacy of Prince Hall Freemasonry but declared that "I took my obligations to white men, not to negroes. When I have to accept negroes as brothers or leave Masonry, I shall leave it." In response to this statement, Prince Hall Masons in Louisiana denounced "the animosity which burned in the breast of this traitor to his country against a wronged and injured people, whom he and his sympathizers would have doomed to unending, unrequited servitude."[89] There can be no doubt that Pike, like most men of his day, was a believer in "white supremacy." He is reported, however, to have given copies of *Morals and Dogma* and a number of other writings on Scottish Rite Masonry to Thornton A. Jackson, Grand Commander of the Scottish Rite, Southern Jurisdiction (Prince Hall Affiliated). This being the case, it indicates that he had no objection to black Masons existing as a separate organization, as long as they were not integrated with white Masons.[90]

The enemies of Freemasonry in the nineteenth- and twentieth-centuries have made extensive use of the writings of Albert Pike. They have often given the impression that Pike spoke for all Freemasons, then and now. This was never the case. Pike was never a Grand Master of any Grand Lodge, let alone of all Grand Lodges. As Grand Commander of the Scottish Rite, Southern Jurisdiction, he held authority over only one of many Supreme Councils. He never sought to speak for all members of the Southern Jurisdiction, much less for all Masons. In his "Preface" to *Morals and Dogma,* he expressed his support for liberty in religious thought:

> The teachings of these Readings are not sacramental, so far as they go beyond the realm of Morality into those of other domains of Thought and Truth. The Ancient and Accepted Scottish Rite uses the word "Dogma" in its true sense of doctrine, or *teaching;* and is not *dogmatic* in the odious sense of that term. Every one is entirely free to reject or dissent from whatsoever herein may seem to him to be untrue or unsound. It is only required of him that he shall weigh what is taught, and give it fair hearing and unprejudiced judgment.[91]

Morals and Dogma was basically the expression of Pike's personal opinions and was never meant to be absolutely binding on all Scottish Rite Masons. This book is replete with quotations from the Bible and evidence indicates that Pike desired to direct people to the Bible rather than away from it.[92] An essay on Jesus is found on pages 718-21 with pro-Christian sentiments expressed.[93]

Anti-Masons have often sought to link Freemasonry with Satanism. Invariably, when they make this effort, the name of Albert Pike appears. Responsibility for the claim that Pike was a Satanist lies with Gabriel Jogang Pages, who was born in the south of France in 1854 and later adopted the pen name of Leo Taxil. Early in his career, Taxil sought to fan the flames of anti-Catholicism which swept over Europe after the dogma of Papal Infallibility was decreed by the First Vatican Council in 1870.[94] It appears that, after the period of Catholic-baiting ran its course, he sought to capitalize on the rising anti-Masonic hysteria. Thus, he went through the motions of penance and was "reconciled" to the Catholic Church. He then wrote a number of anti-Masonic books and pamphlets. He fabricated a story of an international Masonic conspiracy led by Pike. He presented an incredible forgery in the form of a speech and written order allegedly delivered by Pike to French Freemasons for Bastille Day on 14 July 1889.[95] He claimed that, in this speech, Pike declared:

> That which we must say to the world is that we worship a god, but it is the god that one adores without superstition. To you, Sovereign Grand Inspectors General, we say this, that you may repeat it to the brethren of the 32nd, 31st and 30th degrees: The Masonic Religion should be, by all of us initiates of the higher degrees, maintained in the Purity of the Luciferian doctrine. If Lucifer were not God, would Adonay and his priests caluminate him?
>
> Yes, Lucifer is God, and unfortunately Adonay is also god. For the eternal law is that there is no light without shade, no beauty without ugliness, no white without black, for the absolute can only exist as two gods; darkness being necessary for light to serve as its foil as the pedestal is necessary to the statue, and the brake to the locomotive.
>
> Thus the doctrine of Satanism is a heresy, and the true and pure philosophical religion is the belief in Lucifer, the equal of Adonay; but Lucifer, God of Light and God of Good, is struggling for humanity against Adonay, the God of Darkness and Evil.[96]

Taxil presented this obvious political statement inspired by his own vested interests in 1894—three years after Pike's death. He back-dated it to

1889 and forged the signature of "Albert Pike, Sovereign Pontiff of Universal Freemasonry."[97] His influence in Catholic circles became widespread and he was given a personal audience with Pope Leo XIII. However, on 19 April 1897, he acknowledged his fraud before a large crowd in Paris. Having obtained financial security, he lived in retirement at his stately country home until his death in 1907.[98]

Pike's "Lucifer Statement" has been repeatedly revealed as a forgery. Despite this fact it has been quoted extensively by the enemies of Freemasonry in their efforts to prove their claim of a link between Masonry and Satanism.[99] Such is the case with the followers of Lyndon LaRouche, who also have made much of the claim that Pike was involved with the Ku Klux Klan, in their efforts to remove his statue. Their earlier efforts were inspired by the article "The Ku Klux Klan and Regular Freemasonry" by Joseph A. Walkes, Jr.[100] Since then, a number of demonstrations have been held by LaRouche's followers at the statue site, demanding removal. Resolutions have been presented to city councils in Washington, D. C. and other cities in support of the removal. In response, the Supreme Council for the Southern Jurisdiction (Caucasian) developed an Official Position Paper entitled "Should the Statue of Albert Pike Be Removed?" In this paper, Scottish Rite leaders stated that, notwithstanding certain racist statements made by Pike, in keeping with his time, it was improbable that Pike had been involved with the Ku Klux Klan.[101] Books which made a connection between Pike and the Klan were declared to be based on secondary sources and, therefore, unreliable.[102]

One book not cited by the Supreme Council was Carl A. Raschke's *Painted Black*. This work associates Pike directly and Lévi indirectly with the Klan. Raschke described Pike as "one of the original architects of the Ku Klux Klan" and Lévi's "most notable apostle in America." He attributed the white robes, cross burnings, conical hats, and such titles as "grand dragon" and "imperial wizard" to "the strange lore developed by Lévi."[103] Raschke gave no hint as to his sources for this information in his book. I have found no evidence to support such a claim or the idea that Lévi embraced anything resembling "white supremacy." In his commentary on the Tarot Trump called the Empress, Lévi wrote: "Discern the Father Spirit and Mother Spirit, and recognize the sex aspect of the two breaths, and the soul of their movements; learn how the black female seeks the caresses of the white male, and why the white male does not disdain the dark woman. The white man is Day, or the Sun; the black woman refers to Night, and the Moon."[104]

The movement of LaRouche's followers to remove Pike's statue has given birth to a counter-movement involving Freemasons, black as well as white. White Scottish Rite Masons, in the above Position Paper, acknowledged Pike's racism but not his Klan membership. They concluded:

To impose the 1990s concept of racial relations upon the concept of racial relations prevalent in 1865-1871 shows a lack of historical perspective. If we condemn Albert Pike and demand removal of his statue because he *may* have been a member of the Ku Klux Klan, when do we condemn and remove the statues of George Washington, Thomas Jefferson, and many other Americans who are known to have owned slaves?

Albert Pike was a great man, a Renaissance man of his time, a man who lived in the South in an era now faded into history. His statue was erected in Washington, D. C., over 90 years ago because of his many accomplishments as a teacher, poet, editor, lawyer, philosopher, philanthropist, author, and fraternalist. He was not being honored for his service on behalf of the Confederacy, but in spite of it, and he had been pardoned by the president of the United States for his service and actions as a Confederate general. He spoke his mind freely, and what he said those days voiced the general opinion of most persons of that bygone era. It is certain from his writings and actions that if Pike were alive in today's society, he would neither think or write as persons did then. This is a new era in which the antagonisms of old are healing.[105]

Joseph A. Walkes, Jr., the most prolific Prince Hall Masonic writer of all time, was early drawn into the statue controversy, with LaRouche's followers making extensive use of his writings. He received telephone calls from all over the United States, was interviewed by radio and newspaper reporters, and was contacted by Masonic historians, requesting his views on Albert Pike and the statue controversy. Despite his many writings critical of Pike, Walkes eventually realized that, if the statue comes down, Masonry as a whole will suffer and Prince Hall Masons have nothing to gain. Thus, he wrote: "My love for Freemasonry outweighs all other considerations. I would rather the statue remain in place than harm the gentle craft. I have labored for more than twenty years to bring American Freemasonry together and have each other respect the two systems, Caucasian and Prince Hall. If the removal of the statue would in any way harm Freemasonry, then I say let it stay in place."[106] Another very influential Prince Hall Mason, Howard L. Woods, Past Grand Master of Prince Hall Masons in Arkansas, declared:

There is no love lost between Prince Hall Masons and the memory of Albert Pike, Masonic Historian, writer, alleged ritualist for the Ku Klux Klan, but, if Freemasonry is to remain the bulwark of free-thinking people, then, "Let the statue remain!"

Like the natures he wrote about, Albert Pike showed the light and dark sides of his own soul, when with one breath he spoke of his willingness to give up his Freemasonry rather than recognize the Negro as a "Masonic Brother" and with another breath, declared that every man should be free, for a free man is an asset, while a slave is a liability. Mankind is that way, and as long as the statue stands, America and Freemasonry will survive.

Let the statue be torn down and America and Freemasonry will be in jeopardy, for one would have to wonder, "What would be next?" As a Prince Hall Mason, an African American, and supposedly free-thinker, I can see a higher power than the mortal mind of Albert Pike guiding his pen as he wrote such beautiful words of life without an occasional helping hand from someone "bigger than you or I."

Let the statue stand, even if it is proven that Albert Pike did write the ritual for the Ku Klux Klan; more ignoble deeds have been done by others without sacrifice of their historic heroism.

Let the statue stand as a reminder that the good and evil of men are in equilibrium within us, and we all should strive for perfection now and in the future, not in the past. Let the statue stand![107]

Summation

While Carl A. Raschke overstated the case when he called Albert Pike an "apostle" of Éliphas Lévi, Pike was certainly the primary agent for transmission of Lévi's ideas in nineteenth-century America. Pike's influence on Freemasonry was profound. This applies not only to white Masons, but also to their black counterparts. The latter have always recognized his writings as being Masonically authoritative, notwithstanding their denunciation of his racism. For over a hundred years, he has been a primary target for the enemies of Freemasonry. Today, a major division between Masons and anti-Masons can be recognized as the two take their stands on the issue of the Pike statue. This in itself reflects the influence that Lévi, through Pike, has had on American religious thinking. Although Lévi was not the only influence on Pike's thinking, he was one of the primary influences. This is obvious when one takes into account Pike's extensive use of Lévi's writings.[108] An authentic understanding of Pike's thought and its influence in America necessitates an adequate understanding of Lévi.[109] Current controversies surrounding Freemasonry and other movements demonstrate the importance of both Pike and Lévi to the contemporary scene. I must conclude that

Lévi's Kabbalistic thought has largely been introduced to the American scene through the writings of Albert Pike.

Endnotes

1. Raschke, *Painted Black*, 37.
2. John J. Robinson, *A Pilgrim's Path: Freemasonry and the Religious Right* (New York: M. Evans and Company, 1993), 41. Robinson was highly esteemed among Masons and praised for contributing more to Masonry during the last few years of his life than most Masons contribute during a lifetime. His first book, *Born in Blood: The Lost Secrets of Freemasonry*, appeared in 1989. The sequel, *Dungeon, Fire and Sword: The Knights Templar in the Crusades*, was published two years later. He completed the manuscript for his last book, *A Pilgrim's Path*, in 1992. Ironically, he was not a Mason at the time. His value as a non-Masonic defender of the fraternity delayed his application for membership. He received his first degree in the fall of 1992. Complications of cancer prevented his return to the lodge. Ohio Grand Master Ray Evans conferred the remaining degrees in the hospital. Likewise, he received the 33rd degree from Scottish Rite Grand Commander Robert Ralston in the hospital on 3 September 1993—only three days before his death; see Pete Normand, "Memoriam, John J. Robinson, 1925-1993," *American Masonic Review* 3 (Winter 1993): 12.
3. Robert Lipscomb Duncan, *Reluctant General: The Lift and Times of Albert Pike* (New York: E. P. Dutton and Company, 1961), 14.
4. Ibid., 15.
5. Ibid, 15-16.
6. lbid., 17-18.
7. Ibid., 19.
8. Thjd., 19-20.
9. Ibid., 20-21.
10. Ibid., 20-21.
11. Richard W. Thorne, "Albert Pike Memorial Address," *The New Age* 82 (January 1974):5.
12. Ibjd
13. Duncan, *Reluctant General*, 50.
14. Ibid., 66.
15. Ibid., 83-84. *The New Age* was first published by the Supreme Council of the Southern Jurisdiciton of the Scottish Rite of Freemasonry in 1903 as a continuation of *The Bulletin*, a newsletter launched by Pike during his tenure as Grand Commander. *The New Age* was last published under that name in December 1989. During the following month, the name was changed to *The Scottish Rite Journal*. According to the former editor, the 1903 name was

Lévi in America: Albert Pike

adopted for the following reason: "Coming close to the turn of the century, the exact wording of the title was, no doubt, selected to indicate the start of a new and prosperous era for Scottish Rite Masonry in America—which it was." In 1990, the name was changed as a result of unwanted associations with the New Age Movement in the mind of the general public; see John W. Boettjer, "What's In a Name?" *The Scottish Rite Journal* 1 (January 1990): 16.

16. Ibid., 78. Ten children were born to this union, but only three of them outlived both parents. In 1857, Albert and Mary Ann Pike separated. Mary Ann eventually went insane. She died on 14 April 1876. Their daughter Lillian lived with her father and cared for him during his last years; see ibid., 134-35.

17. Ibid., 89.
18. Thorne, "Albert Pike Memorial Address," 5.
19. Duncan, *Reluctant General*, 132.
20. Ibid.
21. Ibid., 144.
22. John W. Donaldson, "Illustrious Albert Pike," *The New Age* 84 (January 1976): 43. Duncan, *Reluctant General*, 144-45.
24. Thorne, "Albert Pike Memoiral Address," 5.
25. Stewart Sifakis, *Who Was Who in the Civil War* (New York: Facts on File Publishers, 1988), 507.
26. Duncan, *Reluctant General*, 256-57. On 15 March 1862, the *Boston Evening Transcript* called its native son "the meanest, the most rascally, the most malevolent of the rebels" and declared that "it is not presumed that a more venomous reptile than Albert Pike ever crawled the face of the earth"; see Mark C. Cames, *Secret Ritual and Manhood in Victorian America* (New Haven, Conn.: Yale University Press, 1989), 136.
27. Ibid., 136-37. It was an "ironic twist of history" that a portion of the Confederate Cherokees originally under Pike's command were the last Confederates to lay down their arms. Their surrender occurred on 23 June 1865 at Doaksville, Choctaw Nation—over six weeks after General Robert E. Lee's surrender at Appomatox Courthouse; see "Michael A. Boteiho, "Albert Pike and the Confederate Indians," in *Heredom* 2 (1993): 52.
28. Duncan, *Reluctant General*, 256-57.
29. Allen E. Roberts, *House Undivided: The Story of Freemasonry and the Civil War* (Richmond, Va.: Macoy Publishing and Masonic Supply Company, Inc., 1990), 45. This act has often been cited by Masonic historians as one of the great examples of the practice of the Masonic principle of brotherly love amid the horrors of Civil War.
30. Duncan, *Reluctant General*, 262-63.
31. Ibid., 264.
32. Ibid., 264-65.
33. Ibid., 266.

34. Ibid., 266-67. President Johnson was a Freemason. Later, Pike returned to the White House and conferred upon him the Scottish Rite degrees.

35. Ibid., 267. During this period, there arose rumors of Pike's involvement with the Ku Klux Klan.

36. Robinson, *A Pilgrim's Path*, 44.

37. Ibid. Robinson regarded Pike's researches as precursors to master's and doctoral programs in comparative religion; see ibid., 43.

38. Duncan, *Reluctant General*, 270.

39. Ibid., 270-72.

40. Ibid., 272-73. The Rites of Kadosh are related to the 30th degree of the Scottish Rite. Later, Pike's body was exhumed and reinterred at the House of the Temple.

41. "Grand Commander Clausen Rededicates Pike Statue," *The New Age* 86 (March 1978): 33-34.

42. Joseph A. Walkes, Jr., "A Word from the President," *The Phylaxis* 18 (Fourth Quarter 1992): 2-3.

43. Rex R. Hutchens, *A Glossary to Morals and Dogma* (Washington, D. C.: House of the Temple, 1993), 247. During Pike's lifetime, there were no English translations of Lévi's French writings or of Rosenroth's Latin work extant. However, such proved no barrier to Pike, who was adept at learning languages.

44. Albert Pike, *Irano-Aryan Faith and Doctrine as Contained in the Zend-Avesta* (Washington, D. C.: House of the Temple, 1924), 265. The holy book of Zoroastrianism is called the "Avesta." "Zend-Avesta" literally means "Commentary on the Avesta." Thus was this Scripture improperly called by the French Orientalist Anquetil-Duperron, whose usage Pike copied; see Rex R. Hutchens and Donald W. Monson, *The Bible in Albert Pike's Morals and Dogma* (Washington, D. C.: House of the Temple, 1992), 255.

45. Albert Pike, *Lectures of the Arya* (Washington, D. C.: House of the Temple, 1930), 97-98.

46. Pike, *Irano-Aryan Faith and Doctrine*, 349. Pike declared that no study had ever interested him so much as that of the ancient Aryans whom he described as "White men . . . the superior race in intellect, in manliness, the governing race of the world, the conquering race of all other races." Pike insisted that "We owe not one single truth, not one idea in philosophy or religion to the Semitic race"; see Pike, *Lectures of the Arya*, 1-2. He believed that Aryan civilization originated in the Scythian Steppes and saw the doctrines of Plato and Philo as growing out of the "primitive simplicity of a natural and reasonable religion" which characterized the Aryan faith; see Pike, *Indo-Aryan Deities and Worship, as Contained in the Rig-Veda* (Washington, D. C.: House of the Temple, 98. The theory of the "Aryan invasion of India," which was commonly accepted in Pike's day, is rejected by many modern scholars; see Robert L. Uzzel, "Albert Pike's Vedic Studies: A Critical

Analysis," *Hautes Grades: The Transactions of the Scottish Rite Research Institute* (PHA) II (2002): 6-23.

47. Pike, *Irano-Aryan Faith and Doctrine*, 127. Pike understood the Persians and Hindus as descended from two branches of the Aryan race. Thus, he wrote: "The advance of the southwest of one branch, and that to the southeast of the other; of the Irano-Aryans by Bactria, Parthia and Media towards the Persian Gulf, and of the Indo-Aryans across the Hindu Kush and by Kabul to the Indus country on its way to the region of the Ganges and the Indian Ocean"; see Pike, *Lectures of the Arya*, 5.

48. Arthur Edward Waite, *The Holy Kabbalah: A Study of the Secret Tradition in Israel as Unfolded by Sons of the Doctrine for the Benefit and Consolation of the Elect Dispersed Through the Lands and Ages of the Greater Exile* (New Hyde Park, New York: University Books, 1960), 552-53. Waite also charged that Pike had no analytical knowledge of *Kabbalah Denudata*.

49. Albert Pike, *Morals and dogma of the Ancient and Accepted Site of Freemasonry* (Washington, D. C.: House of the Temple, 1969), iii-iv. Both Lévi and Rosenroth were among these "best writers." Another was Godfrey Higgins, author of *Anacalypsis* and *The Celtic Druids*, from which Pike also borrowed extensively and without acknowledgment; see Hutchens, *A Glossary to Morals and Dogma*, 527. In my efforts to explore the Lévi-Pike connection, I am greatly indebted to the research of Hutchens, whose books make many cross-references between *Morals and Dogma* and the writings of Lévi.

50. Pike, *Morals and Dogma*, 14; his source was Lévi, *The History of Magic*, 29.

51. Pike, *Morals and Dogma, 58*; his source was Lévi, *Transcendental Magic*, 273. Lévi stated that there were four rivers but did not name them and de-scribed only two. Pike named and described all four. He made a similar reference to the rivers Pison and Gihon in a later passage; see Pike, *Morals and Dogma*, 76; his source was Lévi, *Transcendental Magic*, 273.

52. Ibid., 96-97; his source was Lévi, *The History of Magic*, 92.

53. Ibid., 97; his source was Lévi, *The History of Magic*, 98.

54. Ibid., 102; his source was Lévi, *The History of Magic*, 161.

55. Ibid., 102-03; his source was Lévi, *The History of Magic*, 168.

56. Ibid., 103-04; his source was Lévi, *The History of Magic*, 183-84.

57. Ibid., 104; his source was Lévi, *The History of Magic*, 196-97.

58. Ibid 305-06; his source was Lévi, *The History of Magic*, 46. At this point, Pike broke with the text and wrote about "justice and mercy," instead of repeating Lévi's discussion of the "mysteries of sexual love." In the next paragraph, Pike returned to Lévi.

59. Ibid., 306; his source was Lévi, *The History of Magic*, 47. In this passage, Pike spoke of faith as "the veiled Isis." This reference was not contained in Lévi's text.

60. Ibid., 321; his source was Lévi, *The History of Magic,* 236. In a previously quoted passage, Pike spoke of "the false Lucifer of the legend"; see ibid., 102, derived from Lévi, *The History of Magic,* 161. It appears that both writers were well aware that "Lucifer" is not an appropriate name for Satan. In doing his research for *A Pilgrim's Path,* Robinson was surprised to learn the incorrect nature of the King James Version's translation of Isaiah 14:12 as "How art thou fallen from heaven, 0 Lucifer, son of the morning! How art thou cut down to the ground, which didst weaken the nations!" The original Hebrew text referred not to a fallen angel at all but, rather, to a fallen Babylonian king. "Lucifer" is a Latin word probably inserted in the Hebrew text by a scribe. In the New English Bible, Isaiah 14:12 reads "How art thou fallen from heaven, bright morning star." According to Robinson, when Pike, over a century ago, spoke about the "Luciferian path" or the "energies of Lucifer," he was referring to "the morning star, the light bearer, the search for light; the very antithesis of dark, satanic evil"; see Robinson, *A Pilgrim's Path,* 47-50. Probably the first of the Church Fathers to regard "Lucifer" as a reference to Satan was Jerome; see Hutchens and Monson, *The Bible in Albert Pike's Morals and Dogma,* 102. By the time of John Milton's *Paradise Lost,* the connection was so strong that many believed it to be Scriptural in origin; see Hutchens, *A Glossary to Morals and Dogma,* 269.

61. Pike, *Morals and Dogma,* 321. He wrote that "Inspiration is not of one Age nor of one Creed. Plato and Philo also were inspired."

62. Ibid.; his source was Lévi, *The History of Magic,* 61.

63. Pike, *Morals and Dogma,* 727-28; his source was Lévi, *Transcendental Magic,* 81-82. Pike deleted Lévi's reference to "the Cups and Swords of the Tarot" among the emblems under which the doctrine was concealed.

64. lbid., 731; his source was Lévi, *Transcendental Magic,* 3.

65. Ibid., 731; his source was Lévi, *Transcendental Magic,* 4-5. Pike omitted the following words of Levi: "Furthermore, the antipathy and even open war of the Official Church against all that belongs to the realm of Magic, which is a kind of personal and emancipated priesthood, is allied with necessary and even with inherent causes in the social and hierarchic constitution of Christian sacerdotalism. The Church ignores Magic—for she must either ignore it or perish, as we shall prove later on."

66. Ibid., 73 1-32; his source was Lévi, *Transcendental Magic,* 5-6.

67. Ibid., 732-33; his source was Lévi, *Transcendental Magic,* 17-18.

68. Ibid., 776-77; his source was Lévi, *Transcendental Magic,* 355-56. This passage demonstrates that Pike accepted, without question, the connection Lévi made between Kabbalah and Tarot.

69. Ibid., 778-79; his source was Lévi, *Transcendental Magic,* 357-59. At the end, he quoted Lévi's claim that the Templars gave divine honors to Baphomet. Pike had great admiration for the Templars, claiming that they symbolized the promise of liberty of conscience and a new orthodoxy which

Lévi in America: Albert Pike

would be "the synthesis of all the persecuted creeds." He regarded as absurd the claim that "men of intellect adored the monstrous idol called Baphomet, or recognized Mahomet as an inspired prophet"; see Pike, *Morals and Dogma*, 818.

70. Ibid., 792; his source was Lévi, *Transcendental Magic*, 225.
71. Ibid., 8 15-16; his source was Lévi, *The History of Magic*, 207-08.
72. Ibid 816; his source was Lévi, *The History of Magic*, 208.
73. Ibid., 816-17; his source was Lévi, *The History of Magic*, 208.
74. Ibid., 817; his source was Lévi, *The History of Magic*, 210.
75. Ibid., 817. Here, Pike declared that the anti-Gnostic position attributed to this apostle in the First Epistle of John was "a misrepresentation, or misunderstanding at least, of the whole Spirit of that Evangel"; see 1 John 4:1-3.
76. Ibid., 817; his source was Lévi, *The History of Magic*, 210-11.
77. Ibid., 822-23; his source was Lévi, *The History of Magic*, 260-61.
78. Ibid., 823; his source was Lévi, *The History of Magic*, 291-92.
79. Ibid., 823; his source was Lévi, *The History of Magic*, 301.
80. Ibid., 823; his source was Lévi, *The History of Magic*, 302.
81. This chapter concerns the 30th degree, Knight Kadosh., whose theme is vengeance.
82. Ibid., 823; his source was Lévi, *The History of Magic*, 309-10. Lévi did not identify the "Regent" as the "Duc d'Orleans." Pike omitted part of the description given by Lévi of acts of vengeance, such as those of "a hideous and gigantic being, covered with a long beard," who smote with sabre, axe, and club, declaring "Behold, this is for the Albigenses and the Vaudois; this is for Saint Bartholomew and this is for the exiles of the Cerenne
83. Pike, *Morals and Dogma*, 823-24; his source was Lévi, *The History of Magic*, 310-11. Pike omitted the following interesting description of Lévi: "At the very moment when Louis XVI suffered under the axe of revolution, the man with a long beard — that wandering Jew; significant of vengeance and murder — ascended the scaffold and, confronting the spectators, took the royal blood in both hands, casting it over the heads of the people, and crying with his terrible voice: "People of France, I baptize you in the name of Jacques and of liberty"; see ibid., 310. Lévi believed it was quite significant that Rousseau and de Molay had the same first name; see ibid., 309.
84. Pike, *Morals and Dogma*, 841; his source was Lévi, *History of Magic*, 29.
85. This chapter concerns the 32nd degree, Sublime Prince of the Royal Secret, whose theme is equilibrium, a concept prominent throughout Lévi's works.
86. Pike, *Morals and Dogma*, 843; his source was Lévi, *The History of Magic*, 130.
87. Hutchens, *A Glossary to Morals and Dogma*, 83.

88. Prince Hall Freemasonry began with the initiation of a black man named Prince Hall into a military lodge near Boston, Massachusetts on 6 March 1775. Since then, his fraternity has played an important role in black America. Until recent years, Prince Hall Masons were denied recognition by white Masons. The Masonic "color line" is slowly breaking down.

89. Joseph A. Walkes, Jr., "The Ku Klux Klan and Regular Freemasonry," *The Phylaxis* 18 (Fourth Quarter 1992): 5.

90. Joseph A. Walkes, Jr., *Black Square and Compass: 200 Years of Prince Hall Freemasonry* (Richmond, Virginia: Macoy Publishing and Masonic Supply Company, Inc., 1979), 141-42. There are also unconfirmed reports that Thornton A. Jackson was the personal barber of Albert Pike; see Joseph A. Walkes, Jr., *History of the Shrine: Ancient Egyptian Arabic Order Nobles of the Mystic Shrine, Inc., Prince Hall Affiliated, A Pillar of Black Society, 1893 -1 993* (Detroit, Michigan: Ancient Egyptian Arabic Order Nobles of the Mystic Shrine, Inc., Prince Hall Affiliated, 1993), 65.

91. Pike, *Morals and Dogma,* iv.

92. Hutchens and Monson, *The Bible in Albert Pike's Morals and Dogma,* 3.

93. Ibid., 6.

94. Robinson, *A Pilgrim's Path,* 52.

95. Ibid., 55-57. In discussing the "Catechism of tbe Officiating Mistress" of the Egyptian Rite of Adoption, Taxil distorted passages from Éliphas Lévi's *Dogme et rituel de la Haute Magie* ; see Waite, *Devil Worship in France; or, The Question of Lucifer; a Record of Things Seen and Heard in the Secret Societies According to the Evidence of Initiates* (London: G. Redway, 1896), 60. He represented Lévi as a member of an occult association known as Knights Kadosh; see ibid., 68.

96. Robinson, *A Pilgrim's Path,* 58.

97. In Freemasonry, there has never been such an office as "Sovereign Pontiff."

98. Ibid., *58-59.*

99. During the 1890s, Taxil declared tolerance in religion to be "Satanic"; see Waite, *Devil Worship in France,* 53. During the 1990s, similar claims were made by James Holly, the leading anti-Mason among Southern Baptists.

100. This article originally appeared in The *Phylaxis* 8 (First Quarter 1982), but did not come to the attention of the LaRouche organization until it was reprinted in the edition of *News Quarterly* (Spring 1992), a publication of Scottish Rite Masons (Prince Hall Affiliated). The article was printed a third time in *The Phylaxis* 18 (Fourth Quarter 1992), along with several articles submitted by LaRouche's followers. The Phylaxis Society is an organization of Prince Hall Freemasons involved in Masonic research founded in 1973 by Walkes, who served as president of the society from 1973 to 2003. Bro. Walkes' death on 4 March 2006 was a great loss to Freemasonry as a whole.

101. "Should the Statue of Albert Pike Be Removed?" *The Phylaxis* 19 (First Quarter 1993): 4-6.This paper stated that it would have been difficult for Pike to have served as Grand Dragon of Arkansas during the late 1860s due to the fact that he ceased to be a resident of Arkansas in 1865 and was living in Memphis, Tennessee under a conditional pardon which required him to be a peaceful citizen; see ibid., 7.

103. Raschke, *Painted Black,* 37.

104. Lévi, *The Magical Ritual of the Sanctum Regnum,* 8. It is hard to imagine Pike making such a statement! Many white Southerners of his day practiced miscegenation while verbally denouncing it. It is not known whether he was among this group.

105. "Should the Statue of Albert Pike Be Removed?" 6. The healing of antagonisms is evident in Freemasonry. Since October 1989, the Caucasian Grand Lodges of Connecticut, Nebraska, Wisconsin, Washington, Colorado, Minnesota, North Dakota, Idaho, Wyoming, California, Massachusetts, Vermont, Wyoming, Ohio, Kansas, New Mexico, Maine, New Hampshire, Arizona, South Dakota, Hawaii, Utah, Alaska, Michigan, Pennsylvania, Oregon, Illinois, Indiana, Rhode Island, District of Columbia, Montana, Nevada, Iowa, New York, Virginia, Missouri, Maryland, Oklahoma, and Deleware have exchanged fraternal recognition with Prince Hall Grand Lodges. This trend can be expected to continue. One day, we may see an end to the contradiction of a "color line" in an organization dedicated to the Fatherhood of God and Brotherhood of Man!

106. Joseph A. Walkes, Jr., "Letter," *The Phylaxis* 18 (Fourth Quarter 1992): 7.

107. Quoted in Allen E. Roberts, "Let the Beauty of Freemasonry Into Your Heart," *The Phylaxis* 19 (First Quarter 1993): 10.

108. It is equally obvious that Lévi had no influence on Pike's views on race. When one considers the fact that racial problems have never been as paramount in France as in America, this is understandable.

109. Such understanding involves recognition of differences as well as similarities. To me, it is significant that Pike was a Freemason for over forty years while Lévi left the lodge after the members failed to give him the positive response he expected. Also, Pike was very hostile to the Roman Catholic Church, while Lévi was a Catholic deacon who never completely left the church and was reconciled to it shortly before his death. Politically, Pike was a conservative, while Lévi was a socialist. A final difference should be noted. In response to the question "Did the Templars worship Baphomet?" Pike and Lévi reached opposite conclusions.

CHAPTER IV

Lévi in America: Religious Movements

Literary research indicates that the Kabbalistic thought of Éliphas Lévi has been influential in a number of American religious movements. In this chapter, Lévi's influence in Theosophy, Anthroposophy, Rosicrucianism, the Order of the Temple of the Orient, the Order of the Temple of Astarte, the Builders of the Adytum, the Fraternity of the Hidden Light, and the Church of Mercavah will be explored.

Theosophy

Theosophy[1], in modern times, is a phenomenon within a variety of movements in which the imprint of Éliphas Lévi can be clearly seen.[2] The principal founder of the Theosophical Society is recognized to be Madame Helena Petrovna Blavatsky, who was born in 1831 in Ekaternoslav (present-day Dnepropetrovsk) of noble Russian parentage. From childhood, she exhibited paranormal powers, a tempestuous personality, and unconventional behavior.[3] It is traditionally held that her occult quest began at an early age in the library of her maternal great-grandfather, Prince Paul Vasilyevitch Dolgoronki, where she found hundreds of books on alchemy, magic, and related matters. By the age of fifteen, she read many of these volumes with the keenest interest. She claimed that the library contained a manuscript given to one of her ancestors by the celebrated sixteenth century mystic Count de Saint-Germaine which alluded to "the thorough metamorphosis of nearly the whole of the European map, beginning with the French Revolution."[4] Paul Johnson contends that this manuscript—regardless of its origin—influenced her imagination with the idea of mysterious adepts manipulating occult undercurrents of European politics, undercurrents in which she could play a part.[5] Her great grandfather was a prominent Freemason and Rosicrucian. In his library, she may have been exposed to Russian Rosicrucianism's legend of a worldwide network of Masters and a secret link with Tibet. Such ideas could have had great influence on her interpretation of her later encounters with genuine spiritual teachers of diverse traditions.[6] While still in her teens, she met Prince Aleksandr Golitsyn, a Freemason, magician, and seer, whose grandfather had predicted that a "new universal church," distinct from the Eastern Orthodox tradition, would arise in Russia.[7] In later years, there is indication that she saw the Theosophical Society as playing the role of this "new universal church." Blavatsky was married at the age of seventeen, but soon left her husband and traveled to Europe, the Americas, Egypt, and India.[8] In 1851, while in Cairo, she met Albert Leighton Rawson, who would play an important role in early Theosophy.[9] Rawson was probably the subject of a "Confession" she wrote many years later, stating: "I <loved> one man deeply, but still more I loved occult science, believing in magic, wizards, etc. I wandered with him here and there, in Asia, in America, and in Europe."[10] In old Cairo, the pair disguised themselves as Muslims in order to learn the techniques of snake charming.[11] Blavatsky continued her travels and, during a stop in Paris, met with the Grand Secretary of the Masonic Grand Orient of France, who was amazed at "her knowledge of all the secrets of the degrees in one branch to the Thirty-third, and in another to the Ninety-fifth."[12] She regarded Tibet as one of her most important experiences. There, she claimed, she encountered an "Ascended Master" who had long appeared in her dreams.[13] With a strong belief that she had been appointed to introduce Eastern wisdom to the Western world, she arrived in New York City in 1873.[14]

The name of the society was selected by the first librarian, Charles Sotheran, an Englishman who settled in New York in 1874. Sotheran was a member of various Masonic bodies, including the Scottish Rite, Shrine, Rite of Memphis, and Rite of Swedenborg. He probably borrowed the word "theosophy" from the latter rite, where it has extensive use. He was also a Rosicrucian and was described by Blavatsky as "one of the most learned members of the Society Rosae Crucis." He introduced her to a number of scholars whose names appear in her writings.[15] He had a network of contacts in both secret societies and leftist politics.[16]

In 1877, Blavatsky's first book *Isis Unveiled* (two volumes) was published.[17] Up to this time, an Egyptian atmosphere had prevailed within the society. At a meeting on 7 September 1875, a lecture was delivered by Civil War veteran and inventor George Felt on "The Lost Canon of Proportion of the Egyptians." At the time, he was involved in research on connections between the Egyptian Zodiac and the Hebrew Kabbalah. He desired that the Masonic initiation should more resemble the Egyptian Mysteries. He feared, however, that most Masons were not ready for such, as they were not "pure in mind and body." Due to his influence, on 8 March 1876, the Theosophical Society became a secret organization with signs of recognition and an appropriate seal. During this initiatory period, the society showed a close resemblance to fringe Masonic groups.[18]

By the time of the publication of Blavatsky's major work *The Secret Doctrine* in 1888, the Theosophical Society's orientation had shifted from Egypt to India. In the latter two-volume set, Blavatsky expounded three propositions: viz. (1) that there is an omnipresent, eternal, boundless, and immutable Reality, of which spirit and matter are complementary aspects; (2) that there is a universal law of periodicity, or evolution through cyclic change; and (3) that all souls are identical with the universal Oversoul, which is itself an aspect of the unknown Reality.[19] Blavatsky wrote two further books — *The Voice of the Silence* and *Key to Theosophy*. In 1889, both of these were published.[20]

In 1879, Blavatsky and her co-founder Col. William Steele Olcott, a Civil War veteran, attorney, and writer on such subjects as agriculture and insurance, moved to India. In 1882, the international headquarters of the society was moved from New York to Adyar, a suburb of Madras, India, where it remains today.[21] In India, they established *The Theosophist,* a journal dedicated to uniting Eastern spirituality with Western advances in thought. This publication upheld the values of Hindu culture but called for Western education for Indians and condemned such practices as child marriage and the caste system.

Gnostic Bishop Stephan A. Hoeller, a member of Theosophical Society in America, expressed the opinion that Lévi's influence on Blavatsky was as profound as his influence on Albert Pike.[27] However, Blavatsky was much more honest than Pike in acknowledging her debt to Lévi. While there is no evidence that Blavatsky ever met Lévi, she mentioned him in a number of her writings. In her assessment of him, she included both praise and criticism. She described him as "one of the best authorities on certain points among Kabalists."[28] Elsewhere, she called him "that modem Magus."[29] She expressed the following view of his writings: "No other Kabalist has ever had the talent of heaping up one contradiction on the other, of making one paradox chase another in the same sentence and in such flowing language, as Éliphas Lévi."[30] She called him "the most learned if not the greatest of modem Kabalists" but complained that he was "yet too subservient to his Roman Catholic authorities. . . to confess that this devil was mankind and never had any existence outside of mankind."[31] She rejected the goat as an appropriate symbol for Satan and objected to Levi's use of paradoxes and metaphors to explain Roman Catholic dogma.[32] In "A Posthumous Publication" which originally appeared in *The Theosophist* in July 1881, she wrote:

> We are glad to lay before our readers the first of a series of unpublished writings of the late Éliphas Lévi (Abbé Louis Constant), one of the great masters of the occult sciences of the present century in the West... . Éliphas Lévi knew much; far more than the privileged few even among the greatest mystics of modem Europe; hence, he was traduced by the ignorant many. He had written these ominous words. . . "The discovery of the great secrets of true religion and of the primitive science of the Magi, revealing to the world the unity of the universal dogma, annihilates fanaticism by scientifically explaining and giving the reason for every miracle," and these words sealed his doom. .. . <He> died, as his famous predecessors in the occult arts, Cornelius Agrippa, Paracelsus and many others did—a pauper. Of all the parts of the world, Europe is the one which stones her true prophets the most cruelly, while being led by the nose of the false ones must successfully.

... Though personally we are far from agreeing with all his opinions... . we are yet prepared always to lend a respectful ear to the teaching of so learned a Kabalist... we do concur in the verdict of the world of letters that Éliphas Lévi was one of the cleverest, most learned, and interesting of writers upon all such abstruse subjects.[33]

Blavatsky's article "The Kabalah and the Kabalists" was published in May 1892 — one year after her death. In this article, she described Lévi as "a charming and witty writer, who has more mystified than taught in his many volumes on Magic."[34]

Helena Petrovna Blavatsky

The impact of Lévi on early Theosophy is contained in a number of his articles which appeared in *The Theosophist* between March 1884 and April 1887. During this period, most of the issues of this publication, with only a few exceptions, included "Unpublished Writings of Éliphas Lévi." The January 1886 issue also contained "Personal Recollections of Éliphas Lévi. Another Theosophical publication, *The Path*, which was edited by William Quan Judge, published Lévi's "Notes on the Astral Light" in three parts — August 1887, September 1887, and December 1887.[35]

Both Blavatsky and Judge were impressed with the idea of the Astral Light, which was one of Lévi's key concepts. Blavatsky stated that "This all-pervading force was known to the gymnophists, Hindu magicians, and adepts of all countries."[36] She described parallels to the Astral Light in various cultures, including that of the Parsees, the Greeks, the Romans, the ancient Germanic tribes, and the Judeo-Christian tradition.[37] She attributed earthly fertility to harmony between the "currents of the Astral Light and the divine spirit."[38] She cited Lévi when she defined the Astral Light as the "first envelope of the soul" which forms the etheral body which is entirely disengaged at the moment of death.[39] She again employed his approach in the following discussion of the Astral Light:

> The sovereign will is represented in our symbols by the woman who crushes the serpent's head, and by the resplendent angel who represses the dragon, and holds him under his foot and spear; the great magical agent, the dual current of light, the living and astral fire of the earth, has been represented in the ancient theogonies by a ram, or a dog. It is the double serpent of the *caduceus,* it is the Old Serpent of the *Genesis,* but it is also the *brazen serpent of Moses* entwined around the *rau,* that is to say, the generating *lingha.* It is also the goat of the witch-sabbath, and the Baphomet of the Templars; it is the *Hylé* of the Gnostics; it is the double tail of the serpent which forms the legs of the solar cock of the Abraxas, finally, it is the Devil of M. Eudes de Mirville. But in every fact it is the blind force which souls have to conquer to liberate themselves from the bonds of the earth; from this *fatal attraction,* they will be absorbed in the current by the force which has produced them; and *will return to the central and eternal fire.*[40]

In her major work *The Secret Doctrine,* Blavatsky gave further attention to the Astral Light.

Thus, she wrote:

> Most of the Western Christian Kabalists — pre-eminently Éliphas Lévi — in their desire to reconcile the Occult Sciences with Church dogmas, did their best to make of the "Astral Light" only and preeminently the *Pleroma* of the early Church Fathers, the abode of the Hosts of the Fallen Angels, of the "Archons" and "Powers." But the Astral Light, while only the lower aspect of the Absolute, is yet dual. It is the *Anima Mundi,* and ought never to be viewed otherwise, except for Kabalistic purposes.[41]

Whereas, in *Isis Unveiled,* she was highly uncritical of Lévi, this was not the case in *The Secret Doctrine.* In the latter work, she sought to establish her position as an Oriental Occultist in contrast to Levi's position as a Christian Kabbalist. She did not hesitate to point out what she perceived to be contradictions in Lévi's thought. Thus, she wrote:

> That Astral Light which the paradoxical Éliphas Lévi calls in one breath "the body of the Holy Ghost" and in the next "Baphomet," the Androgyne Goat of Mendes"... the "Astral Light"... is the "grand Agent Magique" with him; undeniably, it is so, but—only so far as Black Magic is concerned, and on the lowest planes of what we call Ether, the noumenon of which is simply the older *"sidereal Light"* of Paracelsus; and to say that "everything which exists has been evolved from it, and it preserves and reproduces all forms," as he writes, is to enunciate truth only in the second proposition. The first is erroneous; for if all that exists was evolved *through* (or *via*) it, it is not the astral light. The latter is not the container of all things but only the reflector, at best, of this all.... when the great authority of the Western Kabalists adds that nevertheless, "it is not the immortal Spirit as the Indian Hierophants have imagined"—we answer that he slanders the said Hierophants, as they have said nothing of the kind; while even the Puranic exoteric writings flatly contradict the assertion.[42]

Later in this work, she referred to the currents of the Astral Light as "circulations."[43] In his book *Echoes from the Orient,* William Quan Judge[44] had much to say about the Astral Light, giving credit to Lévi for this perception. Judge found the Astral Light among the most interesting Theosophical concepts. He deemed it "at once devilish and divine" and as the same as the Akasa (ether) by which the Hindu yogis have accomplished amazing feats. Only through the Astral Light, he said, were such phenomena as clairvoyance, clairaudience, mediumship, and seership possible.[45] He accepted Lévi's view that diseased souls mingle impure reflections with the Astral Light and that such mingling has disastrous results.[46] However, he also saw a useful function in the Astral Light's projection of pictures of the appliances, ideas, philosophy, arts, and sciences of long buried civilizations into the brains of living men.[47] He concurred with Lévi that a powerfully sympathetic will could draw the Astral Light into the proper current to manifest itself as an apparition.[48] He concluded: "The light can therefore be impressed with evil or good pictures, and these are reflected into the subconscious mind of every human being. If you fill the astral light with bad pictures, just such as the present century is adept at creating, it will be our devil and destroyer, but if by the example of even a few good men and women a new and purer sort of events are lined upon the eternal canvas, it will become our Divine Uplifter."[49] Blavatsky, like Lévi, referred to herself as an "occultist." She defined this term as "one who studies the various branches of occult science" and understood "occultism" as embracing the whole range of psychological, physiological, cosmical, physical, and spiritual phenomena, including Kabbalah, alchemy, astrology, and all arcane sciences. For further information, she referred her readers to the writings of Lévi.[50] In a discussion of reincarnation, she quoted Lévi's statement that "nature shuts the door after everything that passes, and pushes life onward."[51] She included him among her authorities for her belief *"that the magical power is never possessed by those addicted to vicious indulgences."*[52] She gave a detailed discussion of Levi's views on the law of reciprocal influences between the planets and mineral, vegetable, and animal life, citing his *Dogme et Rituel de la Haute Magie.*[53] She quoted from the latter work in her discussion of Lévi's claim that "the Kabalistic use of the pentagram can... determine the countenance of unborn infants, and an initiated woman might give to her son the features of Nereus or Achilles, as well as those of Louis XV or Napoleon.[54] She quoted a number of passages from Lévi's *La Science des Esprits* in her discussion of life, death, and immortality.[55] Regarding the matter of resuscitation, Blavatsky reflected Lévi's belief that such is possible while the vital organism remains undestroyed and the astral spirit is yet within reach, and that the worship of relics dates from the time among the Hebrews in which it was believed that resuscitation occurred as a result of contact with the bones of Elisha.[56] She quoted *Dogme et Rituel de La Haute Magie,* where Levi wrote: "Death does not exist, and man never steps outside of universal life. Those whom we think dead live still in us, as we live in them. . . . The more one lives for his kind, the less need he fear to die."[57]

Blavatsky discussed Jean Bodin's 1587 work *La Demonomanie, ou traite des Sorciers,* describing it as a most remarkable collection of "bloody and hideous facts; acts of revolting and superstition, arrests, and executions of stupid ferocity," borrowing this expression from Lévi.[58] On the following page, she gave a description of a Black Mass, using Lévi as one of her sources.[59] Later, she cited him again as a source of information about exorcisms performed by Catholic priests during the Middle Ages "with the tacit if not open consent of the Church."[60] She pointed out that there were pre-Christian uses of the cross among neophytes and adepts. In support of this claim, she quoted Lévi's words in *Dogme et Rituel de la Haute Magie,* where his major claim related to "A sign of the cross, *absolutely* and magnificently Kabalistic, which the profanations of Gnosticism made the militant and official Church completely *lose*.[61] In her discussion of the ancient Hebrew manuscript *Sepher Toldos Jeshu,* she cited Lévi's claim in *La Science des Esprits* that Martin Luther used portions of this manuscript published by Porchetus Salvaticus.[62] She quoted from the same work of Lévi in describing a Jewish version of the birth of Jesus allegedly reported in *Sepher Toldos Jeshu* from the narratives of Talmudic authors Sota and Sanhedrin and translated from Hebrew by Lévi.[63] She gave another quote describing an Egyptian initiation and subsequent persecution allegedly experienced by Jesus. She concluded with the following explanation of Lévi: "All this because he revealed to the people the truths which they (the Pharisees) wished to buy for their own use. He had divined the occult theology of Israel, had compared it with the wisdom of Egypt, and found thereby the reason for a universal religious synthesis." [64]

In her discussion of the *sephira* (emanations) on the Kabbalistic Tree of Life, she referred to *Dogme et Rituel de la Haute Magie,* where Lévi placed Chochma as number two and as a male *sephiroth* on the right hand of the Tree.[65] She used the same source for her discussions of the Kabbalistic interpretation of the Hebrew name of God.[66] She presented Lévi's interpretation of Islam when she quoted him as describing the attitude of Muslims toward both Jesus and Christianity: "Jesus of Nazareth was verily a true prophet of Allah and a grand man; but lo! his disciples went insane one day, and made a god of him."[67] She argued that the number seven was preeminent in all esoteric systems, including Western Kabbalah and Eastern Occultism. In support of this claim, she quoted Lévi's description of the number seven as "the key to the Mosaic creation and the symbols of every religion" and mentioned his presentation of a septenary diagram to symbolize the septenary division of man in *The Key of the Mysteries.*[68]

In volume 2 of her major work, Blavatsky tried to put some distance between herself and Lévi when she wrote:

> Does the Western Kabalists—generally an opponent of the Eastern Occultist—require a proof? Let him open Éliphas Lévi's *Histoire de la Magie,* p. 53 and carefully examine his *"Grand Symbole Kabalistique"* of the Zohar. He will find, on the engraving given, a *white* man standing erect and a *black* woman upside down, i. e., standing on her head, her legs passing under the extended arms of the male figure, and protpiding behind her shoulders, while their hands join at an angle on each side. Éliphas Lévi's makes of it, God and Nature; or God, "light," mirrored inversely on "Nature and Matter," darkness. Kabalistically and symbolically he is right; but only as far as emblematical cosmogony goes. Nor has he invented the symbol any more than the Kabalists have: the two figures in white and black stone have existed in the temples of Egypt from time immemorial—agreeable to tradition; and historically— ever since the days of King Cambyses, who personally saw them.[69]

She went into great detail to express disagreement with Levi's approach to cross symbology. She disagreed with his claim that the Church had lost the inner and higher meaning of this symbol, insisting, instead, that the Church never possessed it. She charged Lévi with "pandering to Rome" and declared that "the cross adopted by the Latin Church was phallic from the beginning."[70]

Olcott, who presided over the society from Blavatsky's death in 1891 until his own death in 1907, was introduced by Blavatsky to Lévi's works.[71] He reported that there were numerous books by Lévi in the society's library and expressed the belief that Blavatsky's knowledge was derived from the Astral Light, which he understood as pure magic.[72]

Annie Besant

Annie Besant, a social reformer and Fabian socialist who became a Theosophist in 1889, served as president of the Theosophical Society from Olcott's death in 1907 until her own death in 1933.[74] In her book *Esoteric Christianity*, she mentioned Lévi:

> Alphonse Louis Constant, better known under his pseudonym, Éliphas Lévi, has put rather well the loss of the Mysteries and the need for their reinstitution.... Will the Churches of today again take up the mystic teaching, the Lesser Mysteries, and so prepare their children for the reestablishment of the Greater Mysteries, again drawing down the Angels as Teachers, and having as Hierophant the Divine Master, Jesus? On the answer to that question depends the future of Christianity.[74]

From my research into the literature of Theosophy, I must conclude that Blavatsky was influenced by Lévi in her understanding of the nature of occultism. It appears that his efforts to maintain his position as a Christian Kabbalist contributed to her efforts to more clearly define her position as an

Oriental Occultist. There is also evidence from the writings of Judge, Olcott, and Besant that each of these Theosophists were influenced by Lévi, although to a lesser degree. Lévi was greatly respected by early Theosophists and his writings helped lay the foundation for this movement's teachings.

Anthroposophy

The history of Theosophy, like that of many other religious movements, has been marked by splinter movements. The most important of these is Anthroposophy ("human wisdom"). Literary research indicates that this movement was also influenced by Éliphas Lévi, but not to the extent as was the case with Theosophy.

Dr. Rudolf Steiner

Dr. Rudolf Steiner, the founder of Anthroposophy, was born on 27 February 1861 in Kraljevo on the Muff Island in Croatia, within the Austrian Empire. He spent his early childhood at Pottschach, a station on the Southern Austrian Railway, attended a scientific high school until the age of eighteen, and graduated from a polytechnic college in Vienna. At the age of twenty-two, he began to edit *Goethe's Natural Scientific Writings*. Three years later, he wrote A *Theory of Knowledge Implicit in Goethe's World Conception*. In 1891, he received his Doctor of Philosophy degree from the University of Rostock and, a year later, he published his dissertation under the title of

Truth and Knowledge. In 1894, he published his primary work in philosophy, *The Philosophy of Freedom*, followed immediately by *Friedrich Nietzsche: Battler Against his Time* and *Goethe's Conception of the World*.[75] By the end of his career, his published works totaled over three-hundred and fifty volumes. Among the best known are The *Philosophy of Spiritual Activity, Knowledge of the Higher Worlds and Its Attainment, Theosophy,* and *Occult Science and Outline*.[76]

From an early age, Steiner reportedly had access to spiritual realities, including the experience of a discarnate form of a recently deceased relative, the inner or "etheric" forces within plants, and the living power of geometric forms.[77] However, he did not manifest publicly his occult, clairvoyant capacities until the age of thirty-nine. At this time, he entered a deep spiritual struggle and experienced what he described as "the mystery of Christian redemption." In the light of this, from 1900 onwards, his approach to spiritual science took a more and more Christian orientation.[78]

Despite his Christian tendencies, Steiner was received into the Theosophical Society by Annie Besant in 1902. He became very influential in the organization, serving as General Secretary of the German branch and helping to shape Theosophical thought. Eventually, he was received into the Esoteric School of Theosophy — an inner circle reserved for advanced occultists. At that time, he shared a large part of the society's crucial vision. Within a few years, however, it became clear that there were critical differences between his approach to occult science and that of the leadership of Theosophy.[79] By 1905, his charismatic personality had drawn to him a following of his own. Around 1906, he was installed as Master of a lodge of the Order of the Temple of the Orient. At the time, the latter organization practiced a synthesis of Hindu Tantra, Sufism, Grail mysticism, and Rosicrucianism.[80] On 14 January 1913, the inevitable schism with Theosophy occurred. At that time, Besant withdrew the charter of the German Section. On 2 February 1913, almost three thousand Theosophists — more than one half of the German Section — seceded to form the Anthroposophical Society, based on Steiner's teachings.[81]

While both Theosophy and Anthroposophy seek to overcome materialism and return the spiritual dimension to human life, and both desire to heal the rift between religion and science, differences between these two forms of modern Gnosis need to be noted. According to Theosophist Edouard Schure, the major difference between the two lies "in the supreme role attributed by Anthroposophy to the Christ in human evolution and also in its connection with the Rosicrucian tradition." Rosicrucianism is a Western esoteric tradition and Anthroposophy is a type of "Western Gnosis" or "Christian Theosophy" in contrast to the "Hindu Gnosis" of Blavatsky.[82] According to an authority on both movements: "For those who were unwilling or unable to substitute Mme Blavatsky's Himalayan Mahatmas for the Christ, Steiner formulated the "Christ Impulse," showing Christ to be the axis of human evolution and not just one of the Theosophists' Mahatmas."[83]

During the week of Christmas 1923, Steiner reorganized his followers as the General Anthroposophical Society and officially assumed its leadership. About this time, he laid the foundation for the Goetheanum, an enormous structure which he designed to be built on a hill in Dornach, near Basel, Switzerland. Since then, the Goetheanum has served as the international publishing and esoteric center for the work of the society. He chose the name "Goetheanum" in order to honor Johann Wofgang von Goethe's understanding of the aesthetic principle that form follows function, the same principle that Steiner sought to follow in designing the structure.[84]

Steiner's aim in developing Anthroposophy was to enable human beings to develop their spiritual faculties and thereby to develop a knowledge of the spiritual in the cosmos. He believed this could be done only by a type of thinking which was synonymously active, loving, spiritual, and free. He sought to demonstrate that such thinking is at the core of great advances in science, art, and religion.[85] He regarded himself as an initiate and he defined this term as meaning one sent by the spiritual world to undertake an important work for humanity. He understood his work as involving reversal of the plunge of Western thought and culture into materialism and restoration to the West of the concepts of *karma* and rebirth. Much of his life and work was devoted to efforts to reconcile the polarities of science and art, matter and spirit, and individualism and community.[86] He sought to overcome barriers resulting from differences in race, gender, and age.[87]

In response to an appeal from German and Swiss pastors and theological students, Steiner provided the spiritual foundation for the Movement for Religious Renewal, a church which combined the Protestant emphasis on individual conscience and the Roman Catholic emphasis on tradition and liturgy. He composed this church's liturgy, entitled "The Act of Consecration of Man."[88] In response to the request of a dancer, he developed an art of movement called eurythmy for use as a performing art, a curative work, and a pedagogical tool.[89] In response to the plea of Emil Molt, owner of the Waldorf Astoria Tobacco Factory in Stuttgart, for help in educating children of employees, he developed the Waldorf schools, which sought to reconcile the arts and sciences based on active, heart-felt thinking.[90] In response to requests from physicians for a course of lectures on homeopathic and anthroposophic healing, he classified herbs and other natural substances with their various healing powers. In response to requests from farmers, he developed a biodynamic approach to agriculture, based on supersensible knowledge of the soul-spiritual forces operative in the earth, plant, and animal worlds.[91] He died at the Goetheanum on 30 March 1925.[92]

According to the editor of the *Journal of Anthroposophy*, the

Anthroposophical Society today has approximately sixty thousand members worldwide while the Chicago-based Anthroposophical Society in America has about thirty-five hundred members. The society supports and coordinates work in the arts, agriculture, education, curative education for disabled persons, philosophy, music, and the sciences.[93]

During his years as a Theosophist, Steiner no doubt studied the works of Helena P. Blavatsky and knew about the strong influence of Éliphas Lévi on Blavatsky's thought.[94] On 29 May 1924, he delivered a lecture at the Goetheanum on the "Influence of the Hierarchies and Reflections of the Planetary Beings on Human Life."[95] In this lecture, he presented Lévi as "an example of the way in which karma can be elaborated in the Jupiter-sphere."[96] In doing so, he expressed his lack of respect for the pre--Columbian civilization of Mexico and presented his belief that Lévi had lived there in a previous incarnation. Steiner declared:

> There was a personality who lived in the later period of Mexican civilisation and was connected with the utterly decadent, pseudo-magical Mystery cults of Mexico; with an intense thirst for knowledge he studied everything with close and meticulous exactitude.... Living reality of Being was experienced in the Mexican Mysteries by the personality of whom I am speaking.... In his life between death and rebirth this individuality passed through the supersensible world in such a way that in the development of his *karma* – *this* in turn was the outcome of still earlier incarnations not in Mexico; knowledge that had degenerated into superstition but was nevertheless replete with vitality, saturated with the fruits of older civilizations. In the Jupiter sphere all this assumed the form of wisdom that is in truth automatic, unconscious, when compared with the wisdom man should make his own by individual effort.... The individuality of whom I am speaking was born again in modem civilisation as *Éliphas Lévi*. Éliphas Lévi, therefore, had spent his previous incarnation in the Mexican civilisation, had then passed through the sphere of Jupiter where everything was worked through once again. But Mexican culture is a decadent culture and if you read the books of Éliphas Lévi, to-day you will find evidence of great wisdom spread out as it were over something extremely primitive. And one who has insight into these things will say: all this is Jupiter, but inferior Jupiter.[97]

Research indicates that Lévi's influence on Steiner was not as profound as it was on Blavatsky. However, it is apparent that Steiner read Lévi and, as a result, was able to give the above interesting interpretation of him. There can be no doubt that Anthroposophists in Europe and America have read this lecture and, thus, have knowledge of Steiner's view of Lévi.

Rosicrucianism

Research further indicates the influence of Éliphas Lévi in a number of religious and fraternal organizations which call themselves "Rosicrucians." I have found the study of Rosicrucianism to be quite complex, in view of the fact that this movement has never been marked by a monolithic structure and has no historic founder comparable to Blavatsky or Steiner.[98] J. Gordon Melton dated this religious movement to a fourteenth-century legend and wrote: "The Rose Cross (the juxtaposition of a cross and one or more roses) has, since the early seventeenth century, become one of the most popular occult symbols. From its origin in Germany, it spread throughout the Western world and gathered to it fanciful legends and colorful stories of mystery and adventure. It entered into Freemasonry where various ritual degrees derived their name and meaning from the Rosicrucian legend."[99]

According to the above legend, the order's history began with the birth of Christian Rosenkreuz in Germany in 1378. This reputed founder of this mystical fraternity began his travels in 1393, visiting Syria, Egypt, and Morocco and studying under the masters of the occult arts. Reportedly, he returned to Germany in 1407, organizing three monks from a local cloister into the Rosicrucian Order and, two years later, completed the building of the Spiritus Sanctum—House of the Holy Spirit. He instructed his followers, whose number was increased to eight, until his death in 1484 at the age of 106. He was buried at Spiritus Sanctum but knowledge of his tomb was lost until 1604. According to this legend, the rediscovery of his tomb resulted in the revival and spread of the order he founded.[100] The earliest record of this legend are found in three documents which appeared during the second decade of the seventeenth century: *The Fama Fraternitas of the Meritorious Order of the Rosy Cross* (1614), *The Confession of the Rosicrucian Fraternity* (1615), and *The Chymical Marriage of Christian Rosenkreuz* (1616). It is claimed that the latter manuscript was written by Rosenkreuz himself in 1459. Most scholars of this movement, however, agree that these three docu-ments and the idea of the order itself were the products of a German Lutheran pastor named Johann Valentin Andreae (1586-1654), who envisioned a soci-ety for the reformation of social life and borrowed the symbols of the rose and cross from his family's coat of aims. Regardless of what other sources Andreae employed, there can be no doubt that these works were very influential. Shortly after their appearance, a number of Rosicrucian bodies appeared on the scene, combining a vision of social transformation with the study of alchemy, Kabbalah, and mysticism. At that time, most followers also sought to maintain an orthodox Christian theology.[101]

The legend of the rose and the cross spread quickly outside of Germany. There was a great deal of interest in such in nineteenth-century France, where Éliphas Lévi became a leading authority on this symbolism. Lévi saw the rose as a type of beauty, life, love, and pleasure, a mystical expression of "the secret thought of all protests manifested at the Renaissance."[102] He understood the union of the rose and the cross as a problem of high initiation and wrote: "The conquest of the problem offered by initiation to science, whilst religion was at work to prepare and to establish the universal, exclusive and final triumph of the Cross."[103] In France, the Rosicrucians came into the public eye as part of the "occult heyday" inspired by the writings and teachings of Lévi.[104]

Pascal Beverly Randolph

The oldest Rosicrucian organization in America, the Fraternitas Rosae Crucis, was founded in 1858 by Pascal Beverly Randolph (1825-1875), whose role in reviving magic and occultism in America may be seen as comparable to Lévi's role in Europe.[105] Randolph was born in upstate New York of mixed ancestry. He has often been included in lists of African American authors and, during his lifetime, was called an "octoroon" (one-eighth African descent). However, he never made such a claim for himself, insisting that his ancestry was a mixture of European, Native American, and Madagascan. He worked as a sailor from adolescence to the age of twenty, then learned the dyer's and barber's trades. He read and studied voraciously, taking a special interest in medicine. At times, he worked as a physician, but there is no evidence that he ever earned the Doctor of Medicine degree. He took a great deal of interest in spiritism and reported receiving many messages from the spirit world.[106] He spoke of vision of a coming "Age of God," in which there would be peace on earth and all men would meet without distinction of color, sex, or money.[107]

In 1854, Randolph relocated from upstate New York to New York City, describing himself as a "Clairvoyant and Psychometric" and "intending to devote himself to the examination of disease and to giving delineations of character." He was employed by New York physicians to provide diagnoses while in a state of trance.[108] In May 1855, he traveled to London for a spiritualist convention whose purpose was "to inaugurate the commencement of the millennium."[109] This was the first of a number of trips abroad.

While in Paris in 1856, Randolph visited Lévi at his apartment.[110] Randolph claimed that, during his third trip to Europe in 1858, Lévi installed him in office as the Supreme Grand Master of the Western World and, upon his return to America, he founded Fraternitas Rosae Crucis. He also claimed that, in 1861, he returned to Europe and was initiated into the Order of the Rose, a group headed by Rosicrucian historian Hargrave Jennings; and, traveling to Syria, he was initiated by an Arab secret society called the Ansaireh.[111] He regarded the Eleusinian philosophers as philosophers of sex and the Eleusinian mysteries as sexual in nature.[112] One of his major contributions to occultism was his recognition of a spiritual dimension to sexuality. In such works as The *Ansairetic Mystery, Physical Love, The Golden Secret,* and *Eulis: The History of Love,* he treated sexuality in a more comprehensive manner than most of the writers of his day, dealing with such subjects as a woman's capacity and need for sexual satisfaction.[113] He also wrote a series of pioneering occult texts, including *Dealing with the Dead; Ravalerte, the Rosicrucian's Story,* and *Seership.*[114]

Although Randolph denied having African blood, he felt the full weight of American racism. When he returned from Europe and the Middle East to find America engaged in a bloody Civil War, he made speeches against slavery in the South and worked to enlist black soldiers in the Union Army. After the war, he moved to New Orleans, where he served as principal of a school for black children named for abolitionist William Lloyd Garrison. In September 1866, he was a delegate from Louisiana to the Southern Loyal Convention in Philadelphia. He later moved from New Orleans to Boston and finally settled in Toledo, Ohio, where he fell from an elevated railroad in 1873. Although partially paralyzed and unable to speak for more than five minutes at a time, he could still give discourses while in trance. Despite his disabilities, he was able to make another trip to England that year. From September 1874 to May 1875, he was in California, organizing Rosicrucian societies. Upon his return to Toledo, he experienced a number of domestic problems, accusing his wife of betraying him. On 19 July 1875, he committed suicide after announcing his plans to a neighbor, whose eyewitness account of this tragedy appeared in a local newspaper.[115]

Randolph was succeeded as Supreme Grand Master by former spiritualist Freeman B. Dowd, who had been drawn to the fraternity by Randolph's writings. He retired in 1907 and was succeeded by Edward H. Brown, who served until his death in 1922. Brown was succeeded by Reuben Swinburne Clymer, the founder of Philosophical Publishing Company, which reprinted many of Randolph's books. Clymer established the organization's current headquarters at Beverly Hall in Quakertown, Pennsylvania. He, like Randolph, was a prolific writer.[116] He regarded Lévi, Buiwer-Lytton, and Randolph as "Three of the greatest Initiates." He saw much common ground between Lévi's *The Sorcerer of Meudon*, Buiwer-Lytton's *Zanoni*, and Randolph's *Ravalette*.[117] Upon his death, Clymer was succeeded by his son Emerson M. Clymer.[118] The current Supreme Grand Master is Dr. Gerald E. Poesnecker, who stated in a letter: "While we accept Lévi as a knowledgeable author, he was not a fully developed Initiate and therefore his writings do not have the same significance as some of his more advanced contemporaries."[118]

As stated in chapter two, the Societas Rosicruciana in Anglia (S.R.I.A.) was founded in 1866 by Robert Wentworth Little, a clerk at Freemasons' Hall in London. This order limited its membership to Freemasons.[120] A Scottish branch of this organization was established a few years later.[121] In 1878, a group of American Freemasons traveled to England and were initiated into this order at the college (chapter) at York. They applied to the English body for permission to establish an American branch. Rebuffed, they turned to the Scottish branch, which granted charters for colleges at Philadelphia in 1879 and New York in 1880. These two colleges established a High Council in April 1880 and, thus, became an autonomous American branch. Later that year, additional colleges were established at Boston, Baltimore, and Burlington, Vermont. This body of Rosicrucians is now called Societas Rosicruciana in Civitatibus Foederatis. Like the British parent body, these Rociscrucians have always restricted their membership to Freemasons.[122]

However, not all American Rosicrucians desired such a limited pool of applicants. Some wanted to open Rosicrucian teaching to the non-Masonic public. As a result, in 1907, Sylvester C. Gould, a member of the college at Boston, was joined by other dissenters in establishing the more inclusive Societas Rosicruciana in America. Gould died in 1909 but the leadership was assumed by one of his close associates, Dr. George Winslow Plummer (1876-1944), who incorporated the society in 1912 and, four years later, founded Mercury Publishing Company and began issuing *Mercury*, the official quarterly. Numerous colleges (including one in Sierra Leone) and several study groups were established under the leadership of Plummer. After his death, Plummer was succeeded by his widow, known as Mother Serena (1894-1989). In 1983, Mother Serena was succeeded by Soror Lucia Gorsch, the present Supreme Magus and Imperiatrix.[123] During a telephone interview, the latter individual stated that Plummer (whom she credits with opening the doors of the order to women) read widely and probably read the writings of Lévi. She also stated that the society's library contains five thousand volumes and includes a number of works by Lévi. Regarding the esoteric writers of the late nineteenth and early twentieth centuries, she said "They all borrowed from each other."[124] Grosch was succeeded by Soror Maria Babwahsingh as Imperatrix in 2001.

George Winslow Plummer

Societas Rosicruciana in America was not the only Rosicrucian body founded in 1907. The latter year also marked the establishment of the Rosicrucian Fellowship by Max Heindel. Heindel, who was born Carl Louis Von Grasshoff on 23 July 1865 in Germany. As a steamer engineer, he traveled to America and the Orient. He lived in New York for several years and settled in Los Angeles in 1903. Possessed by a longing for knowledge of the deeper mysteries of life and a means of lifting the burdens of humanity, he joined the Theosophical Society, serving as Vice-President of the Los Angeles Lodge in 1904-05.[125] He began a lecture tour which, in 1907, led him to Germany.[126] According to a staff member of the Rosicrucian Fellowship, Heindel, while in Germany seeking contact with the "Elder Brothers of the Rosicrucian Order," met with Rudolf Steiner, asking him a number of questions which he could not answer.[127] The following account of what then took place is taken seriously by members of the Fellowship:

One day a visitor appeared to him whom he later learned was an Elder Brother of the Rosicrucian Order....
This Being was clothed in his vital body, and offered to impart to him the teachings for which he had spent time and money to find in Germany, but these teachings could only be given after he, Max Heindel, would make a solemn promise never to divulge them (they must be kept secret). Having passed through an unhappy period of soul hunger he was most desirous of sharing his knowledge with others, who like himself were also seeking, he refused to accept anything which he could not pass on to the world. The Teacher left him.

Later the Teacher appeared in his room again and told him that he, Max Heindel, had stood his test. He stated that if he had accepted the offer... to keep the teachings secret from the world, he, the Elder Brother, would not have returned. . . . he was told that the teachings must be given to the public before the close of the first decade of the century, which would be the end of December 1909.[128]

Max Heindel

This experience, reportedly, was the inspiration for his first book, *The Rosicrucian Cosmo-Conception*. He wrote many books, including *Simplified Scientific Astrology* and *The Message of the Stars,* which were influenced by the astrological emphases of Theosophy and were major factors in the re-

Harvey Spencer Lewis

vival of astrology in twentieth-century America. In 1910, he had a vision of a future center on Mount Ecclesia in Oceanside, California. The center, which was dedicated in 1920 — one year after Heindel's death — remains the international headquarters.'[29] There are a number of local chapters but most of the members join by taking mail order courses.'[30]

As a former Theosophist, Heindel greatly admired Helena P. Blavatsky. No doubt he had studied her works and knew of Éliphas Lévi's influence on her as a seeker of truth. He, no doubt, read Levi as one source of universal truths. This is the view expressed by a current member of the Rosicrucian Fellowship staff.[131]

The largest and best known of America's Rosicrucian groups is the Ancient Mystical Order Rosae Crucis (A.M.O.R.C.), which was founded in 1915 by Harvey Spencer Lewis (1883-1939), a writer, artist, and occultist initiated into Rosicrucianism in France in 1909. At the A.M.O.R.C.'s first convention in 1917, delegates approved a plan for offering the organization's teachings to individuals through correspondence courses. Such courses, which are still widely advertised, became the major tool for expansion of the order. Since 1927, the headquarters has been in San Jose, California. Today, the headquarters complex includes Rose-Croix University, a Planetarium, the Rosicrucian Research Library, and the Egyptian Museum.[132] Lewis was a very prolific writer. The order circulates his many books as well as those of his son Ralph Lewis (1904-1987), who succeeded him as

Imperator of the order.[133]

In his book *Rosicrucian Questions and Answers*, H. Spencer Lewis mentioned Éliphas Lévi as "a member of the regular Rosicrucian organization" and described his departure from the Societas Rosicruciana in Anglia as follows:

> Lévi was invited to become a part of the S.R.I.A. in England, and did so with the belief that the founders were really sincere in their desire to delve deeply into Rosicrucian lore, and become neophytes of the Rosicrucian organization. A few years after his acceptance into the S.R.I.A., Lévi evidently felt that his connections therewith were not proper in the face of his affiliation with the regular Rosicrucian Order, or else he discovered reasons for withdrawing. It is indicated that he had many arguments with the founders of the new English society, and disagreed with their viewpoints in many ways, and finally withdrew his membership. The records of the S.R.I.A. state that Lévi incurred their displeasure by the publication of his several books on magic and ritual, but since the books have proved to be excellent and highly endorsed by mystics of many periods, such explanation does not seem to be justifiable. Lévi passed through transition in 1875, and in the last years of his life was not connected with the S.R.I.A. in any way.[134]

In the same work, Lewis mentioned Lévi's reported meeting with Rosicrucian leaders Kenneth R. H. Mackenzie[135] and Pascal Beverly Randolph[136] These passages indicate familiarity with Lévi's life and work. However, it is obvious that the purpose of each passage is to demonstrate the illegitimacy of rival Rosicrucian bodies. He also spoke of Albert Pike as a "Brother" and described him as "a very thorough Rosicrucian student."[137] However, he did not seek to make any connection between the writings of Pike and those of Lévi.

Of the four American Rosicrucian groups examined, the influence of Lévi appears strong in one, clearly present in one, and unclear in the other two. Pascal Beverly Randolph was personally acquainted with Lévi and greatly influenced by him. H. Spencer Lewis read Lévi's books and used his knowledge of Lévi to try to discredit his Rosicrucian rivals. The influence of Lévi on Max Heindel and George Winslow Plummer is less clear. However, their contemporary followers are of the opinion that both men were familiar with Lévi's works, even though they did not choose to quote from them.

Order of the Temple of the Orient

The imprint of Éliphas Lévi is quite vivid in *Ordo Templi Orientis* (Order of the Temple of the Orient), often called "O.T.O." This order was founded in Germany by Karl Kellner (1850-1905) and Theodor Reuss (1855-1923).[138] This organization has a total of one hundred and thirty-eight official bodies (lodges, camps, and oases) worldwide.[139] Over half of these—seventy-three to be exact—are located in the United States. Twenty-two of the American bodies are located in California—the largest concentration in one state.[140]

According to the Grand Treasurer General, the immediate precursor to this organization was the Hermetic Brotherhood of Light, a mystical society founded in the mid-nineteenth century, with branches in Europe and North America, to which Karl Kellner belonged.[141] Karl Kellner was an Austrian paper chemist and industrialist who was reported to be one of the few Europeans of his day with a detailed knowledge of yoga theories and techniques. In 1896, his paper on "Yoga: A Summary of Its Psycho--Physiological Connections" was distributed at the Third International Congress for Psychology in Munich.[142] He desired to establish an "Academia Masonica" where Freemasons could conduct research into Masonic degrees and systems. It appears that a meeting with Reuss convinced him to abandon the name "Academia Masonica" in favor of "Oriental Templars."[143]

Reuss' career was marked by work as a journalist, concert promoter, protagonist for women's liberation, member of revolutionary socialist circles, and leader of a number of Masonic organizations, all of which were considered irregular by mainstream Masonic authorities.[144] He seems to have participated in many aspects of the nineteenth century occult revival. In 1914, he told British Masonic scholar Arthur Edward Waite that he had been well acquainted with Helena P. Blavatsky and had once held a high office in the German branch of the Theosophical Society. In a 1903 article entitled, "What is Occultism and How Does One Develop Occult Powers?," he reported attending a memorial ceremony at Blavatsky's house a few days after her death in May 1891. His major occult interests related to yoga and the theoretical connections between the Hindu concept of *chakras* (nerve centers) and sexuality.[145] In 1895, he claimed to have revived the Order of the Illuminati at Berlin.[146] Eventually, the Illuminati was given a Masonic complexion, in efforts to make it more appealing to new members. It became known as Ludwig Lodge and conferred a variety of degrees. Reuss announced that "Master Masons who are in possession of the St. Andrew's degree and wish to pursue occult studies can be received into the Rosicrucian degree."[147]

Eventually, Ludwig Lodge was superseded by the Masonic Rite of Swedenborg, to which Reuss was introduced by the French occultist Gerard Encausse ("Papus"), who worked this Rite in France but was regarded with suspicion by French Masonic authorities. Papus referred Reuss to William Wynn Westcott, the Rite's Supreme Grand Secretary in England.[48] In December 1901, Reuss met with Westcott in London.[149] On 2 February 1902, Westcott authorized Reuss to establish the Swedenborgian Lodge of the Holy

Grail No. 15 at Berlin and the High Council in Germania of Societas Rosicruciana in Anglia. Reuss not only started these orders but also launched a periodical entitled *Oriflamma,* which he called the "Organ of the German High-grade Freemasons of the Swedenborg Rite and the Order of the Rosicrucians." Not satisfied with these alone, Reuss later applied for and received warrants for the Antient and Primitive Rite of Memphis and Misraim and for the Cerneau version of the Ancient and Accepted Scottish Rite.[150] In 1904, he published a pamphlet entitled "Historical Edition of the *Oriflamma,"* which was addressed to "all who want to learn the truth and real facts of Masonic historical research." In this pamphlet, he sought to demonstrate the historical authenticity of his collection of rites and to prove a direct connection with the medieval crusading order of the Knights Templar. He declared that "Proofs of our connection with the Templars are available, but they are not of a documentary nature. They are only communicated to the initiated."[151] He moved to London in January 1906. By this time, his "Masonic empire" had virtually ceased to exist. Nevertheless, he was able to publish two issues of *Oriflamina* that year. These reflected his desire to admit women to the Rites of Memphis and Misraim and his preoccupation with "sex magic." During the spring, he issued a warrant for a co-educational Memphis and Misraim Lodge to Rudolf Steiner, then Secretary General of the German Branch of the Theosophical Society. Reuss appointed Steiner as Deputy Grand Master.[152]

Eventually, however, the O.T.O. replaced all of the other rites over which Reuss had presided.[153] The contents of the 1912 "Jubilee Edition" of *Oriflamma* were almost entirely devoted to O.T.O. The publication was described as the "Official Organ of the Order of the Oriental Templars and the Sovereign Sanctuary of Ancient Freemasons in Germany. This issue referred to the leader of O.T.O. in England as "the Most Holy, Most Illustrious, Most Illuminated and Most Puissant Baphomet X, Rex Summus of Ireland, Jona, etc." Such an appellation was applied to Aleister Crowley, who would play a crucial role in the organization's future.[154] Crowley claimed that, in the O.T.O. was concentrated the wisdom and knowledge of the following organizations: the Gnostic Catholic Church, the Order of the Knights of the Holy Ghost, the Order of the illuminati, the Order of the Temple (Knights Templar), the Order of Knights of Saint John, the Order of Knights of Malta, the Order of the Knights of the Holy Sepulchre, the Hidden Church of the Holy Grail, the Rosicrucian Order, the Holy Order of the Rose Croix of Heredom, the Order of the Holy Royal Arch of Enoch, the Antient and Primitive Rite of Memphis (97 degrees), the Ancient and Accepted Scottish Rite (33 degrees), the Swedenborgian Rite of Masonry, the Order of the Martinists, the Order of Sat Bhai, the Hermetic Brotherhood of Light, and the Hermetic Order of the Golden Dawn. He asserted that "Our Order possesses the KEY which embraces all masonic and hermetic secrets. It relates to sex magic and this teaching completely explains all masonic symbolism and religious teachings."[155]

Reuss left London right before the outbreak of World War I in 1914 and returned to Berlin, where he briefly worked for German counter-intelligence on the Dutch border. He then moved to neutral territory in Basle, Switzerland. About this time, the O.T.O. sponsored an international "Anti-National Congress" at Monte Yenta near Ascona on Lake Maggiore. The latter retreat center was founded during the early 1900s as the counterpart of a vegetarian "hippie" commune and was patronized by clientele dedicated to the "simple life," including many Theosophists. An anti-Semitic and anti-Masonic critic charged that Reuss had stated the following purposes of the Congress:

> My secret aim for this congress is to bring together land reformers, vegetarians, pacifists . . . from Spain, Italy, Holland, Russia, France, etc. and convert their hitherto poisonous anti-German sentiments into something more fair to Germany . . . The "Anti-Nationalist Co-operative Congress" flag and the draft programme are naturally merely a camouflage. . . Germany should send two Masonic representatives who are men of the world and know the *true* (not the orthodox) history of Freemasonry and its secret political working.[156]

In 1918, Reuss published his translation of Crowley's Gnostic Mass under O.T.O. auspices. He returned to Germany in September 1921 and settled in Munich. He died there on 28 October 1923.[157]

Crowley was Reuss' designated successor as Head of the O.T.O. He served in this capacity from 1923 until his death in December 1947.[158] In accord with his wishes, Karl Germer was his successor, serving until his own death in 1962. Since Germer's lifetime, the organization has experienced a number of conflicts related to leadership. According to the Treasurer General: "Some disturbed individuals wrote to O.T.O. from mental hospitals, that they were the true Head of O.T.O. A significant number of individuals wrote to tell O.T.O. that they were remiss on not accepting the reincarnation of Aleister Crowley as its leader."[159] The current Head has adopted the name of "Hymenaeus Beta." He serves as Frater Superior for the International O.T.O. and United States Grand Master General for the Agape United States Grand Lodge. He lives in Asheville, North Carolina.[160]

As stated in chapter two, Aleister Crowley was greatly influenced by Éliphas Lévi and claimed that he was Lévi reincarnated. In the February 1992 issue of the newsletter of Thelema Lodge in Berkeley, California, the column called "From the History Heap" listed various historical events during the month of February. Regarding February 8, 1810, the article stated: "The man born on this date once wrote, 'that if a man breathes in a certain way upon the back of a woman she will automatically surrender to his will.' He is also reported as being one of Aleister Crowley's previous incarnations. His name, Éliphas Lévi."[161] The same issue includes an article by the Treasurer General, who quoted Lévi a number of times and claimed that the single book which influenced Crowley the most was Lévi's *The Key of the Mysteries*.[162] In this article, he also stated that James G. Frazer's book *The Golden Bough* "merely fleshed out ideas from Lévi" for Crowley and that Lévi appears to have turned Crowley's interest toward such authors as Edgar Allen Poe and William Blake. He also affirmed Lévi's profound influence on the Hermetic Order of the Golden Dawn. Like Crowley, the Treasurer General has problems with Lévi's efforts to maintain a Christian approach to occultism. Thus, he wrote: "A word of caution. In reading Lévi, a strong stomach is one of the requisites. The book is filled with Christian remarks. It is not always possible to get through this veil on a first or even a third reading. Persist. Write in the margin. The hard part is getting past the pseudo-logic and Christian propaganda."[163] No doubt this article is only one example of many articles in O.T.O. publications in which Lévi is the focus. Research indicates that Lévi profoundly influenced Crowley and, through Crowley, the O.T.O.

Order of the Temple of Astarte

Ordo Templi Astarte (Order of the Temple of Astarte, or O.T.A.) was founded by Carroll R. Runyon, Jr. in 1970 and was incorporated in 1971. This order also operates under the name of Church of Hermetic Science and seeks to practice Kabbalistic Magick in the Western tradition.[164] Based on the psychology of Carl Gustav Jung, the order gives the following definition of "magick": "A system of ritual hypnotic induction (conjuration) that calls upon archetypal forms from the unconscious (evocation) and allows them to be visualized (manifestation) whereupon they can be used for numerous purposes ranging from the frankly psychotherapeutic to the more abstract system research and development."[165]

According to Runyon, the O.T.A. operates a system of ritual called Crater Repoa, which is older than the Golden Dawn. This system consists of seven degrees. three of which are currently being worked. The headquarters is in Pasadena, California. Runyon expressed the opinion that Éliphas Lévi's major contribution was his syncretistic blend of Kabbalah and Tarot. He feels that Lévi's major shortcoming was his failure to differentiate between traditional magic and invented magic. He also stated that Crowley was more of a practical magician than Lévi, whose focus was on the theoretical.[166]

Builders of the Adytum

Besides the Theosophical Society, there is probably no organization in America in which the imprint of Éliphas Lévi can be as clearly seen as the Builders of the Adytum (B.O.T.A.). This organization was founded by Dr. Paul Foster Case (1884-1954), who had been initiated into the Hermetic Order of the Golden Dawn in England.[167] Reportedly, Case entered into his life's work at a very early age "due to his recall of past lives as a Qabalistic Initiate and Adept."[168] As a child, he was an avid reader, had a marked musical talent, and soon discovered he could consciously manipulate his dream states and experience extrasensory states of consciousness. At the age of nine, he corresponded with British author Rudyard Kipling, who assured him of the reality of his experiences. At the age of sixteen, he discovered that playing cards were the descendants of Tarot. As a result, he collected every book on Tarot and set of Tarot keys he could find. His extensive research on Tarot led him to the study of Kabbalah. He developed the conviction that he "already knew the Secret Wisdom of Israel" as a result of experiences in previous incarnations. He claimed that his studies in Tarot and Kabbalah were really like a review, preliminary to some greater work. Eventually, he abandoned a successful musical career and, in 1922, established the School of Ageless Wisdom, which is now called the Builders of the Adytum. He became a prolific writer and enthralling speaker in his efforts to fulfill his mission of translating the techniques of Tarot and Kabbalah into terms understandable to the modern mind and to extend the teachings of the Ageless Wisdom.[169]

The purpose of this movement includes teaching and practice of the doctrines of the Oneness of God, the brotherhood of man, and the kinship of all life patterned alter the Ageless Wisdom mystery schools of spiritual training as particularly exemplified by the Kabbalah. The major objective is "the promotion of the welfare of humanity," which is embodied in a seven-point program of universal peace, universal political freedom, universal religious freedom, universal education, universal health, universal prosperity, and universal spiritual unfoldment. The B.O.T.A. curriculum — which is usually taught in correspondence courses — has as its aim the transmutation of personality, based on the conviction that a transformed personality will be able to change its environment. New members are called associate members and receive graded instruction by mail. They are eligible to become Working Builders (full members) affiliated with active chapters. Eventually, they may receive advanced instruction for participation in esoteric work. The headquarters is in Los Angeles. There are approximately fifty study groups and working groups (pronaos) in nineteen states. There are also groups in Canada, Europe, New Zealand, Colombia, and the Caribbean.[170]

Case did not see the teachings of Kabbalah and Tarot as incompatible with true Christianity, which he understood in esoteric terms. Thus, he wrote:

> Many of us have come into the esoteric teachings of Builders of the Adytum because we were unable to accept the traditional dogmas of exoteric Christianity. We do not, and cannot, accept the ordinary theology. We do not idolize any Scripture. We reject the notion of an infallible Bible, just as we reject the notion that there can be an infallible Church or an infallible Pope. Yet, in our quest for freedom, in our passion for liberty, we must not forget that the principles we base our teachings on *include* much that is believed by the traditional churches, and our free use of passages from both the Old Testament and the New, throughout our teachings, the reverence we pay to the name of Jesus Christ, show that even we continue the ancient Oriental tradition of the power of names. [171]

Case understood true, esoteric Christianity as "a Christianity that was never completely lost even during those dark centuries when the real meaning of the Christ Event was sadly distorted and dogmatized by those who corrupted truth to serve selfish and power-hungry ends."[172] In 1935, he predicted a revolution in consciousness, with B.O.T.A. playing a key role in bringing this revolution to pass. Thus, he wrote:

> Most of the world today is in bondage to Mammon, but the time is at

hand when Mammon shall take its proper place as the servant, not the master of man. Millions are enslaved by the machine, but the hour is striking when a revolution greater than that of 1776 shall throw off the shackles of that hateful servitude. The revolution is now in progress. Its field is not the field of battle between armies of men. It is the field of the human soul. It is a revolution in consciousness, overturning the old false standards of value.[173]

Paul Foster Case

Like other occult writers, Case was quite impressed with Lévi's concept of the Astral Light. He called it "an actual force" and quoted Lévi, as follows:

There exists a force which is far more powerful than steam, by means of which a single man, who can master it, and knows how to direct it, might throw the world into confusion and transform its face. It is diffused throughout infinity; it is the substance of heaven and earth. When it produces radiance, it is called light. It is substance and motion at one and the same time; it is a fluid and perpetual vibration. In infinite space, it is ether, or etherized light; it becomes astral light in the stars which it magnetizes, while in organized beings it becomes magnetic light or fluid. The will of intelligent beings acts directly on this light, and by means thereof, upon all nature, which is made subject to the modifications of intelligence.[174]

Case agreed with Lévi that learning to control and direct the Astral Light enables one to become the depository of the power of God.[175] He quoted Lévi's claim that "God creates it eternally, and man, in the image of the Deity, modifies and apparently multiplies it in the reproduction of his species."[176] He saw the Astral Light as analogous to the Hindu concept of *kundalini* (serpent power).[177] For elaboration on the latter doctrine, he referred his readers to the writings of Helena P. Blavatsky, who called it *Fohat*.[178] He urged member of B.O.T.A. to learn more about the Astral Light, charging them:

You can direct its currents. You can learn to use it for every conceivable good end. It is yours to command, yours to employ for the production of revolutionary changes in your personality and your circumstances. You are now part of an organized movement which utilizes these potencies of subconsciousness every day, and every hour of the day. Some of the achievements of persons connected with this movement have been simply astounding. Yet they have been accomplished by persons in no essential respect more gifted than you.[179]

He understood the Astral Light in terms of the "Life-power" which is the substance and working force in every cell of the human body, yet not limited to the cells nor to the structures composing the environment but, according to Lévi, distributed throughout infinity, as the substance of heaven and earth.[180] He used Lévi's term the Astral Light to refer to the "stuff" which composes all forms throughout the universe.[181] He agreed with Lévi's description of this as the First Matter of the alchemists and as the power whose superconscious manifestation is represented by the Tarot Key 0.[182] He wrote:

> Step by step, the progress of science brings the dumb, brute forces of nature under the control of human thought, *expressed in words*. For milleniums *(sic)*, lightning was only a type of swift death, and thunder was mistaken for the voice of an angry God. Today the same lightning carries the human voice in a flash to every part of the world and has endowed human speech with the universal reverberation and success which Éliphas Lévi prophesied when he wrote what would occur when men began to master the subtler force.[183]

He accepted Lévi's view that "all magic is in the will." [184] He quoted Lévi's teaching regarding imagination:

> Imagination is actually as the eye of the soul, and it is therein that forms are delineated and preserved; by its means we behold the reflections of the indivisible world. It is the mirror of visions and the apparatus of magical life. Thereby we cure diseases, modify the seasons, ward off death from the living, and resuscitate those who are dead, because this faculty exalts the will and gives it power over the universal agent.
>
> Imagination is the instrument of the adaptation of the Logos. In its application to reason it is genius, for reason, like genius, is one amidst the complexity of operations. Demons, souls, and the rest, can therefore be really and truly beheld by means of the imagination; but the imagination of the adept is diaphanous, whilst that of the uninitiated is opaque. The light of truth traverses the one as through a crystal window, and is refracted in the other as in a vitreous mass full of scoriae and foreign matter.
>
> The things which contribute most to the errors of the vulgar and the extravagances of the insane are the reflections of depraved imaginations in one another. But the seer knows with an absolute knowledge that the things he imagines are true, and experience invariably confirms his visions. [185]

He concurred with Lévi's view that death and renewal were inseparably linked and that "the life-current of the progress of souls is regulated by a law of development which carries the individual ever upward."[186] He, like Lévi, was greatly impressed by the Pentagram. Thus, he gave the following quotation:

> The Pentagram expresses the mind's domination over the elements and it is by this sign that we bind the demons of the air, the spirits of fire, the spectres of water, and the ghosts of earth. It is the Star of the Magi, the burning star of the Gnostic schools, the sign of intellectual omnipotence and autocracy. It is the symbol of the Word made Flesh.... The sign of the Pentagram is called also the sign of the Microcosm, and it represents what the Kabbalists of the Zohar term the Microprosopus. Its complete comprehension is the key of the two worlds — it is absolute natural philosophy and natural science. Its use, however, is most dangerous to operators who do not perfectly and completely understand it.... All mysteries of magic, all symbols of the gnosis, all figures of occultism, all kabbalistic keys of prophecy, are resumed in the sign of the Pentagram, which Paracelsus proclaims to be the greatest and most potent of all. It is indeed the sign of the absolute and universal synthesis.[187]

Elsewhere, he quoted the same passage and referred to Lévi as "our illustrious Frater and predecessor" and "the French adept." He warned his readers that they could not expect to obtain the complete and perfect understanding of the Pentagram envisioned by Lévi as a result of a few years' study. Such an understanding, he said, would require "several incarnations devoted to investigations and practice." He also concurred with Lévi's warnings against dabblers in occultism and conviction that genuine adepts never make a parade of their powers.[188] In efforts to describe the characteristics of the true Magus, he again quoted Lévi:

> Magic is the divinity of man achieved in union with faith; the true Magi are Men-Gods, in virtue of their intimate union with the divine principle. They are without fears and without desires, dominated by no falsehood, sharing no error, loving without illusion, suffering without impatience, reposing in the quietude of eternal thought. A Magus cannot be ignorant, for magic implies superiority, mastership, majority, and majority signifies emancipation by knowledge. The Man-God has neither rights nor duties, he has science, will, and power. He is more than free, he is master; he does not command, he creates; he does not obey, because nobody can possibly command him. What others term duty, he names his good pleasure; he does good because he wishes to,

and never wills anything else; he co-operates freely in everything that forwards the cause of Justice, and for him sacrifice is the luxury of the moral life and the magnificence of the heart. He is implacable toward evil because he is without a trace of hatred for the wicked. He regards reparatory chastisement as a benefit and does not comprehend the meaning of vengeance.[189]

Case quoted from a sixteenth-century Hebrew manuscript used by Lévi in *Transcendental Magic* which enumerated "The powers and privileges of the man who holds in his right hand the clavicles of Solomon, and in his left the branch of the blossoming almond."[190]

He declared that such powers attributed to an adept were the same as those which, according to Patanjali, the author of the *Yoga-sutras*, are exercised by the perfected yogi.[191] In warning against haste in efforts to master esoteric work, he referred to Lévi's belief that a magician should work as if he had all eternity in which to complete his undertaking.[192] He further stated, with Lévi, that the adept should be a "Master of Compassion" who will, thus, understand the past, present, and future.[193] He declared that "Lévi wrote one thing... for the instructed and another for the uninitiated."[194] He observed that, for Lévi, the existence of the One Reality was an hypothesis necessary for the experience of the beneficent results of conscious contact with the power of this Reality.[195] He recognized that equilibrium was one of Lévi's key concepts and quoted Lévi's words from *Transcendental Magic*: "Equilibrium is the result of two forces, but if these were absolutely and permanently equal, equilibrium would be immobility and consequently the negation of life. Movement is the result of alternated preponderance."[196] On the same theme, he repeated Lévi's advice to "avoid all excesses" and "carry nothing to extremes" in arguing that "only a balanced person can be a practical occultist."[197] He was moved by Lévi's words "The beautiful lives are the accurate ones, and magnificences of Nature are an algebra of graces and splendours."[198]

Case regarded the Tarot as "one of the most wonderful productions of human ingenuity" and stated that it deserved the following words of praise bestowed upon it by Lévi:

> The Tarot is a veritable oracle, and answers all possible questions with clearness and accuracy; so that a prisoner devoid of books, had he only a Tarot of which he knew how to make use, could, in a few years, acquire a universal science, and converse with unequalled doctrine and inexhaustible eloquence. This wheel, in fact, is the key of the oratorical art, and of the great Art of Raymond Lully; it is the true secret of the transmutation of darkness into light; it is the first and most important of all the arcana of the *magnum opus*. By means of this universal key of

symbolism all the allegories of India, Egypt, and Judaea are made intelligible; the Apocalypse of St. John is a Kabbalistic book, the sense of which is exactly indicated by the figures and numbers of the Urim, Thummin, Teraphim and Ephod, all summarized and completed by the Tarot; the sanctuaries of old are no longer full of mysteries, and the signification of the objects of the Hebrew cultus may for the first time be understood.[199]

To Case, the Tarot represented a summary of Kabbalah, alchemy, astrology, and magic—all of which were parts of an ancient psychological system. He regarded Freemasonry as a remnant of this ancient system and regretted the fact that "all too few Masons realize what a treasury they have inherited from the past."[200] He had great respect for Albert Pike, who wrote: "He who desires to attain the understanding of the Grand Word and the possession of the Great Secret. . . must follow, to class his acquisition of knowledge and direct the operation, the order indicated in the alphabet of the TAROT."[201] He was aware of the strong influence of Lévi on Pike, finding it ironic that "though Lévi himself was a nominal Roman Catholic, his doctrine is utilized by Scottish Rite Masonry in the United States, inasmuch as General Albert Pike's *Morals and Dogma*. . . repeats *verbatim* page after page from the French occultist's *Dogma and Ritual*."[202] He was also aware of Lévi's influence on Madame Blavatsky, whom he regarded as "one of the greatest expounders of the doctrine embodied in the TAROT." He described her books *Isis Unveiled* and *The Secret Doctrine* (both of which contain numerous references to Lévi) as "penetrating," "unusual," and reflecting "her profound knowledge of the symbology used in these KEYS."[203]

Perhaps Case's greatest tribute to Lévi is found in his discussion of the work of mathematician Albert Einstein. Thus, he wrote: "Einstein has advanced a theory that gravitation and electro-magnetism are one and the same thing. By reviving this ancient doctrine, known to his Hebrew ancestors, the great mathematician brings closer than ever the revolution in physics Éliphas Lévi predicted back in 1859, and hastens the day when we shall, in truth, return to the transcendent magic of the Chaldeans, which magic is diagrammed on the Tree of Life." [204] It appears that Case saw both Lévi and Einstein as laying the foundation for the revolution in consciousness in which the B.O.T.A. would play a major role.

Fraternity of the Hidden Light

Fraternitas L.V.X. Occulra (the Fraternity of the Hidden Light or F.H.L.) was founded in 1982 by five initiates who felt a strong mandate to unite diverse streams of Western esotericism. Its headquarters are in Covina, California. Members regard their fraternity as the lineal descendant of the American section of the Hermetic Order of the Golden Dawn. The order's objectives include acting as a modern day repository of ancient wisdom, training members for selfless service to humanity, and promulgation of ancient wisdom. Members work through a curriculum of graded instruction and employ rituals to invoke quantum changes in consciousness.[205] The "Threshold" course is designed to guide aspirants in preparation for initiation. This course includes the following subjects:

> The Origins of the Tradition; Wisdom, Power, and Love; the Hierarchy of Light; the Functions of Consciousness; Esoteric Psychology; Fraternal Harmony and Ethics; the Hermetic Qabalah; the Doctrinal Qabalah; the Tree of Life; the Literal and Cosmic Law of Cause and Effect; Meditation; Reincarnation; the Tarot; the Magical Keys to Consciousness; the Inner Power Centers called the *Chakras*; Esoteric Healing Techniques; the Initiatory Path; the Power and Use of Ritual; the Four Great Maxims, To Know, Will, Dare, and Keep Silent; the Great Arcanum; the Seven Hermetic Principles; the Outer Vehicle (Modern History of the Tradition); the Unreserved Dedication; and Initiation.[206]

The order's Steward (leader), Paul A. Clark was initiated into B.O.T.A. by Ann Davies, the successor to Paul Foster Case. He feels that his order's teachings are closer to the original Golden Dawn teachings than those of B.O.T.A. He credits Lévi with being the first person to show connections between the Tarot and the Hebrew alphabet and stated that Tarot and Kabbalah blend well together even if there was originally no historical connection. He said that, for this order, the most important of Lévi's books is *The Key of the Mysteries*. He expressed the opinion that Lévi preceded Carl Jung in recognizing that the Mysteries work in terms of archetypal symbolism.[207]

Church of Mercavah

The Church of Mercavah was founded in 1982 at Baton Rouge, Louisiana by James Ray Montandon, a Kabbalist who read the works of Éliphas Lévi and often stated his respect for "the great mind and fraud of Éliphas Lévi."[208] The founder is now deceased and the church is led by the founder's son, Luther Ray Montandon, who expressed the belief that "fraud" is the only means of communication of occultism from one culture to another. In this context, the word "fraud" does not have its usual negative meaning. The younger Montandon stated that the Church of Mercavah, whose name is derived from the Hebrew word for chariot as expressed in the Vision of Ezekiel, is more non-creedal than Unitarianism. "Each person," he said "must find their own truth." He said that his father was influenced by many teachers, including Éliphas Lévi, Helena P. Blavatsky, Paul Foster Case, and Paramahansa Yogananda.[209] According to a information pamphlet:

> Quite simply, we are a vehicle of worship. We are structured for the use of any and all people with an open mind. We exist for those who wish to express their individual beliefs without having the opinions of others thrust upon them. We are here to serve others.
>
> We are constructed upon universal lines. We are a synthesis of beliefs that transcend all beliefs and creeds. We embrace no dogma, hold all truths sacred, and believe that the sincere search for truth and understanding will be rewarded. . . . Our services are structured, and our liturgy is comprised from many different beliefs and religions. The symbols and the liturgy of the church are much like a mirror in which each man sees the reflection of his own faith.
>
> Our ministers are instructed in many fields, including comparative religion, symbology, philosophy, esoteric philosophy, and many others. They are appointed to be ministers to all people of all religions, and must show a broad base of knowledge in many fields.[210]

Summation

In this chapter, an effort has been made to assess the influence of Éliphas Lévi on the following religious movements: Theosophy, Anthroposophy, Rosicrucianism, Order of the Temple of the Orient, Order of the Temple of Astarte, Builders of the Adytum, Fraternity of the Hidden Light, and Church of Mercavah. From all indications, Lévi greatly influenced Helena P. Blavatsky, the founder of Theosophy, and had some influence on her successors. His influence on Rudolf Steiner, the founder of Anthroposophy, appears to have been limited. Modern Anthroposophists pay little attention to Lévi. His influence is profoundly recognized in the Rosicrucian Fraternity, limited in A.M.O.R.C., and unclear in both Rosicrucian Fellowship and S.R.LA. Aleister Crowley, a leading figure in the O.T.O., made the largest claim of all when he said he was Lévi reincarnated. Most O.T.O. members are aware of this claim and of Lévi's influence on Crowley. Paul Foster Case, founder of B.O.T.A., was as extensively influenced by Lévi as was Blavatsky, Crowley, or Albert Pike. Leaders of O.T.A. and F.H.L. regard Lévi as important to esotericism in general and their movements in particularly, especially give acknowledgement to his blend of Kabbalah and Tarot. The founder of the Church of Mercavah admired "the great mind and fraud of Éliphas

Lévi," and considered "fraud" to be the only way of communicating occultism from one culture to another.

Endnotes

1. This word is derived from two Greek *words – theos*, "God," and *sophia*, "wisdom." It means "wisdom concerning God or things divine." Implicit in this definition is the idea that such wisdom is accessible to the human soul through direct intuition of a supersorial reality. In the West, the concept has a long history, beginning in Pythagorean Greece. In the East, a similar concept can be found, although it has never been called "theosophy." The theosophical worldview, however expressed, rests on a metaphysical foundation that wisdom is reached through insight into the nature of things as they are, rather than through intellectual reasoning; see Emily B. Sellon and Renee Weber, "Theosophy and the Theosophical Society," in Antoine Faivre and Jacob Needleman, eds., *Modern Esoteric Spirituality* (New York: Crossroad, 1992), 311.

2. Lévi's writings were especially important in early Theosophy, before Eastern influences became prominent. This is the view of Shirley Nickolson, Director of the Krotona Institute, which is the California branch of the Theosophical Society in America; cited in Shirley Nicholson, personal letter, 8 November 1994. From its founding in New York City in 1875 – the year of Lévi's death – the Theosophical Society was highly eclectic in its approach to religious truth. Reportedly, it "lit a syncretist bonfire that is still shooting sparks"; see Antoine Faivre, *Access to Western Esotericism* (New York: State University of New York Press, 1994), 39.

3. Emily Sellon, "Blavatsky, H. P." *The Encyclopedia of Religion,* ed. Mircea Eliade (New York: MacMillan Publishing Company, 1987), 2:245.

4. K. Paul Johnson, *The Masters Revealed: Madame Blavatsky and the Myth of the Great White Lodge* (New York: State University of New York Press, 1994), 19.

5. Ibid., 20.

6. Ibid., 22.

7. Ibid., 23.

8. Sellon, "Blavatsky, H. P.," 245.

9. Johnson, *The Masters Revealed,* 25. During the same trip, Rawson accompanied a caravan of pilgrims from Cairo to Mecca, disguised as a Muslim medical student.

10. Ibid., 28. Rawson was born in Chester, Vermont on 15 October 1828. He held Doctorates in Medicine, Divinity, and Letters. He was the author of a number of books and exhibited great proficiency as a linguist. He was also a noted artist, illustrating not only his own books but also those of other authors. Among the best known of the books he illustrated was Robert

Morris' *Freemasonry in the Holy Land, or Handmarks of Hiram's Builders* (New York: Arno Press, 1977). Throughout his life, he was deeply involved in secret societies, including Freemasonry and Rosicruciansim. He claimed to have received initiation from the Druzes of Lebanon and the Adwan Bedouin of Moab; see Johnson, *The Masters Revealed,* 26. He was one of the early members of the para-Masonic organization called the Ancient Arabic Order of Nobles of the Mystic Shrine of North America (popularly known as "Shriners") which was established in New York City in 1872 — three years before the Theosophical Society. He did art work and Arabic translations for the Shriners; see Fred Van Deventer, *Parade to Glory: The Shriners and their Caravan to Destiny* (New York: Pyramid Books, 1964), 43-52. The Shriners have a ritual based on Islam, including a mock pilgrimage to Mecca. Rawson was one of the few Shriners ever to make the real pilgrimage. However, he never embraced Islam. He had remarkable success traveling in the Muslim world in disguise; see Jocelyn Godwin, *The Theosophical Enlightenment* (New York: State University of New York Press, 1994), 280.

11. Ibid., 278-79.

12. Ibid., 280.

13. Sellon, "Blavatsky, H. P.," 245. Blavatsky taught that the "Ascended Masters" were the guardians of an ancient mystery tradition and included all of the great teachers of humanity, all of who were members of the "Great White Lodge," whose site is the Holy City of Shamballah in the Gobi Desert; see Max Heindel, *Blavatsky and the Secret Doctrine* (Santa Monica, California: DeVorss and Company, 1933), 78-82.

14. Sellon, "Blavatsky, H. P." One authority on Theosophy attached great significance to Blavatsky's arrival in the Empire State and wrote: "That both Spiritualism and Theosophy originated in the New York area is not coincidental as it may first appear. New York was the heart of the so-called burned-over district, an area of the American Northeast through which most immigrants were channeled. The "burned-over district" became famous for its revivalists, free thinkers, dissenters, and religious eccentrics of every conceivable stamp. The Seventh Day Adventists, Jehovah's Witnesses, Joseph Smith's Mormonism, and Mary Baker Eddy's Christian Science all emerged from this area, as well as the Transcendentalists and a variety of social utopian groups. That Mme Blavatsky gravitated toward this area and that both Spiritualism and Theosophy had their beginnings there is not the be wondered at"; see Maria Carlson, *"No Religion Higher Than Truth". A History of the Theosophical Movement in Russia, 1875-1922* (Princeton, New Jersey: Princeton University Press, 1993), 212.

15. Johnson, *The Masters Revealed,* 80-85. Sotheran worked as a journalist, bibliographer, and antiquarian. He conducted extensive research into Freemasonry prior to applying for membership. Reportedly, when he took the first degree, "all the arcana required for the last were in his possession." He

rose rapidly through Masonic ranks. He was also quite active in promoting socialism. In the latter capacity, he served as a district delegate for the Knights of Labor and one of the organizers of the Social Democratic Workingman's Party of North America (now the Socialist Labor Party). He was a popular lecturer at the New York Liberal Club.

16. Godwin, *The Theosophical Enlightenment,* 284.

17. Ted Peters, *The Cosmic Self: A Penetrating Look at Today's New Age Movements* (San Francisco, Ca.: Harper San Francisco, 1991), 47-48. Peters described Blavatsky as a "Victorian hippie" who conducted discussion groups called "at-homes," where drug use was common. He claimed that *Isis Unveiled* was influenced by "healthy doses of hashish and a vision of the goddess Isis herself."

18. Godwin, *The Theosophical Enlightenment,* 286-88.

19. Sellon, "Blavatsky, H. P.," 245-46. Rosicrucian leader Max Heindel greatly admired Blavatsky and understood *The Secret Doctrine* as a work which contained the essence of all religions; see Heindel, *Blavatsky and the Secret Doctrine,* 59. He was quite impressed with her concept of the fundamental identity of all souls with the universal Oversoul and with her idea of the obligatory pilgrimage of every soul through the cycle of incarnation; see ibid., 64. He saw himself as a Christian Mystic and Blavatsky as an Oriental Occultist but expressed the belief that her teachings "can make us wise unto salvation"; see ibid., 89.

20. Sellon, "Blavatsky, H. P.," 246.

21. "Introducing You to the Theosophical Society," (Wheaton, Illinois: Theosophical Society in America, 1994), 1. Wheaton, Illinois is the headquarters of the American branch of the original Theosophical Society based in Adyar. However, there are two other groups of Theosophists independent of this group. These arose from schisms following Blavatsky's death in 1891. At that time, there was much controversy as to whether William Quan Judge or Annie Besant would succeed Blavatsky as principal articulator of Theosophical teachings. Thus, in 1894, seventy-five of the American branches seceded to form a new organization under Judge's leadership. Judge died the following year and was succeeded by Katherine Tingley (1847-1929), who led her followers to Point Loma, California, where she instituted a number of experimental and educational programs. This group's headquarters was later moved to Pasadena, California. Another schism occurred in 1909, when Robert Crosbie (1849- 1919), a member of the Point Loma society, organized the United Lodge of Theosophists in Los Angeles. This branch concentrates on the teachings of Blavatsky and Judge, rejecting the works of such "second generation" Theosophists as Besant and C. W. Leadbeater, and seeks to minimize formal organization; see Sellon and Weber, "Theosophy and the Theosophical Society," 3 16-17. According to the Secretary General of the Pasadena group, the three bodies at times jointly represent The-

osophy, as they did at the 1993 Parliament of the World's Religions in Chicago; cited in Kirby Van Mater, letter to the author, 2 December 1994.

22. Sellon and Weber, "Theosophy and the Theosophical Society," 314. Theosophy seeks to promote understanding and brotherhood among peoples of all races, nationalities, philosophies, and religions. Such has been part of the Theosophical worldview since the organization's beginning—at a time when such a belief in human equality was not widely held; see ibid., 328.

23. Sellon, "Blavatsky, H. P.," 246. Blavatsky's positive attitude toward Hinduism is in marked contrast to that of Lévi, who called India "the wise mother of all idolatries" and the Mysteries of India "the Kabbalah of profanation." He charged that Brahmanism plunged the soul into gulfs of madness and claimed the Gnostics borrowed their reveries from the false Kabbalah of India; see Lévi, *History of Magic*, 72. He believed that anarchy was embedded in the Indian caste system.

24. Sellon, Blavatsky, H. P.," 246. Blavatsky spent seven months in the home of Gustave and Marie Gebhard in Elberfield, Germany. As stated in chapter one, they had previously welcomed Lévi as a guest in their home. When they learned of the existence of the Theosophical Society, they wrote to Olcott and soon joined. The Gebhards had seven children, most of who became Theosophists. They probably influenced many of Lévi's German followers to embrace Theosophy in the years following his death; see Cranston, *HPB*, 262. The German Theosophical Society was already functioning by the time of Blavatsky's arrival. On 27 July 1884, Olcott conducted an organizational meeting in Mrs. Gebhard's "occult room." Dr. Hubbe Schleiden was elected the society's first president; see Josephine Ransom, comp. *A Short History of the Thosophical Society* (Adyar, Madras, India: Theosophical Publishing House, 1938), 202.

25. Sellon, Blavatsky, H. P.," 246. It is possible that this journal's name may have been inspired by Lévi. She agreed with Lévi that Lucifer was actually a vehicle of light (literally, "light-bearer") and "a mediating force diffused throughout creation; that it serves for creation and destruction." She held that the "light in question is of the nature of fire, that is warming and vivifying in its purest use, but that it burns, dissolves, and destroys in its excess"; see Helena P. Blavatsky, *The Secret Coctrine: The Synthesis of Science, Religion and Philosophy* (New York: Theosophical Publishing Company, Ltd., 1888), 2:511. Her source was Lévi, *History of Magic,* 159. In the October/November 1890 issue *of Lucifer,* she published an article entitled "Psychic and Noetic Action," in which she wrote: "Too close association with the 'Old Terrestrial Serpent' is infectious. The odic and magnetic currents of the Astral Light often incite to murder, drunkenness, and immorality, and as Éliphas Lévi expresses it, the not altogether pure natures can be driven headlong by the blind forces set in motion in the *Light* — *by* the errors and sins imposed on its waves"; see George Robert Stow Mead, ed. *Five Years of*

Theosophical, Historical, and Scientific Essays Selected from "The Theosophist" (New York: Arno Press, 1976), 37.

26. Sellon, "Blavatsky, H. P.," 246. It is interesting that Blavatsky outlived Albert Pike by one month. She was aware of his work, describing him as "perhaps the greatest authority of the day, among American Masons"; see Helena P. Blavatsky, *Isis Unveiled: A Master-Key to the Mysteries of Ancient and Modern Science and Theology,* (Pasadena, California: Theosophical University Press, 1950), 2:377. There is no evidence that Blavatsky and Pike ever met.

27. Stephan A. Hoeller, telephone conversation with author, 26 December 1994.

28. Helena P. Blavatsky, *Isis Unveiled: A Master-Key to the Mysteries of Ancient and Modern Science and Theology* (Covina, California: Theosophical University Press, 1950), 1:395.

29. Ibid., 1:511.

30. Helena P. Blavatsky, *Isis Unveiled: A Master-Key to the Mysteries of Ancient and Modern Science and Theology* (London: Theosophical Publishing Company, Ltd., 1888), 1:196.

31. Blavatsky, *The Secret Doctrine,* 2:506-07.

32. Ibid, 2:5 10.

33. Helena P. Blavatsky, *Kabalah and Kabalism* (Los Angeles, Ca.: Theosophy Company, n.d.), 44-45. This work is a collection of reprints of Blavatsky's journal articles.

34. Ibid., 15.

35. "Selected Titles," Computer Printout, 8 November 1994. Provided by Kirby Van Mater, Secretary-General, Theosophical Society, Pasadena, California.

36. Blavatsky, *Isis Unveiled,* 1:113.

37 Ibid., *1:125.*

38. Ibid., 1:247.

39. Ibid., 1:281.

40. Ibid, 1:137; her source was Levi, *Transcendental Magic,* 242. Here, both Lévi and Blavatsky mentioned Abraxas, an important Gnostic symbol. According to Bishop Hoeller: "In contrast to Helios, the god of light, and the Devil, god of darkness, Abraxas appears as the supreme power of being in whom light and darkness are both united and transcended.... The most frequently mentioned explanations of the symbols embodied in the Abraxas figure are as follows. The head of the rooster symbolizes vigilant wakefulness and is related to both the human heart and to universal heart, the sun, the rising of which is invoked by the matutinal clarion call of the chanticleer. The human torso is the embodiment of the principle of logos, or articulated thought, which is regarded as the unique power of the human being. The legs shaped like snakes indicate prudence whereby the dynamic

rulership of universal being governs its own all powerful energies. The shield held in the right hand is symbolic of wisdom, the great protector of all divine warriors. The whip, held in the left hand, denotes the relentless, driving power of life that spurs all existence on. The four white horses drawing the chariot, represent the tetramorphic forces whereby the universal libido or psychic energy expresses itself, variously called the four ethers of the power of the sun, the four elements of earth, water, fire and air, and in Jungian psychological terms, the four functions of human consciousness, sensation, feeling, thinking and intuition"; see Hoeller, *The Gnostic Jung and the Seven Sermons to the Dead*, 84-86. For a detailed study of Abraxas, see Robert L. Uzzel, "Abraxas: From Ancient Gnosis to Contemporary Culture, with Overtones in Freemasonry," *Lux e Tenebris* (1997): 1-69.

41. Blavatsky, *The Secret Doctrine,* 1:196.

42. Ibid., 1:254.

43. Ibid., 2:74.

44. After Blavatsky and Olcott moved to India, the Theosophical Society flourished in America under the leadership of Judge (1851-1896), a New York attorney who served as General Secretary for the American section. He was a good organizer, administrator, speaker, and writer. The society experienced rapid growth under his leadership. He presided over the Theosophical Congress at the World's Parliament of Religions in Chicago in 1893. His books include *Letters That Have Helped Me, The Ocean of Theosophy,* and *Practical Occultism;* see Sellon and Weber, "Theosophy and the Theosophical Society," 316.

45. William Quan Judge, *Echoes from the Orient: A Broad Outline of Theosophical Doctrines* (Covina, Ca.: Theosophical University Press, 1944), 84.

46. Ibid., 87.

47. Ibid., 87-88.

48. Ibid., 89.

49. Ibid., 91.

50. Blavatsky, *Isis Unveiled,* 1:xxxii. During Blavatsky's lifetime, words such as "occult" and "occultism" had much more positive connotations than they do today. Thus, contemporary Theosophists have sought to distance themselves from such terms. According to a Theosophy promotional brochure: "In recent times. . . the words *occult* and *occultism* have been given new, debased, and even sinister meanings. They are often connected with such phenomena as devil worship, animal sacrifice, drugs, ghosts, fortune telling, and a variety of other things... . The "occult" section in a bookstore is likely to include books dealing with a hodgepodge of subjects—some respectable, some foolish, and some trashy, if not actually wicked. With this new meaning of occult. . . Theosophy has nothing to do. The Theosophical view is that the devil of popular lore is a myth and a misunderstanding of a symbol. Theosophy also teaches that the first step to spiritual progress is a

clean life"; see "Cults, the Occult and Theosophy" (Wheaton, Ill.: Theosophical Society in America, n.d.), 1-2.
51. Blavatsky, *Isis Unveiled*, 1:179.
52. Ibid., 1:218.
53. Ibid., 1:3 14.
54. Ibid., 1:395.
55. Ibid., 1:480-84.
56. Ibid., 1:485.
57. Blavatsky, *Isis Unveiled*, 2:343.
58. Ibid., 2:55. The English title is *Demonomania, or Treatise on the Sorcerers*.
59. Ibid., 2:56.
60. Ibid., 2:66.
61. Ibid., 2:87.
62. Ibid., 2:127.
63. Ibid., 2:201.
64. Ibid., 2:202.
65. Ibid., 2:215.
66. Ibid., 2:398.
67. Ibid., 2:480.
68. Blavatsky, *The SecretDoctrine*, 1:241.
69. Ibid., 2:360.
70. Ibid., 562.
71. Godwin, *The Theosophical Enlightenment*, 303.
72. Madon Meade, *Madame Blava:sky: The Woman Behind the Myth* (New York: G. Putnam's and Sons, 1980), 159.
73. Carlson, *"No Religion Higher Than Truth"*, 32.
74. Annie Besant, *Esoteric Christianity, or the Lesser Mysteries* (London: Theosophical Publishing House, 1918), 119.
75. Robert A. McDermott, "Rudolf Steiner and Anthroposophy," in Faivre and Needleman, *Modern Esoteric Spirituality*, 290.
76. Robert A. McDermott, "Steiner, Rudolf," in *Encyclopedia of Religion*, ed. Mircea Eliade (New York: MacMillan Publishing Company, 1987), 14:47. In *Theosophy*, Steiner sought unsuccessfully to give the term "theosophy" a broader meaning to the general public than the one popularized by Blavatsky.
77. Ibid., 47-48.
78. McDermott, "Rudolf Steiner and Anthroposophy," 29 1-92.
79. Carlson, *"No Religion Higher Than Truth"*, 32.
80. Dan Merkur, *Gnosis: An Esoteric Tradition of Mystical Visions and Unions* (New York: State University of New York Press, 1993), 61. In 1914, Steiner left the Order of the Temple of the Orient; see Faivre, *Access to Western Esotericism*, 9. At the time of his association, the order had not yet adopted the anti-Christian teachings of Aleister Crowley.
81. Carlson, *"No Religion Higher Than Truth"*, 33.

82. Ibid. While Theosophy expands more extensively into the area of metaphysical hierarchies, Anthroposophy has developed more from an anthrophenomenological basis.

83. Ibid.

84. McDermott, "Rudolf Steiner and Anthroposophy," 292.

85. Ibid., 289.

86. Ibid., 291.

87. Ibid., 306.

88. Ibid., 295.

89. Ibid., 293.

90. Ibid., 294.

91. Ibid., 295.

92. McDermott, "Steiner, Rudolf," 48.

93. Hilmar Moore, letter to the author, 18 January 1995.

94. Bishop Hoeller expressed the opinion that eighty per cent of Steiner's ideas were derived from Blavatsky and that Lévi influenced Steiner through Theosophy; Stephan A. Hoeller, telephone conversation with author, 26 December 1994.

95. Rudolf Steiner, *Karmic Relationships: Esoteric Studies*, trans. George Adams, rev. M. Cotterell, C. Davy, and D. S. Osmond ((London: Rudolf Steiner Press, 1974), 2:8.

96. Ibid., 192.

97. Ibid., 192-94.

98. As previously pointed out, there are three distinct groups of Theosophists. However, each group holds Blavatsky in high esteem as their founder, differing as to who was her proper successors. All Anthroposophists hold Steiner in high esteem. In contrast, Rosicrucianism is marked by a number of competing organizations. I know of no instance in which rival groups have jointly represented Rosicrucianism in a manner similar to the cooperation among Theosophists at the Parliament of the World's Religions in Chicago in 1993. Most of the time, the relations between various Rosicrucian groups has not been good. At times, the "war of the roses" has been quite bitter.

99. J. Gordon Melton, *Encyclopedic Handbook of Cults in America*, rev. ed. (New York: Garland Publishing, Inc., 1992), 96

100. Ibid. Few historians take seriously the accuracy of this account. Even if such a person did live, separating fact from fiction regarding his life is extremely problematic. Dealing with a legendary founder is quite different from dealing with historic persons like Blavatsky and Steiner.

101. Ibid. Rosicrucianism, like other movements of the time, seems to have arisen from a milieu where there was much concern for justice and equality in human society and a dissatisfaction with the position of established leaders of church and state related to such matters.

102. Lévi *The History of Magic,* 263.
103. Ibid., 264.
104. McIntosh, *The Rosicrucians,* 104.
105. 1bid., 99.
106. Godwin, *The Theosophical Enlightenment,* 248.
107. Ibid., 250.
108. Ibid., 250-51. A century later, this method was popularized by psychic Edgar Cayce.
109. Ibid., 253.
110. 1bid., 254. For an account of this visit, see chapter two.
111. Melton, *Encyclopedic Handbook of Cults in America,* 99.
112. Godwin, *The Theosophical Enlightenment,* 260.
113. 1bid., 257.
114. Melton, *Encyclopedic Handbook of Cults in America,* 99.
115. Godwin, *The Theosophical Enlightenment,* 257-59.
116. Melton, *Encyclopedic Handbook of Cults in America,* 99-100.
117. Clymer, *Book of Rosicruciae,* 69.
118. Melton, *Encyclopedic Handbook of Cults in America,* 100.
119. Gerald E. Poesnecker, letter to the author, 8 January 1995.
120. Howe, *The Magicians of the Golden Dawn,* 26.
121. Melton, *Encyclopedic Handbook of Cults in America,* 98.
122. Ibid., 100.
123. Ibid., 101. Mother Serena published many of her husband's books and pamphlets after his death.
124. Lucia Gorsch, telephone conversation with author, 23 January 1995. A perusal of several of Plummer's books revealed no specific mention of Lévi.
125. Manly P. Hall, "Biography of Max Heindel," in Heindel, *Blavatsky and the Secret Doctrine,* 19-20.
126. Ibid., 22.
127. Gloria Hayes, telephone conversation with the author, 23 January 1995.
128. Hall, "Biography of Max Heindel," 22-23.
129. Melton, *Encyclopedic Handbook of Cults in America,* 103.
130. Ibid., 104.
131. Gloria Hayes, telephone conversation with the author, 23 January 1994. A perusal of several of Heindel's books revealed no specific mention of Lévi.
132. Melton, *Encyclopedic Handbook of Cults in Americas* 102.
133. 1bid., 102-03.
134. H. Spencer Lewis, *Rosicrucian Questions and Answers, with Complete History of the Rosicrucian Order* (San Jose, California: Ancient Mystical Order Rosae Crucis, 1993), 145-46.
135. Ibid., 145.
136. Ibid., 157.

137. Ibid., 148.

138. Faivre, *Access to Western Esotericism*, 91.

139. "O.T.O. Official Bodies Worldwide Directory: Revised September 1994," *The Magical Link*, Spring-Summer 1994, 14. This directory lists O.T.O. bodies in Bosnia--Hercegovina but notes "No mail response due to war." Regarding Yugoslavia, it states "Listings temporarily suspended due to present climate of religious persecution."

140. Ibid.

141. Bill Heidrick, letter to the author, 31 December 1994.

142. Howe and Möller, "Theodor Reuss," 30.

143. Ibid., 31.

144. Ibid., 28.

145. Ibid., 30.

146. Ibid., 31. The original Order of the Illuminati was suppressed in Bavaria in 1784. It has been called a "quasi-Masonic" association because it infiltrated Freemasonry yet was never officially recognized by any Masonic body. The founder, Adam Weishaupt, was a professor at the University of Ingolstadt with an ambitious plan for modernization of German society who proposed to bring his goals to pass by utilizing the secrecy and social discipline of the Masonic lodges. Weishaupt was especially attracted to the existence within German Freemasonry of defined grades of illumination and the doctrine of obedience to unknown superior authorities. He recruited a number of men who held important positions in the German government and society. He sought to employ Masonic secrecy to achieve leftist political objectives. Although the Illuminati never gained much power, they were considered at least a potential threat by German conservatives; the suppression was the result; see Partner, *The Murdered Magicians*, 125-26.

147. Howe and Möller, "Theodor Reuss," 32. Contemporary O.T.O. members claim that H. Spencer Lewis, founder of A.M.O.R.C., was once a seventh degree member of O.T.O. Bill Heidrick, letter to the author, 31 December 1994.

148. Ibid., 33.

149. Ibid. A decade earlier, the two men had met in Theosophical Society circles. 156.

150. 1bid., 34.

151. 1bid., 36.

152. Ibid., 37-38. In his autobiography, The *Story of My Life,* Steiner went to great lengths to minimize the significance of his previous connection with Reuss and claimed that "this symbolic−cultural section of the anthroposophical movement came to an end in the middle of 1914."

153. 1bid., 37.

154. 1bid., 38-39. For detailed information on Crowley, see chapter two.

155. 1bid., 39.

156. Müller von Hansen, *The Protocols of the Elders of Zion* (Berlin, 1919), as quoted in ibid., 40. This work has been translated into English a number of times. Victor Marsden's translation *The Protocols of the Meetings of the Wise Men of Zion* (Chicago: Patriotic Publishing Company, 1934) has been quite influential in anti-Semitic circles. It is unclear whether Howe and Möller used the German original or a translation.

157. Ibid.

158. Bill Heidrick, letter to the author, 31 December 1994.

159. 1bid.

160. "Ordo Templi Orientis," *The Magical Link,* Spring-Summer 1994, 15.

161. "From the History Heap," *Thelema Lodge, O.T.O.*, February 1992, 9.

162Bill Heidrick, "From the Out Basket," *Thelema Lodge, O.T.O.*, February 1992, 7. Crowley translated Lévi's original French work into English.

162. Bill Heidrick, "From the Out Basket," *Thelema Lodge, O.T.O,,* February 1992, 7. Crowley translated Lévi's original French work into English.

163. Ibid., 8.

164. J. Gordon Melton, *Encyclopedia of American Religions,* 4th ed. (Detroit, Michigan: Gale Research, Inc., 1993), 824. Aleister Crowley was responsible for the spelling 'magick.'

165. Ibid.

166. Carroll R. Runyon, Jr., telephone conversation with author, 1 February 1995.

167. Stephan A. Hoeller, telephone conversation with author, 26 December 1994.

168. Paul Foster Case, *Highlights of Tarot, with Coloring Instructions* (Los Angeles, Ca.: Builders of the Adytum, 1989), 4.

169. Paul Foster Case, *The True and Invisible Rosicrucian Order: An Interpretation of the Rosicrucian Allegory and an Explanation of the Ten Rosicrucian Grades* (York Beach, Me.: Samuel Wiser, Inc., 1981), 333. Regarding the title of this book, an active member of this organization wrote to me: "There are many groups which call themselves Rosicrucians and B.O.T.A. is not connected in any way with them. However, B.O.T.A. could be said to be the outer manifestation of the True and Invisible Rosicrucian Order." Soror V, letter to the autor, 16 January 1995.

170. Melton, *Encyclopedia of American Religions,* 819. The B.O.T.A. center in Paris is located at 19 rue Turgot—not far from the place where Levi lived; cited in Soror V, letter to the author, 16 January 1995.

171. Paul Foster Case, *The Name of Names* (Los Angeles, Ca.: Builders of the Adytum, 1981), 5-6.

172. Ibid.

173. Paul Foster Case, *The Great Seal of the United States: Its History, Symbolism and Message for the New Age* (Santa Barbara, Ca.: J. F. Rowy Press, 1935),

22.

174. Lévi, *The Mysteries of Magic*, 75-76.; quoted in Case, *The True and Invisible Rosicrucian Order*, 192.

175. Ibid., 209.

176. Ibid., 223.

177. Ibid., 300.

178. Paul Foster Case, *The Book of Tokens: Twenty-two Meditations on the Ageless Wisdom*, 14th ed. (Los Angeles, Ca.: Builders of the Adytum, 1989), 95.

179. Paul Foster Case, *Seven Steps in Practical Occultism* (Los Angeles, Ca.: Builders of the Adytum, 1938), 2:4.

180. Ibid., 4:3.

181. Paul Foster Case, *Tarot Fundamentals* (Los Angeles, Ca.: Builders of the Adytum, 1938), 18:5.

182. Paul Foster Case, *Tarot Interpretation* (Los Angeles, Ca.: Builders of the Adytum, 1938), 22:1.

183. Paul Foster Case, *Introduction to Tarot* (Los Angeles, Ca.: Builders of the Adytum, 1938), 5:2.

184. Case, *The True and Invisible Rosicrucian Order*, 261.

185. Lévi, *The Mysteries of Magic*, 74-75; quoted in Case, *The True and Invisible Rosicrucian Order*, 289.

186. Case, *Tarot Interpretation*, 23:2.

187. Lévi, *The Mysteries of Magic*, 202, 206; quoted in Case, *The True and Invisible Rosicrucian Order*, 140.

188. Case, *The Tree of Life*, 22:1.

189. Lévi, *The Mysteries of Magic*, 55; quoted in Case, *The True and Invisible Rosicrucian Order*, 284.

190. Lévi, *Transcendental Magic*, 10-11; quoted in Case, *Thirty-two Paths of Wisdom* (Los Angeles, Ca.: Builders of the Adytum, 1938), 1:7-8.

191. Ibid., 1:8.

192. Ibid.,, 4:6.

193. Ibid., 9:6.

194. Case, *Tarot Interpretation*, 14:1.

195. Case, *Thirty-two Paths of Wisdom*, 2:3.

196. Levi, *Transcendental Magic*, 213; quoted in Case, *Tarot Fundamentals*, 25:1.

197. Case, *Tarot Interpretation*, 23:2.

198. Case, *The True and Invisible Rosicrucian Order*, 214.

199. Levi, *Transcendental Magic*, 394; quoted in ibid., 112.

200. Case, *Highlights of Tarot*, 12-13.

201. Pike, *Morals and Dogma*, 777; quoted in ibid., 13. According to Case, "These words are given added significance when you consider that the essential meaning of the Grand Word is MAN, and that the Great Secret is the

power of controlling the forces of man's inner life."

202. Paul Foster Case, *The Tarot: A Key to the Wisdom of the Ages* (Richmond, Va.: Macoy Publishing and Masonic Supply Company, 1947), 1.

203. Case, *The Tree of Life,* 22:1.

204. Ibid., 8:1.

205. Melton, *Encyclopedia of American Religions,* 821.

206. Paul A. Clark, *The Threshold: A Guide to Initiation* (Covina, Ca.: Fraternity of the Hidden Light, 1986), 2.

207. Paul A. Clark, telephone conversation with author, 24 January 1995.

208. Luther Ray Montandon, letter to the author, 4 December 1994.

209. Luther Ray Montandon, telephone conversation with author, 13 March 1995. Yogananda (1893- 1952) was a Hindu guru who founded the Self-Realization Fellowship; see Paramahansa Yogananda, *Autobiography of a Yogi* (Los Angeles, Ca.: Self-Realization Fellowship, 1946).

210. "Introduction to the Church Mercavah" (Baton Rouge, La.: Church of Mercavah, n.d.), 1.

CHAPTER V

Éliphas Lévi within the *Zeitgeist* of the Nineteenth Century and Its Relevance to the Twentieth and Twenty-First Centuries

In this final chapter, the significance Éliphas Lévi within the *zeitgeist*[1] of the nineteenth century will be considered in an effort to give added significance to its relevance to the twentieth and twenty-first centuries. In chapter one, Lévi was described as a noted French writer in the field of medieval Hebrew Kabbalah. It was pointed out that he has been called "the last of the magi" and has been given much credit for the revival of interest in magic and mysticism which occurred during the nineteenth century.[2] Of him it was stated that a great deal of modem occult terminology and practice could be attributed.[3] Also significant is the fact that his life spanned the "heart years" of the nineteenth century, with him being implicated in most of the major movements and currents of that time.[4] In light of this research, a description of the significance of his conceptual thought on Kabbalah will be made in regard to each of the modem esoteric groups researched in this book. This study will also highlight themes and issues that will provide data and scope for further investigation and research. In this final analysis, I will seek to demonstrate that truly Éliphas Lévi should be regarded as the Masonic and French connection of the American mystery tradition.

Éliphas Lévi Within the *Zeitgeist* of the Nineteenth Century

As stated in chapter one, Lévi has been given credit for coining the term "occultism."[5] In his *Dogme et rituel de la haute magie,* he wrote: "We have dared to dig into the old sanctuaries of occultism."[6] In this work, he sought to unite science and religion by demonstrating the unity of universal dogma in the secret doctrines of the Hebrews, Egyptians, and Chaldeans. His approach to knowledge, like that of other occultists, was inspired by the Renaissance. He followed the German philosopher Immanuel Kant in affirming the universality of reason. He was critical of both Aristotelian distinctions and the medieval division between nature and revelation. In the foundation he laid, he initiated the efforts of occultists to transfigure a world in which revelation was submitted to criticism. However, such criticism was aimed not at denying revelation but at rendering it obvious. This distinguished the nineteenth-century occultists from the eighteenth-century ideologues.[7] Lévi was the most widely read of all French occult writers. After the appearance of his books, the number of French writings on occult themes increased dramatically.[8]

Lévi's contemporary Ferdinand Denis (1798-1890) was a connoisseur of ancient manuscripts at Bibliotheque Sainte-Geneviève in Paris. Denis justified the occult sciences in terms of the social function of all knowledge and argued that the solitary inquirer, persecuted because of the incomprehension of the general population, had to take shelter in secrecy. He contended that a different kind of knowledge needed to be transmitted from ancient initiations through the sects of the Middle Ages to modem societies.[9] His views appear to share much in common with those of Lévi, who believed that all esoteric systems were rooted in Kabbalah.[10] Such "sects of the Middle Ages" included the Knights Templar who, according to Lévi, were custodians of secret knowledge and whose real crime was betrayal of the great secret to the profane through Masonic lodges organized by Jacques de Molay while in prison awaiting execution.[11]

Nineteenth-century intellectual currents were marked by "a voyage into the strange world of the European past."[12] The nineteenth century was the Age of the Ancient Near East and of the Indo-European Awakening.[13] Lévi believed that the *Zohar,* one of the most important of the Kabbalistic books, contained the lost knowledge of the ancient world.[14] During his lifetime, the idea that the study of religion involved comparison gained wide acceptance.[15] Lévi believed that there was a relationship between all religions and that this relationship was veiled in Kabbalah, from which all religions issued and into which all would return.[16]

During the 1860s, as Americans were fighting the Civil War, Europeans were developing evolutionary concepts which they applied to religious studies. Max Müller suggested that there might be a "science of religion" which would do justice to both religion and science. It was during this decade that the discipline of comparative religion developed.[17] This discipline developed from the comparisons which were necessary in the attempted rapprochement between religion and science.[18] Lévi believed Kabbalah alone could reconcile reason with faith, power with liberty, and science with mystery.[19] He rejected the notion that there was anything pre-scientific about Kabbalah, which he regarded as the oldest and truest science.[20] Such a claim has not generally been made by Jewish scholars of Kabbalah. Thus, Gershom Scholem has charged Lévi with "supreme charlatanism."[21]

The motif of progress was quite prominent among many nineteenth-century thinkers, both religious and secular. The Judeo-Christian idea of progress was rooted in the Hebrew scriptures, which taught that God had chosen a nation and people to fulfill His promise to move history toward a specific end. This idea was shared by nineteenth-century political, business, and religious leaders, to some extent in Europe but more so in America.[22]

The nineteenth-century notion of progress was given its most concrete expression at the World's Columbian Exposition, which was held in Chicago in 1893.[23] Col. George R. Davis, director of the Exposition, saw this event as a celebration of the ceaseless, irresistible march of civilization. He predicted the coming of a time when people would learn "the nearness of man to man, the Fatherhood of God, and the brotherhood of the human race."[24] Associated with the Exposition were twenty congresses, whose planners were possessed by a bold vision for the "establishment of a universal fraternity of learning and virtue," coupled with the affirmation of the human capacity to move forward.[25]

The congress with the most lasting effects was the World's Parliament of Religions, which was held 11-27 September 1893, primarily at two assembly halls in the present Art Institute on Michigan Avenue in Chicago. Each hall accommodated three thousand people and each was full at every session. The idea of the parliament was first proposed by Charles Carroll Bonney, an influential lawyer, civic leader, and firm believer in progress.[26] Bonney was a member of the Church of the New Jerusalem, better known as the Swedenborgians, a church whose American membership numbered 7,095 in the 1890 census.[27] Martin E. Marty well described the nineteenth-century notion of progress as exemplified by Bonney and his church:

> Bonney welcomed attendees in the name of the Church of the Holy City, the Church of Reconciliation. Its creed was also modernist: "It comes to reconcile reason and faith, science and religion, miracle and law, revelation and philosophy, the teachings of sacred scripture and the results of modern research. Bonney seemed plausible as he opened the congress by announcing that it would stand in human history, like a new Mount Zion, and begin "a new epoch of brotherhood and peace."
> ... Bonney was an essentialist who believed that there were common essentials by which everyone must be saved, in all the religions.[28]

Bonney viewed the parliament as "a friendly conference <based on> the golden rule of Christ: a royal feast to which the representatives of every faith were asked to bring the richest fruits and rarest flowers of their religion."[29] This feast was attended by American Protestants, Catholics, Jews, and humanists. It included quite a few women. Many delegates were surprised to learn that they had Asian counterparts overseas.[30]

As a result of the parliament, individuals like Chicago Unitarian Jenkins Lloyd Jones and naturalist Paul Carus looked forward to an age of global religious unity on the platform of universal progress, while liberal missionary George Candlin wrote that the parliament marked "a bright dawn of Gospel morning for the world, for all the world."[31] Fifty years earlier Éliphas Lévi experienced a prophetic vision of "anarchy, strife, and babble of conflicting voices" that characterized his time being "a prelude to the transfiguration of human society." In this vision, he saw the apocalyptic downfall of the old order, the downfall of Satan, and the dawning of a new day.[32] He envisioned a society in which antisocial behavior would be treated as an illness and every branch of learning would be part of the science of God, with religious understanding seen as "analysis and synthesis of love in all its forms."[33]

Whether or not the parliament participants read Lévi, there can be no doubt that his visions of the 1840s anticipated the idealistic spirit of the 1890s. Rev. George A. Gordon of Boston's Old South Church was greatly impressed by the parliament. In the mid-1890s, he proclaimed that a vision of a kingdom of the Spirit which would appropriate the wealth of all faiths had arisen in his day.[34] Such a vision resembles the visions of the reign of the Paraclete which characterized the generation of European occultists influenced by Lévi. Rev. John Henry Barrows, pastor of the First Presbyterian Church of Chicago, served as permanent chairman of the World's Parliament of Religions.[35] He called Jews "Old Testament Christians" and Christians "New Testament Jews."[36] While Lévi never used such terminology, he rejected all notions that God's covenant with Israel had been nullified. He insisted that Jesus came not to destroy but to fulfill the secret tradition of the Jews.[37]

Barrows was certain that the God Whom Jews and Christians worship had something to do with all the religions of the world. He asked, "Why should not Christians be glad to learn what God has wrought through Buddha and Zoroaster, through the sages of China, and the prophets of India and the prophet of Islam?" He searched for "a spiritual root of all human progress" in the science of comparative religion.[38] Here it is important to note that Lévi predicted the reconciliation of science and religion, with the letter giving place to the spirit and a "great universal religion" ushered in.[39] He called Jesus "the new and eternal Solomon."[40] Barrows, like Lévi, saw no conflict between being both a Christian and a seeker of universal religious truth. In his address at the closing session of the parliament, Barrows stated: ""I desire that the last words which I speak to this parliament shall be the name of Him to whom I owe life and truth and hope and all things, who reconciles all contradictions, pacifies all antagonisms, and who from the throne of His heavenly kingdom directs the serene and unwearied omnipotence of redeeming love-Jesus Christ, the Saviour of the world.""[41] He envisioned a "perpetual parliament on high <in which> the people of God will be satisfied."[42]

Barrows further called comparative religion "the highest study to which the human mind can now devote its energies." While the parliament did not initiate the study of comparative religion in America, it did provide a strong stimulus for such study in American colleges, universities, and theological seminaries.[43] According to John J. Robinson, the researches of Albert Pike—which focused on Éliphas Lévi and other authors—were precursors to such academic study of comparative religion.[44] Both Pike and Madame Blavatsky died two years before the parliament. It seems quite likely that if, in 1893, both had been living and able to attend, they would have had much to contribute.[45]

In a book prepared for the centennial of the parliament, Richard Hughes Seager wrote:

> The World's Parliament of Religions of 1893 was infused with the optimistic progressivism and postmillennial hope that was a conspicuous feature of the religious landscape in many quarters at the turn of the century. Most parties looked forward to the dawn of a new era, a better era, with the dawn of the twentieth, perhaps the Christian century. The Parliament is a valuable witness to this era, an era before the schism between the fundamentalists and liberals in the old Protestant mainstream, before the triumph of ultramontanism and antimodernism and the rise of Zionism and conservatism in the Catholic and Jewish communities, respectively. It was an era in which the confidence of the Western, Christian nations had not yet been shattered by World War I and the great empires not yet dismantled by the twentieth-century wars of liberation.[46]

In the above passage Seager referred to postmillennialism, an approach to the Apocalypse (Revelation) associated with nineteenth-century liberalism. It is interesting to compare this approach to that of Lévi, who rejected the literal approach of premillennialism and declared that any New Testament interpreter ignorant of Kabbalah was incapable of understanding the Apocalypse, which is clearly a Kabbalistic book.[47]

The World's Parliament of Religions was a fitting finale to many of the nineteenth-century developments in religious thought which were inspired by the idea of progress. Although Éliphas Lévi died eighteen years before the parliament, many of his writings reflect some of the same ideals as expressed by the leaders of the parliament. Such a comparison helps place his thought within the nineteenth-century *zeitgeist*.

A marked feature of America during the nineteenth century was the rise of fraternalism. Freemasonry and other fraternal orders experienced much growth during this period. Freemasonry took its present form in England during the early eighteenth century.[48] It was brought to America by the early colonists, with Freemasons playing a major role in the establishment of the new republic. The order survived the anti-Masonic hysteria of the early nineteenth century. During the Civil War, Freemasons fought on both sides. There are many documented cases of the display of the Masonic principle of brotherly love across enemy lines during this time.[49] During Reconstruction, Masonic elements entered the rituals of organizations with diverse political aims, including the Ku Klux Klan and the Union League. [50]

The last decades of the nineteenth century marked the "Golden Age of Fraternity." In an 1897 study, W. S. Harwood estimated that, of America's adult male population of 19,000,000, approximately 500,000 were members of one or more fraternal orders. Harwood insisted that men joined not primarily for social or business reasons but because they felt a "strange and powerful attraction to the ritual."[51] In her study of Freemasonry in the late nineteenth and early twentieth centuries, Lynn Dumenil argued that, during the nineteenth century, Masonic rituals contributed significantly to sociological function. She presented the Masonic lodge as a "spiritual oasis" and "sacred asylum" in a rapidly changing and increasingly heterogeneous world. She recognized the centrality of ritual to the fraternal experience. Rituals, she said, separate men from the outside world by placing them securely amongst brothers of the lodge.[52] Recent historians have concluded that fraternal rituals were "part of the very fabric" of the cultural life of many individuals during the late nineteenth century.[53] This indicates how fraternal rituals were an integral part of the *zeirgeist* of nineteenth-century America. Noteworthy is that American Masons who were initiated into the "higher degrees" of the Scottish Rite participated in rituals written by Albert Pike. Many of these obtained copies of Pike's *Morals and Dogma*. Those who actually read this book were exposed to many of the ideas Pike borrowed from Éliphas Lévi.

It was pointed out in chapter one how numerology played an important role in Lévi's thought. For example, he interpreted the number thirteen as symbolic of death, birth, property, inheritance, society, family, war, and treaties.[54] In the years following the treaties that ended the Civil War, many Americans were intrigued by this number. The following developments need to be noted:

> In the spring and summer of 1870, the "13" craze swept New York City... As much as anything else, the craze over "13" could be attributed to the aftermath of the War between the States, a flouting of all omens of ill-luck in an effort to forget.... Among the luncheon tables set for thirteen guests was one of the second floor of Knickerbocker Cottage located at 426 Sixth Avenue, a popular bistro... patronized largely by members of the Masonic fraternity. . . . <At the time> Masonry was prosperous. ... . <In> this great city that was developing at the mouth of the Hudson and even then—five years after Appomatox—was still celebrating the end of the bloodiest war in history. Parts of the Confederacy were still prostrate and sometimes starving but in New York the only problem was to find new worlds to conquer. The French Empire was about to crumble before Bismarck and Victor Emanuel would soon take over Rome and, in effect, restrict the temporal power of the Papacy to the Vatican grounds. But neither event would interrupt

the flow of the finest wines and brandies to a city that was literally "living up" the preservation of the Union.[55]

These Masons who sat down for lunch at exactly 12:13 p.m. each day at tables of thirteen were among the organizers of the Ancient Arabic Order of Nobles of the Mystic Shrine, the para-Masonic organization popularly called "Shriners."[56]

During the 1890s, Masons were among those Americans who were influenced by the idea of progress. Many Masons attended the World's Columbian Exposition and those who took seriously Masonic teachings regarding religious toleration also took an interest in the World's Parliament of Religions.[57] Nineteenth-century American fraternalism, like the World's Parliament of Religions, was greatly influenced by ideas of progress and religious toleration.[58] Both the fraternal orders and the parliament were important expressions of the nineteenth-century *zeitgeist*.

Lévi's apocalyptic visions are not dissimilar to the ideas of progress and postmillennial eschatology which developed in the years after his death. His views on the common root of all religions have much in common with the approach to religious pluralism associated with the parliament and with American fraternalism.[59] His thought clearly features within the *zeitgeist* of his time. It is in this context that his influence is to be appreciated and evaluated.

Éliphas Lévi's Relevance to the Twentieth and Twenty-First Centuries

Éliphas Lévi's writings demonstrate a great deal of relevance for an understanding of various theological, social, and political developments during the twentieth and twenty-first centuries. This applies both to his early writings under his real name of Alphonse Louis Constant and his later works under his better known pen name of Éliphas Lévi. Despite changing emphases, a basic unity runs throughout his works. According to Thomas A. Williams: "Constant's occultism does not represent a complete break with previous experiences and beliefs. It is simply a new codification of them."[60]

In February 1844, his book *La Mère de Dieu* was published. In this book, woman, idealized in the Blessed Virgin Mary, leads souls to salvation and shows humankind the way of ultimate, secular regeneration. He expressed the belief that human beings would be redeemed by Mary, the Mother of God and the fullest representation of woman's pure and holy life. He saw the orgy of strife, faction, greed, war and inhumanity as being resolved through the love of Mary, as society exchanged the old Adam for the new Christ. He envisioned a new order rising from the destructive years, which leveled old values and opened the way for the Holy Spirit, which he saw as feminine.[61] Although this book received a hostile reaction from Catholic officials at that time, its message is consistent with that of Catholic visionaries throughout history and with contemporary feminist aspirations. A great deal of Christian idealism entered into the deliberations of the Second Vatican Council, which was one of the most important events of the 1960s. At Saint Peter's Basilica in Rome, on 21 November 1964, the following prayer was formulated:

> Let the entire body of the faithful pour forth persevering prayer to the Mother of God and Mother of men. Let them implore that she who aided the beginnings of the Church by her prayers may now, exalted as she is in heaven above all the saints and angels, intercede with her Son in the fellowship of all the saints. May she do so until all the peoples of the human family, whether they still do not know their Savior, are happily gathered together in peace and harmony into the one People of God, for the glory of the Most Holy and Undivided Trinity.[62]

The same document quoted Saint Irenaeus statement that 'the knot of Eve's disobedience was untied by Mary's obedience. What the virgin Eve bound through her unbelief, Mary loosened by her faith."[63] Lévi went further than Irenaeus in presenting Mary and Eve as archetypes revealed extensively in human destiny. Such discussion of archetypal symbolism also antedated the analytical psychology of Carl Gustav Jung.[64]

Jungian psychology is relevant to an understanding of Lévi's writings on Kabbalah and Tarot. Noteworthy also is the fact that Lévi appears to have been the first person in history to link these two mystical systems, which were apparently of independent origin.[65] Notwithstanding this, Jung's theory of synchronicity explains the legitimacy of such a connection.[66] Today, leaders of both the Order of the Temple of Astarte and the Fraternity of the Hidden Light see Lévi's syncretistic blend of Kabbalah and Tarot as his most important contribution.[67]

To Lévi, harmony consisted in equilibrium subsisted by the analogy of opposites.[68] Papus gave Lévi credit for solving the most obscure problems of Kabbalah based on the law that "harmony results from the analogy of opposites."[69] Papus was a leader of the Hermetic Order of the Golden Dawn, an organization which drew much inspiration from Lévi.[70] Paul Foster Case was initiated into the Golden Dawn in England. He later founded the Builders of the Adytum (B.O.T.A.). Paul A. Clark was initiated into the Builders of the Adytum by Ann Davies, the successor to Case. He later founded. the Fraternity of the Hidden Light. The rituals of the latter organization are allegedly closer to the Golden Dawn than those of the B.O.T.A.[71] Thus, while the Golden Dawn no longer exists, a number of organizations perpetuate the influence of its rituals and symbols.

Through Albert Pike's *Morals and Dogma,* the ideas of Éliphas Lévi reached a wider audience than the French magus ever envisioned. This is true despite the fact that there is no evidence that Pike ever met Lévi or acknowledged him as the primary source of his writing on Kabbalah. Pike seemed especially impressed with Lévi's views on equilibrium, a concept that plays a major role in Scottish Rite Masonry today. Another important concept which Pike borrowed from Lévi was that of an initiatory society which would be the sole depository of all religious and social secrets with the power to create religious and secular rulers. Such a claim was preparatory to a discussion of the Knights Templar as an order of monks initiated into the mysteries of Kabbalah who had become a menace to both church and state. It was in this regard that Pike extracted a large portion of the chapter entitled "Some Famous Persecutions' in Lévi's *The History of Magic.*[72] This highlights how the writings of Lévi and Pike have influenced twentieth-century Masonic writers to view the Knights Templar as victims of persecution and oppression, and Jacques de Molay as a martyr to a just and righteous cause. It is doubtful if the Templars would have been able to play such a prominent role in Masonic ritual today had it not been for the writings of Lévi.[73]

Contemporary perceptions of Freemasonry, for good or ill, have been shaped to a large extent by what Albert Pike said or was accused of having said. The current generation of Masonic scholars acknowledge Pike's contributions notwithstanding his limitations. This is especially the case with Rex Hutchens, whose writings are full of words of praise for Pike's wisdom, but also accompanied by words of criticism for his errors. Hutchens has written the most comprehensive studies of *Morals and Dogma* to date. In these studies, he has gone into great detail to describe the sources from which passages in Pike's best known work were derived. He wrote of Lévi: "In 1855 and 1856, he produced *The Doctrine of Transcendental Magic* and The *Ritual of Transcendental Magic,* now available in English translated by A. E. Waite. It was from the originals of these works, as well as the subsequent *History of Magic* (1860), that Pike extracted portions of *Morals and Dogma.*"[74] Thus, during the 1990s, the writings of Hutchens have' made the Lévi-Pike connection known to a wider audience of Scottish Rite Masons.

According to Bishop Stephan A. Hoeller, the influence of Lévi on Madame Blavatsky was as profound as it was on Pike.[75] Today, this fact is well known to many informed Theosophists. Lévi's teachings, especially regarding the Astral Light, were influential not only on Blavatsky but also on her successors, including William Steele Olcott, William Quan Judge, and Annie Besant. As contemporary Theosophists study their works, they become aware of the influence of Lévi. It is evident that Lévi's relationship to American Theosophy was probably more widespread than it was to

Freemasonry. This can be established by the fact that it was not merely confined to one individual, as in the case of Pike.

The influence of Blavatsky can be seen today not only in Theosophy but also in the New Age Movement. According to one of Blavatsky's contemporary disciples: "H. P. Blavatsky, or Theosophy as expressed in her books, have influenced 'New Age' groups of all kinds. Many have made a mish-mash of the philosophy of Theosophy, Masters (Adepts) etc., taking only what was appealing to them."[76] It is highly probable that Lévi has had some indirect influence by way of Blavatsky in some of these groups.[77]

Bishop Hoeller expressed the opinion that 80 percent of Rudolf Steiner's ideas were derived from Blavatsky and that Lévi influenced Steiner through Theosophy.[78] Steiner presented Lévi as "an example of the way in which *karma* can be elaborated in the Jupiter-sphere," claiming that Lévi had lived in the pre-Columbian civilization of Mexico during a previous incarnation.[79] Evidence indicates that Steiner was influenced by Lévi but to a lesser extent than Blavatsky and Lévi's influence on Anthroposophy is present but much less evident than in Theosophy.

Johann Valentin Andreae envisioned a society for the reformation of social life and borrowed the symbols of the rose and cross from his family coat of arms. Shortly after the appearance of his books, a number of Rosicrucian bodies appeared on the scene, combining a vision of social transformation with the study of alchemy, Kabbalah, and mysticism.[80] In France, Rosicrucianism came into the public eye as part of the "occult heyday" inspired by the writings and teachings of Lévi.[81]

The role of Pascal Beverly Randolph in reviving magic and occultism in America may be analogous to the role of Lévi in Europe.[82] Randolph, who visited with Lévi in Paris, shared with the French magus the experience of apocalyptic visions. Randolph envisioned a day in which there would be peace on earth and all people would meet without distinction of color, sex, or money.[83] It appears that Levi's greatest influence in American Rosicrucianism is found in the Rosicrucian Fraternity founded by Randolph. Lévi has also received acknowledgements from Reuben Swinburne Clymer and Gerald E. Poesnecker, two of Randolph's successors.[84]

There is no doubt that H. Spencer Lewis, founder of the Ancient Mystical Order Rosac Crucis (A.M.O.R.C.), had read Lévi. It is equally clear that his primary aim in his use of Lévi's writings was to discredit rival Rosicrucian leaders.[85] For this reason, it is unclear whether Levi's teachings play a prominent role in the lessons studied by A.M.O.R.C. members today.

According to contemporary members of the Societas Rosicruciana in America and the Rosicrucian Fellowship, both George Winslow Plummer and Max Heindel probably read Lévi.[86] Lévi's influence in these two branches of American Rosicrucianism, however, appears limited in view of the fact that neither interpreter of the Rosy Cross quoted from the French magus.

For this reason, most members of these organizations do not pay a great deal of attention to Lévi.

According to Bill Heidrick, Treasurer-General of the Order of the Temple of the Orient (O.T.O.), Lévi greatly influenced Aleister Crowley and, through Crowley, influenced this organization. Like Crowley, Heidrick also rejected Lévi's Christian approach to occultism.[87] O.T.O. publications contain numerous references to Lévi. It is common knowledge among O.T.O. members that Crowley claimed to be Lévi reincarnated.

James Ray Montandon, the founder of the Church of Mercavah, often stated his respect for "the great mind and fraud of Éliphas Lévi" and expressed the belief that fraud had a positive dimension, as it was the only means of communication of occultism from one culture to another.[88]

Other than Theosophy, no organization in America has been as influenced by Lévi to the extent of the B.O.T.A.[89] Paul Foster Case, who founded this order, was, like Blavatsky, evidently impressed with Lévi's concept of the Astral Light. To Case, Tarot represented a summary of Kabbalah, alchemy, astrology, and magic, all of which were parts of an ancient psychological system. He regarded Freemasonry as a remnant of this ancient system and regretted the fact that "all too few Masons realize what a treasury they have inherited from the past."[90] He had great respect for Albert Pike, and was aware of Lévi's influence on him.[91] He was also aware of Lévi's influence on Blavatsky, whom he regarded as "one of the greatest expounders of the doctrine embodied in the TAROT."[92] In a very significant passage, Case spoke of both Éliphas Lévi and Albert Einstein. He wrote: "Einstein has advanced a theory that gravitation and electromagnetism are one and the same thing. By reviving this ancient doctrine, known to his Hebrew ancestors, the great mathematician brings closer than ever the revolution in physics Éliphas Lévi predicted back in 1859, and hastens the day when we shall, in truth, return to the transcendent magic of the Chaldeans, which magic is diagrammed on the Tree of Life."[93]

Such a "revolution in physics" has been confirmed in recent years by developments in quantum theory, according to which scientific discoveries can be in perfect harmony with spiritual aims and religious beliefs.[94] Quantum physics has been described as "organic," "holistic," and "ecological" and regards all phenomena as integral parts of an inseparable, harmonious whole.[95] Like ancient Indian devotees of Shiva as Nataraja, quantum physicists depict universal processes as a cosmic dance, with the rhythmic patterns determined by the molecular, atomic, and nuclear structures. Thus, the universe must be grasped dynamically as it moves, vibrates, and dances.[96] Quantum theory depicts phenomena moving at very high speeds and takes into account Einstein's theory of relativity. According to Einstein, space and time are inseparably linked. According to Zen Buddhist scholar D. T. Suzuki: "fact of pure experience, there is no space without time, no time without space."[97] Quantum physicists have recognized the ways that Eastern mystics have developed for the intuitive experience of the reality of space-time. Many of these scientists have studied ancient Hindu, Buddhist, and Taoist texts and recognized much truth in conceptions of the world in terms of movement, flow, and change.[98]

Dr. Fritjof Capra expressed the goal of quantum physics as follows:

> Mystical experience is necessary to understand the deepest nature of things, and science is essential for modern life. What we need, therefore, to cope fully with life is a dynamic balance between mystical intuition and scientific analysis.
>
> So far this balance has not been achieved in our society.... I believe that the world view implied by modem physics is inconsistent with our present society, which certainly does not reflect the harmonious interrelatedness we observe in nature. To achieve such a state of dynamic balance, a radically different socioeconomic structure will be needed — a cultural revolution in the true sense of the word. The survival of our whole civilization may depend on whether we can bring such a change. It will depend, ultimately, on our ability. . . to experience the wholeness of nature and the art of living with it in harmony.[99]

Many years earlier, Éliphas Lévi wrote: "Let the physicists seek and find out; ever will the Kabalist explain the discoveries of science."[100] This might be interpreted as indication of the impact of Lévi's thought on contemporary developments in quantum physics.

The major objectives of B.O.T.A. include "the promotion of the welfare of humanity," which is embodied in a seven-point program of universal peace, universal political freedom, universal education, universal health, universal prosperity, and universal spiritual unfoldment. The great aim is transformation of personality, based on the belief that a transformed personality can contribute to a transformed environment.[101] This is consistent with the ideals of Éliphas Lévi, who sought to instruct his students in methods of personal transformation and whose visions of a transformed society have been discussed.

In 1935, Paul Foster Case predicted a revolution in consciousness, with B.O.T.A playing a key role. In keeping with this, he wrote:

> Most of the world today is in bondage to Mammon, but the time is at hand when Mammon shall take its place as the servant, not the master of man. Millions are enslaved but the hour is striking when a revolution greater than that of 1776 shall throw off the shackles of that hateful servitude. The revolution is now in progress. Its field is not the field of

battle between armies of men. It is the field of the human soul. It is a revolution in consciousness, overturning the old false standards of value.[102]

Thirty-five years later, in a national best seller, Yale Law Professor Charles A. Reich wrote:

> There is a revolution coming. It will not be like the revolutions of the past. It will originate with the individual and with culture, and it will change the political structure only as its final act. It will not require violence to succeed, and it cannot be successfully resisted by violence.
>
> This is the revolution of the new generation... It is both necessary and inevitable, and in time it will include not only youth, but all people in America...
>
> The revolution is a movement to bring man's thinking, his society, and his life to terms with the revolution of technology and science that has already taken place. Technology demands of man a new mind—a higher, transcendent reason—if it is to be controlled and guided rather than to become an unthinkable monster....
>
> At the heart of everything is what we shall call a change in consciousness.[103]

The counter culture of the 1960s which Reich praised as a revolution in consciousness encountered a barrage of criticism from social scientists, journalists, and. historians. Some dismissed it as a creation of old radicals and tired bohemians. While most observers saw the counter culture as generated by the youth culture, some saw inspiration in an earlier generation of opponents of the status quo. The most prominent names mentioned in this regard were Karl Marx, Herbert Marcuse, Sigmund Freud, Norman 0. Brown, William Blake, and the Eastern mystics.[104] During the same decade, encounter groups and other methods of realizing human potential became more widespread. Esalen Institute in Big Sur, California became a popular center for these practices. A historian of Esalen described the hippie phenomenon as "a wild-eyed younger cousin of the human potential movement."[105] Whereas there is no direct evidence that Éliphas Lévi influenced these movements to any extent, the many people involved in these movements undoubtedly were seeking answers to the kinds of questions which are central to Lévi's thought. More conservative critics have compared the counter culture to the antinomian and Gnostic heresies of the early church.[106] Yet even in these are found the seeds of that which is analogous to Lévi.

The writings of Case and Reich reflect the longings for personal and social transformation on the part of many idealists in various decades of the twentieth and twenty-first centuries. Such longings are not dissimilar to the longings experienced during the nineteenth century by Éliphas Lévi and Pascal Beverly Randolph. A key element in Lévi's ideal society was the development of a divine science.[107] He believed that the primary source for such a science was Kabbalah, from which all religions issue and into which all would return.[108]

Notwithstanding the reality of numerous causes for discouragement, there is still hope in the aspirations of those who believe that personal and social transformation is possible. In response to a 1985 letter, Bishop Hoeller, a modern spokesman for Gnosticism, wrote:

> Yes, the war for greater consciousness ever goes on. One of the naive mistakes of the counter-culture of the sixties was the assumption that this war could be won by one fell swoop as it were by ushering in a new age. It has not worked. Still, significant advances have been made and the gains will not be lost.... Progress is never unidirectional and linear. It proceeds rather like taking two steps forwards and one step backward and thus being still a step ahead. Action is always followed by reaction, and eventually a state of creative balance comes about.[109]

Summation

In all periods of history, there have been seekers after light and wisdom who have believed that greater consciousness was possible and that such consciousness could lead to personal and social transformation. During the "heart years" of the nineteenth century, Éliphas Lévi was just such a person. His writings inspired many individuals and groups during his lifetime with the perception of such a hope and they continue to do so today. His approach to magic and mysticism has found a ready audience not only among occultists of various types but also among diverse groups, including social conservatives like Albert Pike and American youth seeking liberation and expanded consciousness through counter culture activity. As long as the desire for esoteric spirituality remains in the human consciousness, Éliphas Lévi's life and work will endure.

Endnotes

1. This word is derived from two German *words – zeit* ('time") and *geist* ("spirit'). *Zeitgeist* refers to the spirit of the time; the general intellectual and moral state or the trend of culture and taste characteristic of an era.
2. McIntosh, *Éliphas Lévi and the French Occult Revival*, 129.
3. Butler, *Practical Magic and the Western Mystery Tradition*, 15.
4. Williams, *Éliphas Lévi: Master of Occultism*, 2.
5. Giles, *The Tarot*, 28. The word *occulte* ("hidden") first appeared in French in 1120 in *Psauteir d'Oxford*. By 1633, the word was applied to the secrets of antiquity and the Middle Ages; see Jean-Pierre Laurrant, "The Primitive Characteristics of Nineteenth-Century Esotericism," in *Modern Esoteric Spirituality*, ed. Antoine Faivre and Jacob Neddleman (New York: Crossroad, 1992), 287.
6. Lévi, *Transcendental Magic*, 3. Virtually all historians agree that the revival of European occultism was sparked by the publication of Lévi's original French work in 1856.
7. Laurant, "The Primitive Characteristics of Nineteenth-Century Esotericism," 280.
8. McIntosh, Éliphas Lévi and the French Occult Revival, 17
9. Laurant, "The Primitive Characteristics of Nineteenth-Century Esotericism," 280.
10. Lévi, *The History of Magic*, 98.
11. Partner, *The Murdered Magicians*, 65-66.
12. Eric J. Sharpe, *Comparative Religion: A History*, 2nd ed. (La Salle, Ill.: Open Court Publishing Co., 1986), 20.
13. Ibid., 21.
14. Gilbert, "Foreword," in Lévi, *The Book of Spelndours*, 9.
15. Sharpe, *Comparative Religion* , xi. Oxford scholar Max Müller's *Introduction to the Science of Religion* (1873) is regarded as the foundation document of comparative religion in the English-speaking world. It seems reasonable that Lévi would have concurred with Müller's claim regarding religions that "he who knows one knows none." The scientific study of religion was a product of the Enlightenment; see Joseph M. Kitagawa, "The History of Religions in America," in *The History of Religions: Essays in Methodology*, ed. Mircea Eliade and Joseph M. Kitagawa (Chicago, Ill.: University of Chicago Press, *1959)*, 17.
16. Waite, *The Holy Kabbalah*, 493-95.
17. Sharpe, *Comparative Religion,* 28. From 1861 to 1862, Albert Pike fought the Civil War. During the remainder of the war and the remainder of his life, he contributed to the discipline of comparative religion. He read Max Müller and praised his writings; see Pike's writings, *Morals and Dogma*, 619, and *Indo-Aryan Deities and Worship*, 414.

18. Sharpe, *Comparative Religion*, 32.

19. Lévi, *Transcendental Magic*, 19.

20. Ibid., 95.

21. Scholem, *Kabbalah*, 203.

22. Joseph M. Kitagawa, "The 1893 World's Parliament of Religions and Its Legacy," in *A Museum of Faiths: Histories and Legacies of the 1893 World's Parliament of Religions* (Atlanta, Ga.: Scholars Press, 1993), 174. The idea of a chosen nation and people was important to Lévi, who extended this notion to his native France at the time of the Franco--Prussian War in 1871. He saw France as the future savior of civilization and was deeply hurt by the defeat of France in this conflict; see McIntosh, *Éliphas Lévi and the French Occult Revival*, 136. Lévi never visited America. One can only speculate as to his reaction to the notion of America as a type of new Israel with a destiny to be the leader of the world. Such an idea became more pronounced in the years following his death.

23. Kitagawa, "The 1893 World's Parliament of Religions and Its Legacy," 173. The World's Columbian Exposition, as a celebration of scientific, technological, and cultural achievement, was the culmination of a series of exhibits and fairs. This series included the Crystal Palace Exhibition at Hyde Park in London (1851), the Crystal Palace Exhibition in New York (1853), the Centennial Exposition in Philadelphia (1876), and the Paris Exhibition (1889). The Chicago fair has been described as "the last major exhibition of the nineteenth century" and "the crowning symbol of the achievement of Western civilization during the great century"; see ibid., 174. In 1893, Chicago was rebuilding from the devastation of the Great Fire. William Rainey Harper was serving as the first president of the new University of Chicago. He had a vision of a "second Reformation of Christianity through scholarship"; see ibid., 182.

24. Martin E. Marty, "A Cosmopolitan Habit in Theology," in *A Museum of Faiths*, 166.

25. Kitagawa, "The 1893 World's Parliament of Religions and Its Legacy," 188-89.

26. Ibid., 175.

27. Marty, "A Cosmopolitan Habit in Theology," 168. The Church of the New Jerusalem was founded by Swedish mystic Emanuel Swedenborg (1688-1772). Swedenborg was trained as a scientist but, after a profound religious crisis in 1743-44, abandoned his scientific work due to a sense of divine mission to teach mankind the true meaning of the scriptures. His study of the human body as the kingdom of the soul led to his development of a "doctrine of correspondence," according to which all phenomena of the physical world have their spiritual correspondences. This doctrine was his main instrument for uncovering the hidden meaning of scripture. He developed an anthropomorphic theological system, with the spiritual world

populated by deceased human beings grouped together according to their innermost affections into heavenly or infernal societies. He regarded Jesus as the highest manifestation of humanity as *divinwn humanwn*. The first Swedenborgian congregation was organized in England in the late 1780s. The doctrines of Swedenborg were introduced into America during the same decade. The most important center of movement today is the New Church Academy in Bryn Athyn, Pennsylvania; see Inge Jonsson, "Swedenborg, Emanuel," in *The Encyclopedia of Religion,* ed. Mircea Eliade (New York: MacMillan Publishing Company, 1987), 14:192-93. Éliphas Lévi made a number of references in his writings to Swedenborg, whom he called "the most sincere and the mildest among the prophets of false illuminism"; see Levi, *The History of Magic,* 290.

28. Marty, "A Cosmopolitan Habit in Theology," 168.

29. *The Monist 5* (April *1895):* 323-24; quoted in Kitagawa, "The 1893 World's Parliament of Religions and Its Legacy," 176. Paul Carter described the parliament as the finale to a century marked by church schisms, the rise of the social gospel, and the emergence of evolutionary and other naturalistic philosophies. All of these facts, he argued, helped.. shatter the "united front of the ante-bellum Protestant mainstream." He presented the event as "a grand and exotic punctuation point to a wonderful somewhat chaotic century"; see Paul Carter, *The Spiritual Crisis of the Gilded Age* (Dc Kalb, Ill.: Northern Illinois University Press, 1971), 199-221. In Carter's chronicle of nineteenth-century phenomena, he omitted occultism.

30. Richard Hughes Seager, "Pluralism and the American Mainstream: The View from the World's Parliament of Religions," in *A Museum of Faiths,* 213. According to Seager "The American tours of Vivekananda, Dharmapala, Majumdav, and others, the founding of the Vedanta Society, the first American Wesak, the arrival of D. T. Suzuki in Illinois, the various Pacific migrations, and all the subsequent events that lead eventually to the 1960s. . . the Asians were the men who came to dinner, tarried over cognac and cigars, and then never went away." At the parliament, Islam was represented only by Alexander Russell "Muhammad" Webb, an American convert from Protestantism. The only African Americans on program were Fannie Barrier Williams, a Chicago Unitarian; and Bishops Daniel Alexander Payne and Benjamin William Arnett of the African Methodist Episcopal Church; see Robert L. Uzzel, "AMEs at the Fair: African Methodism and the World's Columbian Exposition of 1893," *The A.M.E. Church Review* 101 (July-September 1985): 8-16.

31. Seager, "Pluralism and the American Mainstream," 214.

32. Williams, *Éliphas Lévi: Master of Occultism,* 27-28.

33. Ibid., 145.

34. George A. Gordon, *The Christ of To-Day* (Boston: Houghton Mifflin, 1895), p. 20; cited in Marty, "A Cosmopolitan Habit in Theology," 165.

35. Kitagawa, "The 1893 World's Parliament of Religions and Its Legacy," 181.

36. Ibid., 183.

37. Lévi, *The Book of Splendours*, 15.

38. Kitagawa, "The 1893 World's Parliament of Religions and Its Legacy," 184.

39. Lévi, *The Great Secret*, 99.

40. Lévi, *The Key of the Mysteries*, 55.

41. Kitagawa, "The 1893 World's Parliament of Religions and Its Legacy," 185.

42. Ibid., 189. Ninety years later, Kitagawa wrote: "Now all these leaders have joined the heavenly parliament leaving behind precious memories of a grandiose vision, an undaunted spirit, and a profound dedication to the search for truth in religion—indeed, noble legacies that we are proud to inherit."

43. Ibid., 185. The popularity of comparative religion during the first quarter of the twentieth century was aided by the spirit of nineteenth-century liberalism that was still strong. This spirit affirmed the oneness of humanity and had an optimistic vision of social progress. The study of comparative religion, like the liberal spirit that inspired it, declined during the 1930s due to the impact of neo-orthodox theology, the Great Depression, and the impending war.

44. Robinson, *A Pilgrim's Path*, 43.

45. Freemasonry had no official representative at the parliament, probably because the order is a fraternity and not a religion. No doubt many individual Masons were present. Swami Vivekananda, whose proclamation that "all religions are One" received much media attention, was once a member of a lodge in Calcutta, India. Later, however, he called for "no esoteric backguardism, no secret humbug, nothing should be done in a corner"; see George Mason Williams, *The Quest for Meaning of Swami Vivekananda: A Study of Religious Change* (Chico, Ca.: New Horizons Press, 1974), 15-16. Theosophy was represented at the parliament by Annie Besant and William Quan Judge. The latter regarded Lévi's Astral Light as among the more interesting Theosophical concepts; see Judge, *Echoes from the Orient*, 84-89. During the years after the parliament, there was conflict between Theosophy and the Vedanta Society established by Vivekananda. The latter Hindu had no interest in promoting the "mystic East" view of India presented by Besant. Vivekananda, at times, castigated "the Indian grafting of American Spiritualism." He rejected the popular notion that occultism was the best of what India had to offer America; see Steven F. Walker, "Vivekananda and American Occultism," in *The Occult in America: New Historical Perspectives*, eds. Howard Kerr and Charles L. Crow (Urbana, Ill.: University of Illinois Press, 1983), 163-65. During the parliament, a seventeen-year-old Nebraska

youth named E. E. Dickinson heard Vivekananda speak and desired to be taught by him. Vivekenanda said to him: "No, my son, I am not your guru. Your teacher will come later. He will give you a silver cup. He will pour out to you more blessings than you are now able to hold." Eventually, Dickinson became a member of the Self-Realization Fellowship. When, in December 1936, Paramahansa Yogananda gave him a silver cup for a Christmas gift, Dickinson interpreted the action as a fulfillment of Vivekananda's words. Yogananda was born on 5 January 1893. Thus, he was eight months old at the time of the parliament. According to members of the Self-Realization Fellowship: "Vivekananda was apparently aware that Yogananda was again in incarnation, and that he would go to America to teach the philosophy of India"; see Yogananda, *The Autobiography of a Yogi,* 543-45. As stated in chapter four, Yogandanda, along with Lévi, Blavatsky, and Case, greatly influenced James Ray Montandon, founder of the Church of Mercavah.

46. Richard Hughes Seager, ed. *The Dawn of Religious Pluralism: Voices from the World's Parliament of Religions, 1893* (La Salle, Ill.: Open Court Publishing Company, 1993), 10.

47. Lévi, *The Mysteries of the Qabalah,* 271.

48. Most Masonic historians trace the origins of speculative Freemasonry to the operative Masons who built cathedrals during the Middle Ages. However, there are other theories. In recent years, a number of books have sought to establish a direct link between Freemasonry and the Knights Templar see John J. Robinson, *Born in Blood: The Lost Secrets of Freemasonry* (New York: M. Evans and Company, 1989); Michael Baigent and Richard Leigh, *The Temple and the Lodge* (New York: Arcade Publishers, 1989); and Andrew Sinclair, *The Sword and the Grail. Of the Grail, the Templars and a True Discovery of America* (New York: Crown Publishers, Inc., 1992).

49. Many such cases are recorded in Allen E. Roberts' book *House Undivided.*

50. See Walkes, "The Ku Klux Klan and Regular Freemasonry," and *Documents Relating to Reconstruction,* ed. Walter L. Fleming (Morgantown, W. Va.: West Virginia University Press, 1904).

51. W. S. Harwood, "Golden Age of Fraternity," *North American Review* 164 (May 1897): 620-23.

52. Lynn Dumenil, *Freemasonry and American Culture, 1880-1939* (Princeton, N. J.: Princeton University Press, 1984), 32-42.

53. Mark C. Carnes, *Secret Ritual and Manhood in Victorian America* (New Haven, Conn.: Yale University Press, 1989), 12. According to French sociologist Emile Durkheim, ritual forms arise in response to transformation in the underlying structure of society; see ibid., 13.

54. Lévi, *The Key of the Mysteries,* 45.

55. Van Daventer, *Parade to Glory,* 11-15.

56. Ibid., 15. Among the early Shriners was Albert Rawson, a Theosophist and traveling companion of Madame Blavatsky. The Shrine was organized

in New York in 1872—three years before the Theosophical Society; see chapter four.

57. 0n 24 April 1893, Monroe C. Crawford, Grand Master of the Caucasian Grand Lodge of Illinois, sent a letter to all of the grand lodges with whom his grand lodge was in fraternal correspondence, inviting them to participate in "a Fraternal Congress of Masons in the year of the great Columbian Exposition to begin on 14 August 1893 in the Preceptory of Oriental Consistory, Ancient and Accepted Scottish Rite, which was housed in Chicago's Masonic Temple; see *Proceedings of tile Grand Lodge of Illinois, A.F.&AM.* (1893), 19-21. Delegates from several states attended this meeting; see ibid., 44. Two years earlier, T. H. Smith, Grand Master of the Prince Hall Grand Lodge of Illinois, appointed a committee to open a headquarters in Chicago to receive and entertain visiting brethren attending the exposition and to hold a Masonic Congress; see *Proceedings of the Most Worshipful Prince Hall Grand Lodge of Illinois, F.&A.M.* (1891), 157. The Masonic Congress was held 21-23 August 1893 in Chicago. It was the forerunner to what is now called the Conference of Grand Masters, Prince Hall Masons; see Walkes, *Shrine History*, 14. White Shriners from Chicago's Medinah Temple attended the fair and were impressed by the Turkish exhibits and the beautiful Oriental dancers. The Oriental band, which is a standard feature of Shrine temples today, was inspired by the musicians who accompanied these dancers; see Van Deventer, *Parade to Glory*, 153-54. It is possible that some costumes currently worn by Shriners were inspired by the dress of Arabs and Turks at the fair; see ibid., 105. Prince Hall Masons in Chicago at the time of the fair organized what became known as the Ancient Egyptian Arabic Order of Nobles of the Mystic Shrine; see Walkes, *Shrine History*, 15-54.

58. In making this statement, I am not ignoring the fact that, throughout much of their history, American fraternal orders have been known not only for their mystical symbolism but also for their social conservatism. I believe the words of Gershom Scholem are relevant here. Scholem observed: "All mysticism has two contradictory or complementary aspects: the one conservative, the other revolutionary. How can a mystic be a conservative, a champion and interpreter of religious authority? How is he able to do what the great mystics of Catholicism, such Sufis as Ghazzali, and most of the Jewish Kabbalists did? The answer is that these mystics seem to rediscover the sources of traditional authority.. ... The mystic's experience tends to confirm the religious authority under which he lives... He contributes not only to the conservation of the tradition, but also to its development. Seen with new eyes, the old values acquire new meaning. . . a mystic's understanding and interpretation of his own experience may even lead him to question the religious authority he had hitherto supported"; see Gershom Scholem, *On the Kabbalah and Its Symbolism*, trans. Ralph Manheim (New York: Schocken Books, 1965), 7-9. The same principle may be applied to the

relationship of Freemasonry to civil authority. American Freemasonry has been noted for social conservatism. However, experiences in Europe and Latin America demonstrate that Masonic rituals can also inspire revolutionary activity.

59. The parliament was strongly opposed by many fundamentalist Christians. Today, many within the latter group criticize Freemasonry for admitting Christians and non-Christians on an equal basis.

60. Williams, *Éliphas Lévi: Master of Occultism*, 145.

61. Ibid., 22-25.

62. "Dogmatic Constitution on the Church," in *The Documents of Vatican II*, ed. Walter M. Abbott (Baltimore, Md.: America Press, 1966), 96.

63. Ibid., 88.

64. Williams, *Éliphas Lévi: Master of Occultism*, 26.

65. Hoeller, *The Royal Road*. 1.

66. Ibid., 26. Jung defined synchronicity as the meaningful coincidence or equivalence of a psychic and physical state or event which have no causal relationship to one another, or of similar or identical thoughts or dreams occurring at the same time but in different places; see Carl Gustav Jung, *Memories, Dreams, Reflections*, ed. Aniela Jaffe and tans. Richard and Clara Winston, rev. ed. (New York: Random House, 1963), 400.

67. Carroll R. Runyon, Jr., telephone conversation with author, 1 February 1995; and Paul A. Clark, telephone conversation with author, 24 January 1995.

68. *Lévi, Transcendental Magic*, 179.

69. Papus, "The Doctrines of Éliphas Lévi." in Lévi, *The Book of Splandours*, 146. The analogy of opposites was also important to Jung, who wrote: "Nothing so promotes the growth of consciousness as this inner confrontation of opposites"; see Jung, *Memories, Dreams, Reflections*, 345.

70. Howe, *The Magicians of the Golden Dawn*, 26. There was a legend that Lévi was a member of this order, despite the fact that he died thirteen years before its founding.

71. Clark, telephone conversation with author, 24 January 1995.

72. Pike, *Morals and Dogma*, 8 15-16; his source was *The History of Magic*, 207-08.

73. There is no mention of the Knights Templar in the foundation order of Masonry, which is called the Blue Lodge. The highest degree of the York Rite is called the "Knights Templar." The setting for the Thirtieth Degree of the Scottish Rite is the tomb of Jacques de Molay. On 18 March 1919, the Order of DeMolay was established in Kansas City, Missouri as an auxiliary to Freemasonry for young men ages fourteen to twenty-one. The date of the founding was deliberately selected in commemoration of the execution of Jacques de Molay on 18 March 1314; see Herbert Ewing Duncan, *Hi, Dad!: A Story about Frank S. Land and the Order of DeMolay* (Kansas City, Mo.:

International Supreme Council, Order of DeMolay, 1970), 29. Michael Baigent and Richard Leigh detect a strange irony in this order "issuing from the heart of 'middle America', dedicated to fostering personal and civic virtues in generations of American youth, yet named after a medieval French knight executed for blasphemy, heresy, sodomy, necromancy, and assorted other forms of misconduct"; see Baigent and Leigh, *The Temple and the Lodge*, 267. To avoid torture, de Molay confessed to all charges except sodomy. Later he retracted his confessions. Such retraction was punishable by death.

74. Hutchens and Monson, *The Bible in Albert Pike's Morals and Dogma*, 243-44. This book, along with Hutchens' *A Glossary to Morals and Dogma*, were of inestimable value in the cross-referencing of the works of Lévi and Pike in preparation of this book.

75. Hoeller, telephone conversation with author, 26 December 1994.

76. Kirby Van Mater, letter to the author, 21 December 1994.

77. In the course of research for this book, over one hundred letters were written. Many of them were sent to various New Age organizations and/or publications, most of which did not respond. Those that did respond denied any direct influence of Lévi. The director of the New Age World Religious and Scientific Research Foundation wrote: "I am acquainted with Éliphas Lévi's books, and have read some of his work some years ago, <yet> his books have not influenced my studies or organization in any way whatsoever"; see Rev. Victoria E. Vandertuin, letter to the author, 10 November 1994. The director of Meditation Groups for the New Age denied any particular influence from Lévi but stated: "Éliphas Lévi, to my mind, is a part of the continuous flow of the Ancient Wisdom, and to that extent he may have had some impact on all that followed"; see Frances Adams Moore, letter to the author, 7 November 1994. Other organizations which do not acknowledge any influence nevertheless maintain copies of his books in their libraries and/or bookstores. According to Bishop Hoeller, members of the New Age Movement are "three of four generations removed from Lévi"; Hoeller, telephone conversation with author, 26 December 1994.

78. Ibid.

79. Steiner, *Karmic Relationships*. 2:192.

80. Melton, *Handbook of Cults in America*, 96.

81. McIntosh, *The Rosicrucians*, 104.

82. Ibid., 99.

83. Godwin, *The Theosophical Enlightenment*, 248. The visions of Randolph, who did not share Lévi's pro-Catholic sympathies, made no reference to the Mother of God. No doubt Randolph's experiences with racial discrimination influenced his views on eschatology.

84. Clymer described Lévi as one of the three "greatest Initiates"; see Clymer, *The Book of Rosicruciae*, 69. Poesnecker regarded him as "a

knowledgeable author" but not "a fully developed Initiate"; see Gerald E. Poesnecker, letter to the author, 8 January 1995.

85. Lewis, *Rosicrucian Questions and Answers*, 145-46, 157.

86. Soror Lucia Gorsch, telephone conversation with author. 23 January 1995, regarding Plummer, and Gloria Hayes, telephone conversation with author, 23 January 1995, regarding Heindel.

87. Heidrick, "From the Out Basket." 8.

88. Luther Ray Montandon, telephone conversation with author.

89. Case, *The True and Invisible Rosicrucian Order*, 300. Case saw the Astral Light as analogous to the Hindu concept of *kundalini* (serpent power). He referred to the writings of Blavatsky, who called this power *Fohar*, see Case, *The Book of Tokens*, 95.

90. Case, *The Highlights of Tarot*, 12-13.

91. Case, *The Tarot: A Key to the Wisdom of the Ages*, 1.

92. Case, *The Tree of Life*, 22:1.

93. Ibid.

94. Fritjof Capra, "The Tao of Physics: Reflections on the Cosmic Dance," *Saturday Review* 5 (10 December 1977): 21-22.

95. Ibid., 22.

96. Ibid., 23.

97. Ibid., 28. Suzuki was brought to America by his mentor Shaku Söen, who spoke at the World's Parliament of Religions; see Marty, "A Cosmopolitan Habit in Theology," 178-88.

98. Capra, "The Tao of Physics," 28.

99. Ibid. Early in his career, Lévi sought "a radically different socioeconomic structure" in his involvement in socialist politics. While his political activism declined after the Revolution of 1848, there is no evidence that his political views changed. His focus shifted from social to individual transformation; see chapter one. It is debatable, of course, whether the two can be completely separated.

100. Lévi, *The Paradoxes of the Highest Science*, 100.

101. Melton, *Encyclopedia of American Religions*, 819.

104. Robert L. Johnson, *Counter Culture and the Vision of God* (Minneapolis, Minn: Augsburg Publishing House, 1971), 25. Few of the critics were familiar with Éliphas Lévi and Paul Foster Case.

105. Walter Truett Anderson, *The Upstart Spring: Esalen and the American Awakening* (Reading, Mass.: Addison-Wesley Publishing Company, 1983), 231. One of the prominent individuals associated with Esalen for many years was Alan Watts, a former Episcopal priest and popularizer of Zen Buddhism in America. While in London during the 1930s, Watts was greatly influenced by Theosophy, which contributed much to the spiritual ferment in Britain of that day; see ibid., 54-55.

106. Johnson, *Counter Culture and the Vision of God*, 29.

107. Williams, *Éliphas Lévi: Master of Occultism,* 145.
108. Waite, *The Holy Kabbalah,* 493-94.
109. Stephan A. Hoeller, letter to the author, 12 December 1985.

Bibliography

PRIMARY SOURCES

French

Chacomac, Paul. *Eliphas Levi, renovateur de l'Occulrisme en France, 1810-1875*. Presentation par Paul-Redonnel; preface de Victor Emile Michilet. Paris: Chacomac frères, 1926.

Lévi, Éliphas. *L'Assomption de lafem,ne; ou Le livre de l'amour*. Paris: A. Le Gallois, 1841.

_____. *Le catechisme de la paix, suivi de quatrains sur le Bible et de la liberré*. Paris: Chamuel, 1896.

_____. *La Clef des Grands mysrères suivant Hénoch, Abraham, Hermé Trismégiste et Salomon*. Paris: G. Bailhière, 1861.

_____. *La dernière incarnation Légendes evangéliques du xixe siècle*. Paris: Librairie socitaire, 1846.

_____. *Dictionnaire de Littérature Chrénenne*. Paris: J. P. Migne, 1851.

_____. *Doctrines religieuses et sociales*. Pans: A Le Gallois, 1841.

_____. *Dogme et rituel de la haute magie*. Paris: G. Baillière, 1856.

_____. *Fables et symboles avec leur explication, ou sont-révélés les grandes secrets de la direction du magnetisme universel et des principes fondementaux du grand oeuvre*. Paris: G. Baillière, 1862.

_____ *Le grand arcane; ou L'occultisme dévoilé*. Paris: Chamuel, 1898.

_____ *Histoire de la magie, avec une exposition clair et precise de ses procédés de ses rites et de ses mystères*. Paris: G. Baillière, 1860.

_____. *Le Livre des larmes ou Le Christ consolateur; essai de conciliation entre l'Eglise catholique er la philosophie moderne*. Paris: Paulia, 1845.

_____. *La Mere de Dieu, épopée religieuse er humanitaire*. Paris: C. Gosselin, 1844.

_____. *Rebelais a la Basmetre*. Paris: Librairie phalansterienne, 1847.

_____. *La science des esprits; révélation du dogme secret des Kabbalistes esprit occulte des evangiles, appreciation des doctrines et des phénomènes spirites*. Paris: G. Baillière, 1865.

_____. *Le sorcier de Meudon*. Paris: A. Bourdilliat et ce, 1861.

_____. *Les trois harmonies*. Paris: Fellens et du four, *1845.* Tristan, Flora. *L'Emancipation de lafemme ou, le testament de la paria*. Paris: Au Bureau de la Direction de la Verité, 1846.

English

Abbott, Walter M., ed. *The Documents of Vatican II*. Baltimore, Md.: America Press, 1966.

Besant, Annie. *Esoteric Christianity, or the Lesser Mysteries*. London: Theosophical Publishing House, 1918.

Blavatsky, Helena P. *Isis Unveiled: A Master-Key to the Mysteries of Ancient and Modern Science and Theology*, vols. 1 and 2. Pasadena, Ca.: Theosophical University Press, 1950.

_____. *Kabalah and Kabalism*. Los Angeles, Ca.: Theosophy Company, n.d.

_____. *The Secret Doctrine: The Synthesis of Science, Religion, and Philosophy*, vols. 1 and 2. New York: Theosophical Publishing Company, Ltd., 1888.

Bulwer-Lytton, Edward George. *The Last Days of Pompeii*. Cutchogue, New York: Buccaneer Books, Inc., 1976.

_____. *Zanoni*. New York: P. F. Collier and Son, 1842.

Capra, Fritjof. "The Tao of Physics: Reflections on the Cosmic Dance." *Saturday Review* 5 (10 December 1977), 21-22.

Case, Paul Foster. *The Book of Tokens: Twenty-two Meditations on the Ageless Wisdom*. 14th ed. Los Angeles, Ca.: Builders of the Adytum, 1989.

_____ *The Great Seal of the United States: Its History, Symbolism and Message for the New Age*. Santa Barbara, Ca., J. F. Rowy Press, 1935.

_____. *Highlights of Tarot, with Coloring Instructions*. Los Angeles, Ca.: Builders of the Adytum, 1989.

_____. *Introduction to Tarot*. Los Angeles, Ca.: Builders of the Adytum, 1938.

_____. *The Name of Names*. Los Angeles, Ca.: Builders of the Adytum, 1981.

_____. *Seven Steps in Practical Occultism*. Los Angeles, Ca.: Builders of the Adytum, 1938.

_____. *The Tarot: A Key to the Wisdom of the Ages*. Richmond, Va.: Macoy Publishing and Masonic Supply Company, 1947.

_____. *Tarot Fundamentals*. Los Angeles, Ca.: Builders of the Adytum, 1938.

_____. *Tarot Interpretation*. Los Angeles, Ca.: Builders of the Adytum, 1938.

_____. *Thirty-two Paths of Wisdom*. Los Angeles, Ca.: Builders of the Adytum, 1938.

_____. *The Tree of Life*. Los Angeles, Ca.: Builders of the Adytum, 1938.

_____. *The True and Invisible Rosicrucian Order: An Interpretation of the Rosicrucian Allegory and an Explanation of the Ten Rosicrucian Grades*. York Beach, Me.: Samuel Weiser, Inc., 1981.

Clark, Paul A. *The Threshold: A Guide to Initiation*. Covina, Ca.: Fraternity of the Hidden Light, 1986.

Clymer, Reuben, Swinburne. *Book of Rosicruciae*. vol. 2. Quakertown, Pa.: Philosophical Publishing Company, 1948.

Bibliography

Crowley, Aleister. *The Book of the Law.* York Beach, Me.: Samuel Weiser, Inc., 1976.

"Cults, the Occult and Theosophy." Wheaton, I11.: Theosophical Society in America, n.d.

"From the History Heap." *Thelema Lodge, O.T.O.,* Febrtrary 1992, 9.

Gordon, George A. *The Christ of To-Day.* Boston: Houghton-Mifflin, 1895.

Harwood, W. S. "Golden Age of Fraternity." *North American Review* 164 (May 1897):620-2

Heidrick, Bill. "From the Out Basket." *Thelema Lodge, O.T.O.,* February 1992, 7.

Heindel, Max. *Blavatsky and the Secret Doctrine.* Santa Monica, Ca.: DeVorss and Company, 1933.

Huysmans, J. K. *Down There.* trans. Keene Wallis. New York: Albert and Charles Born, 1924.

"Introducing You to the Theosophical Society." Wheaton, Ill.: Theosophical Society in America, 1994.

"Introduction to the Church Mercavah." Baton Rouge, La.: Church of Mercavah, n.d.

Judge, William Quan. *Echoes from the Orient: A Broad Outline of Theosophical Doctrines.* Covina, Ca.: Theosophical University Press, 1944.

Lévi, Éliphas. *The Book of Splendours: The Inner Mysteries of Qabalism, Its Relationship to Freemasonry, Numerology and Tarot..* York Beach, Me.: Samuel Weiser, Inc., 1973.

_____. *The Great Secret, or Occultism Unveiled.* York Beach, Me.: Samuel Weiser, Inc., 1975.

_____. *The History of Magic, Including a Clear and Precise Exposition of Its Procedures, Its Rites and Its Mysteries.* ed. and trans. Arthur Edward Waite. York Beach, Me.: Samuel Weiser, Inc., 1970.

_____. *The Key of the Mysteries.* ed. and trans. Aleister Crowley. London: Rider and Company, 1959.

_____. *The Last Incarnation: Gospel Legends of the Nineteenth Century.* trans. Francis George Shaw. New York: William H. Graham, 1848.

_____. *The Magical Ritual of the Sanctwn Regnum.* ed. and trans. William Wynn Westcott. Edmonds, Wa.: Holmes Publishing Group, 1922.

_____ *The Mysteries of Magic: A Digest of the Writings of Éliphas Lévi.* ed. and trans. Arthur Edward Waite. New Hyde Park, N. Y.: University Books, 1974.

_____. *The Mysteries of the Qabalah, or the Occult Agreement of the Two Testaments, as Contained in the Prophecy of Ezekiel and the Apocalypse of Saint John.* Wellingborough, U. K.: Aquarian Press, 1974.

_____. *The Paradoxes of the Highest Science.* Boise, Id.: Kessinger Publishing Company, 1992.

_____. *Transcendental Magic: Its Doctrine and Ritual.* ed. and trans. Arthur Edward Waite. York Beach, Me.: Samuel Weiser, Inc., 1968.

Lewis, H. Spencer. *Rosicrucian Questions and Answers, with Complete History of the Rosicrucian Order.* San Jose, Ca.: Ancient Mystical Order Rosae Crucis, 1993.

Mead, George Robert Stow, ed. *Five Years of Theosophical, Historical, and Scientific Essays Selected from "The Theosophisr".* New York: Amo Press, 1976.

"O.T.O.Official Bodies Worldwide Directory: Revised September 1994." *The Magical Link,* Spring-Summer 1994, 14.

"Ordo Templi Orientis." *The Magical Link,* Spring-Summer 1994, 15.

Pike, Albert. *Indo-Aryan Deities and Worship, as Contained in the Rig-Veda.* Washington, D. C.: House of the Temple, 1930.

_____. *Irano-Aryan Faith and Doctrine as Contained in the Zend-Avesra.* Washington, D. C.: House of the Temple, 1924.

_____. *Lectures of the Arya.* Washington, D. C.: House of the Temple, 1930.

_____. *Morals and Dogma of the Ancient andAccepted Rire of Freemasonry.* Washington, D. C.: House of the Temple, 1969.

Reich, Charles A. *The Greening of America.* New York: Bantam Books, 1970.

Scholem, Gershom. *Kabbalah.* New York: New American Library, 1974.

_____. *On the Kabbalah and Its Symbolism.* trans. Ralph Manheim. New York Schocken Books, 1965.

"Selected Titles." Computer Printout. Pasadena, Ca.: Theosophical Society, 8 November 1994.

Steiner, Rudolf. *Karmic Relationships: Esoteric Studies.* trans. George Adams. rev. M. Cotterell, C. Davy, and D. S. Osmond. vol. 2. London: Rudolf Steiner Press, 1974.

Von Hausen, Muller. *The Protocols of the Meetings of the Wise Men of Zion.* trans. Victor Marsden. Chicago, Ill.: Patriotic Publishing Company, 1934.

Waite, Arthur Edward. *The Brotherhood of the Rosy Cross, Being Records of the House of the Holy Spirit in Its Inward and Outward History.* New Hyde Park, N. Y.: University Books, 1961.

_____. *Devil Worship in France; or, the Question of Luc4fer; a Record of Things Seen and Heard in the Secret Societies According to the Evidence of Initiates.* London: G. Redway, 1896.

_____. *The Holy Kabbalah: A Study of the Secret Tradition in Israel as Unfolded by Sons of the Doctrine for the Benefit and Consolation of the Elect Dispersed Through the Lands and Ages of the Greater Exile.* New Hyde Park, N. Y.: University Books, 1960.

_____. *Shadows of Life and Thought: A Retrospective Review in the Form of Memoirs.* London: Selwyn and Blount, 1937.

Westcott, William Wynn. *An Introduction to the Study of the Kabalah, with Eight Diagrams.* London: John M. Watkins, 1926.

Bibliography

SECONDARY SOURCES

Anderson, Walter Truett. *The Upstart Spring: Esalen and the American Awakening*. Reading, Mass.: Addison-Wesley Publishing Company, 1983.

Baigent, Michael and Leigh, Richard. *The Temple and the Lodge*. New York: Arcade Publishers, 1989.

_____and Lincoln, Henry. *Holy Blood, Holy Grail*. New York: Dell Publishing Company, 1983.

Bessel, Paul "Prince Hall Recognition Details," http://bessel.org/masrec/pha.htm, 1-24.

Billington, James H. *Fire in the Minds of Men: Origins of the Revolutionary Faith*. New York: Basic Books, Inc., 1980.

Boettjer, John W. "What's In a Name?" *The Scottish Rite Journal* 1(January 1990): 15-18.

Botelho, Michael A. "Albert Pike and the Confederate Indians." *Heredom* 2 (1993): 52.

Butler, W. E. *Practical Magic and the Western Occult Tradition*. Wellingborough, U. K.: Aquaran Press, 1986.

Carlson, Maria. *"No Religion Higher Than Truth": A History of the Theosophical Movement in Russia, 1875-1922*. Princeton, N. J.: Princeton University Press, 1993.

Carnes, Mark C. *Secret Ritual and Manhood in Victorian America*. New Haven, Conn.: Yale University Press, 1989.

Carter, Paul. *The Spiritual Crisis of the Gilded Age*. DeKaib, Ill.: Northern Illinois University Press, 1971.

Clegg, R. I. "More Leaves from a Freemason's Note-Book." *American Freemason* (May 1913): 312-16.

Cranston, Sylvia. *HPB: The Extraordinary Life and Influence of Helena Blavatsky, Founder of the Modern Theosophical Movement*. New York: G. P. Putnam's Sons, 1993.

Dan, Joseph. *Jewish Mysticism and Jewish Ethics*. Seattle, Wa.: University of Washington Press, 1986.

Donaldson, John W. "Illustrious Albert Pike." *The New Age* 84 (January 1976): 43-45.

Dumenil, Lynn. *Freemasonry and American Culture, 1880-1939*. Princeton, N. J.: Princeton University Press, 1984.

Duncan, Herbert Ewing. *Hi, Dad!: A Story about Frank S. Land and the Order of DeMolay*. Kansas City, Mo.: International Supreme Council, Order of DeMolay, 1970.

Duncan, Robert Lipscomb. *Reluctant General: The Life and Times of Albert Pike*. New York: E. P. Dutton and Company, 1961.

Edwardes, Michael. *The Dark Side of History: Magic in the Making of Man*. New York: Stein and Day, 1977.

Eliade, Mircea and Kitagawa, Joseph M., eds. *The History of Religions: Essays in Methodology.* Chicago, Ill.: University of Chieago Press, 1959.

"Éliphas Lévi was a Freemason—Briefly," www.freemasonry.bcy.ca/biography/esoterica/levi_e/levi_notes.html, 1-2.

Epstein, Isidor. *Judaism: A Historical Perspective.* New York: Penguin Books, 1959.

Faivre, Antoine. *Access to Western Esotericism.* New York: State University of New York Press, 1994.

Faivre, Antoine and Needleman, Jacob, eds. *Modern Esoteric Spirituality.* New York: Crossroad, 1992.

Farren, David. *Living with Magic.* New York: Simon and Schuster, 1974.

Fleming, Walter L., ed. *Documents Relating to Reconstruction.* Morgantown, W. Va.: West Virginia University Press, 1904.

Giles, Cynthia. *The Tarot: History, Mystery, and Lore.* New York: Paragon House, 1992.

Godwin, Jocelyn. *The Theosophical Enlightenment.* New York: State University of New York Press, 1994.

"Grand Commander Clausen Rededicates Pike Statue." *The New Age* 86 (March 1978): 33-34.

Hoeller, Stephan A. *The Enchanted Life.* Hollywood, Ca.: Gnostic Society, n.d.

_____. *The Gnostic Jung and the Seven Sermons to the Dead.* Wheaton, Ill: Theosophical Society in America, 1982.

_____. *The Royal Road: A Manual of Kabalistic Meditations on the Tarot.* Wheaton, Ill.: Theosophical Society in America, 1975.

_____. *The Tao of Freedom: Jung, Gnosis and a Voluntary Society.* Rolling Hills Estates, Ca.: Wayfarer Press, 1984.

Howe, Ellic. *The Magicians of the Golden Dawn: A Documentary History of a Magical Order, 1887-1923.* York Beach, Me.: Samuel Weiser, Inc., 1987.

_____. and Möller, Helmut. "Theodor Reuss: Irregular Freemasonry in Germany, 1900-23." *Transactions of Quatuor Coronati Lodge* 91(16 February 1978): 28-42.

Hutchens, Rex R. *A Glossary to Morals and Dogma.* Washington, D. C.: House of the Temple, 1993.

_____ and Monson, Donald W. *The Bible in Albert Pike's Morals and Dogma.* Washington, D. C.: House of the Temple, 1992.

"Israel ben Eliezer Ba'al Shem Tov." *Encyclopedia Judaica.* Jerusalem: Keter Publishing House, Ltd., 1971. 9:1050.

Johnson, K. Paul. *The Masters Revealed: Madame Blavatsky and the Myth of the Great White Lodge.* New York: State University of New York Press, 1994.

Johnson, Robert L. *Counter Culture and the Vision of God.* Minneapolis, Minn.: Augsburg Publishing House, 1971.

Bibliography

Jonsson, Inge. "Swedenborg, Emanuel." *The Encyclopedia of Religion.* ed. Mircea Eliade. New York: MacMillan Publishing Company, 1987. 14:192-93.

Jung, Carl Gustav. *Memories, Dreams, Reflections.* ed. Aniela Jaffé. trans. Richard and Clara Winston. New York: Random House, 1963.

Kerr, Howard and Crow, Charles L. *The Occult in America: New Historical Perspectives.* Urbana, Ill.: University of Illinois Press, 1983.

McDermott, Robert A. "Steiner, Rudolf." *Encyclopedia of Religion.* ed. Mircea Eliade. New York: MacMillan Publishing Company, 1987. 14:47.

McIntosh, Christopher. *Éliphas Lévi and the French Occult Revival.* London: Rider and Company, 1972.

_____ *The Rosicrucians: The History, Mythology and Rituals of an Occult Order.* Wellingborough, U. K.: Aquarian Press, 1987.

Meade, Marion. *Madame Blavatsky: The Woman Behind the Myth.* New York: G. P. Putnam's and Sons, 1980.

Melton, J. Gordon. *Encyclopedia of American Religions.* 4th ed. Detroit, Mich.: Gale Research, Inc., 1993.

Encyclopedic Handbook of Cults in America. rev. ed. New York: Garland Publishing, Inc., 1992.

Minkin, Jacob S. "Baal Shem, The." *The Universal Jewish Encyclopedia.* ed. Isaac Landman. New York: Universal Jewish Encyclopedia, Inc., 1940. 2:3-4.

Morris, Robert. *Freemasonry in the Holy Land, or Handmarks of Hiram's Builders.* New York: Arno Press, 1977.

Normand, Pete. "In Memoriam, John J. Robinson, 1925-1993." *American Masonic Review.* 3 (Winter 1993): 12.

Moss, John B. and Noss, David S. *A History of the World's Religions.* 9th ed. New York: MacMillan Publishing Company, Inc., 1994.

Partner, Peter. *The Murdered Magicians: The Templars and their Myth.* Rochester,Vt.: Inner Traditions, International, 1987.

Peters, Ted. *The Cosmic Seif: A Penetrating Look at Today's New Age Movements.* San Francisco, Ca.: Harper San Francisco, 1991.

Pierrot, Jean. *The Decadent Imagination, 1880-1900.* Chicago, ifi.: University of Chicago Press, 1981.

Ransom, Josephine, comp. *A Short History of the Theosophical Society.* Adyar, Madras, India: Theosophical Publishing House, 1938.

Raschke, Carl A. *The Interruption of Eternity: Modern Gnosticism and the Origins of the New Religious Consciousness.* Chicago, Ill.: Nelson-Hall, 1989.

_____. *Painted Black: From Drug Killings to Heavy Metal, the Alarming True Story of How Satanism is Terrorizing Our Communities.* San Francisco, Ca.: Harper and Row, 1990.

Roberts, Allen E. *House Undivided: The Story of Freemasonry and the Civil War.* Richmond, Va.: Macoy Publishing and Masonic Supply Company, Inc., 1990.

_____. "Let the Beauty of Freemasonry Into Your Heart." *The Phylaxis* 19 (First Quarter 1993): 10.

Robinson, John J. *Born in Blood: The Lost Secrets of Freemasonry*. New York: M. Evans and Company, Inc., 1989.

Dungeon, Fire and Sword: The Knights Templar in the Crusades. New York: M. Evans and Company, Inc., 1991.

_____. *A Pilgrim's Path: Freemasonry and the New Religious Right*. New York: M. Evans and Company, Inc., 1993.

Seager, Richard Hughes, ed. *The Dawn of Religious Pluralism: Voices from the World's Parliament of Religions, 1893*. LaSalle, Ill.: Open Court Publishing Company, 1993.

Sellon, Emily. "Blavatsky, H. P." *Encyclopedia of Religion*. ed. Mircea Eliade. New York: MacMillan Publishing Company, 1987. 2:245-46.

Sharpe, Eric J. *Comparative Religion: A History*. 2nd ed. LaSalle, Ill.: Open Court Publishing Company, 1986.

"Should the Statue of Albert Pike Be Removed?" *The Phylaxis*. 19 (First Quarter 1993): 4-6.

Sifakis, Stewart. *Who Was Who in the Civil War*. New York: Facts on File Publishers, 1988.

Sinclair, Andrew. *The Sword and the Grail: Of the Grail, the Templars and a True Discovery of America*. New York: Crown Publishers, Inc., 1992.

Stewart, Louis. *Life Forces: A Contemporary Guide to the Cult and Occult*. Kansas City, Mo.: Andrews and McMeel, Inc., 1980.

Symonds, John. *The Magic of Aleister Crowley*. London: Frederick Müller, Ltd., 1980.

Thorne, Richard W. "Albert Pike Memorial Address." *The New Age* 82 (January 1974):4-6.

Uzzel, Robert L. "Abraxas: From Ancient Gnosis to Contemporary Culture, with Overtones In Freemasonry." *Lux e Tenebris*, 1997, 1-56.

_____. "Albert Pike's Vedic Studies: A Critical Analysis."

_____. "Albert Pike's Vedic Studies: A Critical Analysis." *Hautes Grades: The Transactions of the Scottish Rite Research Institute* (PHA) II (2002): 6-23.

_____. "AMEs at the Fair: African Methodism and the World's Columbian Exposition of 1893." *The A.M.E. Church Review* 101 (July-September 1985): 8-16.

_____. "The Divine Feminine and the Demonic Feminine: A Message for all Good Men and Masons." *Hautes Grades: The Transactions of the Scottish Rite Research Institute* (PHA) III (2003): 5-54.

Van Deventer, Fred. *Parade to Glory: The Shriners and their Caravan to Destiny*. New York: Pyramid Books, 1964.

Walkes, Jr., Joseph A. *Black Square and Compass: 200 Years of Prince Hall Freemasonry*. Richmond, Va.: Macoy Publishing and Masonic Supply Company, Inc., 1979.

Bibliography

―――――. *History of the Shrine: Ancient Egyptian Arabic Order Nobles of the Mystic Shrine, Inc., Prince Hall Affiliated, A Pillar of Black Society, 1893-1993.* Detroit, Mich.: Ancient Egyptian Arabic Order Nobles of the Mystic Shrine, 1993.

―――――. "The Ku Klux Klan and Regular Freemasonry." *The Phylaxis* 18 (Fourth Quarter 1992): 5.

―――――. "Letter." *The Phylaxis* 18 (Fourth Quarter 1992): 7.

―――――. "A Word from the President." *The Phylaxis* 18 (Fourth Quarter 1992): 2-3.

Williams, George Mason. *The Quest for Meaning of Study of Religious Change.* Chico, Ca.: New Horizons Press, 1974.

Williams, Thomas A. *Éliphas Lévi: Master of Occultism.* University, Ala.: University of Alabama Press, 1975.

Wilson, Collin. *The Mammoth Book of the Supernatural.* ed. Damon Wilson. New York: Carroll and Graf Publishers, Inc., 1991.

―――――. *The Occult: A History.* New York: Random House, 1971.

Yogananda, Paramahansa. *Autobiography of a Yogi.* Los Angeles, Ca.: Self-Realization Fellowship, 1946.

Ziolkowski, Eric J., ed. *A Museum of Faiths: Histories and Legacies of the 1893 World's Parliament of Religions.* Atlanta, Ga.: Scholars Press, 1993.

UNPUBLISHED MATERIAL

Clark, Paul A. Telephone conversation with author, 24 January 1995.
Dalton, D. M. Letter to author, 9 November 1994.
Gilbert, Robert A. Letter to author, 28 May 1994.
Gorsch, Lucia. Telephone conversation with author, 23 January 1995.
Hayes, Gloria. Telephone conversation with author, 23 January 1995.
Heidrick, Bill. Letter to author, 31 December 1994.
Hoeller, Stephan A. Letter to author, 12 December 1985.
―――――. Telephone conversation with author, 26 December 1994.
Montandon, Luther Ray. Letter to author, 4 December 1994.
―――――. Telephone conversation with author, 13 March 1995.
Moore, Hilmar. Letter to author, 18 January 1995.
Poesnecker, Gerald E. Letter to author, 8 January 1995.
Reich, Charles A. Telephone conversation with author, 14 March 1995.
Runyon, Jr., Carroll R. Telephone conversation with author, 1 February 1995.
Van Mater, Kirby. Letter to author, 2 December 1994.

Glossary

Albigenses — Religious movement in medieval Europe regarded as heretical by Roman Catholicism. The Albigenses made up about half the population of Languedoc in the southeast of France. They believed that Yahweh, the God of the Old Testament, was an evil god who had created only material things; while Jesus Christ, the God of the New Testament, had created only spiritual things. As they believed human flesh was evil, they denied that Jesus ever had a human body. They condemned many Catholic practices. They were the targets of the Albigensian Crusade.

Alchemy — Outwardly, a material process of transformation of base metals into gold; but, inwardly, a spiritual process directed at knowing the center of all things. The transmutative process is seen as an integral part of the Great Work, which is a material and spiritual realization. Man is the true subject of the alchemist's work. The Philosopher's Stone could allegedly transform base metals into gold. Christian alchemists identified this stone with Christ the Chief Cornerstone.

Androgyne — A single being coupling the male and female powers and energies, also called hermaphrodite. Gnostic literature is full of phrases suggesting that a humanity in which the masculine and feminine are reunited would achieve omnipotence, eternal life, and the Kingdom of God. The figure of the androgyne, representing the conjunction of opposites, plays an important role in alchemy. The myth of the androgyne gripped the imagination of the nineteenth century.

Apocalyptic — Literally "uncovering" or "revealing." This term is applied to a class of literature in the Judeo-Christian tradition with reference to past, present, and future. Apocalyptic is an important type of mystical and visionary literature. It was nearly all produced under stress and with a sense of urgency, showing the interaction of good and evil and the ultimate triumph of good. As symbolic expressions of ultimate truths, apocalyptic visions retain their fascination and challenge.

Kabbalah — The root meaning is "received." The Jewish Kabbalah is understood as the received (handed down) divinely inspired tradition of the mystical understanding of God and the universe.

Martinism — Esoteric movement led by French mystic Marquis Louis Claude de Saint-Martin (1743-1803).

Glossary

Mercavah — The throne-chariot of Ezekiel 10, a major topic of Jewish mysticism; the throne-world as seen as the true center of all mystic contemplation.

Mesmerism — Teachings of Franciscus Antonius Mesmer (1733-1815), a German physician. and mystic who taught that a mysterious fluid emanated from the stars, filling the universe and, if a proper balance between this fluid and the body was not maintained, disease would result. He used suggestion to cure illnesses and said that a healing fluid emanated from his brain, nerves, and will, which he called "animal magnetism."

Occultism — The study of the supernatural, hidden, secret, and mysterious; belief in knowledge communicated by way of initiation. This term was coined by Éliphas Lévi. During his lifetime, it did not have the sinister meaning attached to it today. Levi was never involved in devil worship or black magic.

Pantheism — The doctrine that God and the universe are synonymous, that God is everything and everything is God.

Pentacle — A five-pointed star formed by five straight lines connecting the vertices of a pentagram.

Sephiroth — Divine emanations (flowings) on the Kabbalistic Tree of Life.

Trimurri — Trinity of Hindu deities consisting of Brahma (Creator), Vishnu (Preserver), and Shiva (Destroyer). All three play essential roles in the cosmic process. Thus, Shiva is not seen as evil, since his destruction is followed by re-creation.

Vaudois — Religious movement, also known as the Waldenses. This group was founded in medieval France by Peter Waldo as an attempted return to primitive Christianity. They were especially strong in the Alps and were also active in Bohemia, Spain, and elsewhere. They faced severe persecution but inspired a number of later Christian reform movements.

Index

Abraham, 17, 76, 83
Abraxas, 102, 136-37
Achilles, 104
Act of Consecration of Man, 109
Adam, 17, 151
Adonai, 77
Affre, Monsignor, 5
African Methodist Episcopal Church, 161
Age of God, 112-13
Age of the Ancient Near East, 146
Age of Wisdom, 123
Agrippa, Heinrich Cornelius, 6, 53, 100
Albigenses, 95
Alchemy, 39, 46, 53, 104, 111, 154, 155
Allenbach, Adèle, 3, 29
Ambelain, Robert, 61
Amesha Spentas, 75
Analogy of Contraries, 40, 47, 77
Anarchy, 76, 135
Ancient Mystical Order Rosae Crucis (A.M.O.R.C.), 117-18
Ancient of Days, 75
Andreae, Johann Valentin, 111, 154
Anima Mundi, 102
Anquetil-Duperron, 92
Anthroposophy, 98, 107-10, 131, 139, 154
Anti-National Congress, 121
Antinomianism, 157
Antiquaries, Society of, 50
Anubis, 76
Apocalypse (Revelation), 17-19, 21, 22, 25, 37, 46, 76, 78, 81, 82, 129, 149

Appollinaire, Guillaume, 49
Appolonius of Tyana, 14, 34-35, 45, 50, 63, 65
Apuleius, Book of, 76
Aquinas, Thomas, 19
Arcanum, Arcane Sciences, 24-25, 104
Archetypes, 53, 75, 131, 152
Archons, 102
Aristotle, 145
Armistice of 1918, 49
Arnett, Benjamin William, 161
Aryans, 75, 92-93
Ascended Masters, 98, 99, 108, 133, 154
Astral Light, 28, 39, 46, 101-03, 125-26, 153, 155, 162, 167
Astrology, 104, 117, 155
Atheism, 76
Avesta, 92
Baal Shem Tov (Master of the Holy Name), 64
Babwahsingh, Soror Maria, 115
Baigent, Michael, 166
Baphomet, 42, 46, 50, 60, 79, 94-95, 97, 101, 103, 120
Barrows, John Henry, 148
Bartholomew, Saint, 95
Bastille Day, 43, 86
Baudelaire, Charles, 47
Belen (Bel), 77
Ben Yohai, Simeon, 36
Benedictine Abbey at Solemes, 4
Benton, Jr., Thomas H., 72
Bergson, Mina, 53
Besant, Annie, 106-07, 108, 134, 153, 162
Beta, Hymenaeus, 121
Bible, 37, 46, 86

181

Bibliotheque Sdainte-Geneviève, 145
Biodynamic Agriculture, 109
Bismarck, Otto von, 150
Black Mass, 104
Blake, William, 122, 157
Blavatsky, Helena Petrovna, 44, 53, 66, 98-107, 110, 111, 117, 119, 125, 129, 130, 132-39, 148, 153-54, 163, 167
Bodin, Jean, 104
Boehme, Jacob, 51, 53
Bomet, Anna, 16
Bonaparte, Napoleon, 37, 41, 104
Bonney, Charles Carroll, 147
Boston Evening Transcript, 91
Brahman, 75
Brazen Serpent, 102
Breton, André, 49
Brown, Edward H., 114
Brown, Norman O., 157
Buddha, Buddhism, 38, 84-85, 148
Buena Vista, Battle of, 71
Builders of the Adytum (B.O.T.A.), 122-31, 142, 152, 155-57
Bulletin, The, 90
Bulwer-Lytton, Edward, 35, 49, 63, 65, 114
C., Eugenie, 7, 8
Cabalistic Order of the Rosy Cross, 44
Cadiot, Noémi, 7
Cadmus, 18
Café Perocope, 29
Cagliostro, 60, 63, 82
Caithness, Lady, 51
Callié, René, 47

Cambyses, 105
Capra, Fritjof, 156
Cardan, Jerome, 53
Carter, Paul, 161
Carus, Paul, 147
Case, Paul Foster, 123-31, 143, 152, 155-58, 163, 167
Catholic Rosy Cross, the Temple, and the Grail, Order of the, 45
Catholicism
    see Roman Catholicism
Caubert, Jean-Marie Lazare, 11, 33
Cayce, Edgar, 140
Cerenne, 95
Chacornac, Paul, 1-2, 31, 58
Chakras (Nerve Centers), 119
Charity, 37
Charrot, Jacques, 15
Chauliac, M., 15
Choisy-le-roi, 5
Christ Impulse, 108
Christian Science, 133
Civil War, 71-73, 113, 146, 149, 150, 159
Clark, Paul A., 130, 144, 152
Clausen, Henry C., 74
Clement V, Pope, 60, 82
Clymer, Emerson M., 114
Clymer, Ruben Swinburne, 13, 35, 114, 154, 166
College de Juilly, 4
Colonna, Abbé Frère, 2
Communism, 56
Comparative Religion, 146, 159
Congregational Church, 74
Constant, Marie, 8
Crater Repoa, 122

Index

Crescent, 37
Crosbie, Robert, 134
Cross, 20-21, 37, 80, 104, 105, 111, 112
Crowley, Edward Alexander "Aleister", 33, 55-59, 65, 66, 120-22, 131, 138, 141, 155
Curtis, Samuel, 72
Dalton, D. M., 59
Daniel, Book of, 18, 75
Dante, Alighieri, 81-82
Davidson, Peter, 51, 66
Davies, Ann, 16-30, 152
Davis, George R., 146-47
Davis, Jefferson, 72
De Guaïta, Marquis Stanislaus, 44-45, 48
De'Isle-Adam, Philippe Valliers, 47
De Guaïta, Stanislaus, 44, 61, 62
De Gebelin, Court, 38
De Leon, Moses, 36
De Lorris, Guillame, 82
De Mirandola, Pico, 53
De Molay, Jacques, 41-43, 60, 82-83, 95, 146, 153, 165-66
De Molay, Order of, 165-66
De Paul, Vincent, 36
De Payens, Hugues, 81
De Trentanove, Gilbert, 74
Denis, Ferdinand, 145-46
Dharmapala, 161
Dialectical Society, 65
Dickinson, E. E., 163
Dolongoronki, Prince Paul Vasilyevitch, 98
Dowd, Freeman B., 114
Druids, 77, 84, 93
Duc 'd'Orleans, 95

Dumenil, Lynn, 150
Duncan, Robert Lipscomb, 71
Durkheim, Emile, 163
Eastern Orthodoxy, 35, 80, 98
Eddy, Mary Baker, 133
Eden, Garden of, 75
Egypt, 76, 98-99, 104-05
Einstein, Albert, 129, 155
Eliezer, Israel ben
  see Baal Shem Tov
Eleusinian Mysteries, 113
Emanuel, Victor, 150
Encausee, Gerard
  see Papus
Enoch, 18, 53
Enochian Magic, 53
Episcopal Church, 74
Equilibrium, 27-28, 81, 95, 128
Esalen Institute, 157, 167
Esoteric School of Theosophy, 108
Esquiros, Alphonse, 4,7
Ether, 79, 103
Ethiopia, 75
Eurythmy, 109
Evans, Ray, 90
Eve, 152
Exorcisms, 104
Ezekiel, Book of, 19-21, 23, 25, 35, 75, 78, 82, 130
Fascism, 56
Faust, 82
Fauverty, Charles, 7, 33
Felt, George, 99
Feminism, 30, 119, 151-52
Fludd, Robert, 53
France, Anatole, 44, 61
Franco-Prussian War, 15, 160
Fraternalism, 149-51

183

Fraternitas Rosae Crucis (Rosicrucian Fraternity), 112-15
Fraternity of the Hidden Light (F.H.L.), 122-23, 131, 152
Frazer, James G., 122
Freemasonry, 8, 11, 17, 19, 20, 23, 33-34, 39, 41-42, 45-46, 53, 60, 61, 63, 71, 80, 82, 85, 86-89, 96-97, 98, 114, 119, 133, 136, 141, 146, 153-55, 162, 164-65
French Revolution, 43, 82, 98
Freud, Sigmund, 49, 157
Ganneau, 4, 29
Garrison, William Lloyd, 113
Gautier, Judith, 15
Gebhard, Gustave, 14, 35, 135
Gebhard, Marie, 14, 35, 135
Germer, Karl, 121
Gihon River, 75, 93
Gilbert, Robert A., 65
Gnosis, Gnosticism, 24, 37, 38, 41, 46, 59, 78, 80, 81, 95, 102, 104, 108, 127, 157
Gnostic Mass, 121
Gobi Desert, 133
God the Father, 48, 77, 79, 80
Godwin, Jocelyn, 63, 65
Goethe, Johann Wolfgang von, 107-09
Golitsyn, Prince Aleksandr, 98
Gordon, George A., 148
Gorsch, Soro Lucia, 114-15, 140, 167
Gould, Sylvester C., 114
Grail, Holy, 108, 119-20
Grand Orient of France (Masonic), 33, 38

Grasshoff, Carl Louis Von *see* Heindel, Max
Great Depression, 162
Great White Lodge, 133
Great Work (Magnum Opus), 26, 27, 77, 79
Guyon, Madame, 4
Gypsies, 25
Hammer-Purgstall, Joseph von, 60
Hamnett, Nina, 57
Harper, William Rainey, 160
Harris, Frank, 58
Harvard University, 69-70
Harwood, W. S., 150
Hasidic Jews, 34
Hayes, Gloria, 140, 167
Heidrick, Bill, 67, 141, 155
Heindel, Max, 115-17, 118, 140, 154, 167
Henri IV, 43
Hermanubis, 79
Hermes Trismegistus, 18
Hermetic Brotherhood of Light, 119
Hermetic Brotherhood of Luxor, 51, 63
Hermetic Order of the Golden Dawn, 51-54, 59, 62-63, 122, 123, 152, 165
Hermetic Society, 63, 65
Hermeticism, Hermetic Philosophy, 53, 79
Hierarchy, 82
Higgins, Godfrey, 84-85, 93
Hippies, 121, 134, 157
Hiram Abif, 12, 20, 26
Hockley, Frederick, 52-53

Index

Hoeller, Stephan, 23, 38-39, 100, 136, 153, 158
Holly, James, 96
Holy Spirit (Paraclete), 23, 27, 45, 48, 49, 61, 77, 79, 102, 151-52
Holy Trinity, 30, 68, 77, 79, 152
Homeopathy, 109
Homer, 46
Hormiman, Annie, 53
House of the Temple, 73-74
Hugo, Victor, 15
Human Potential Movement, 157
Hutchens, Rex, 84, 93, 153, 166
Hutchinson, Louise, 49, 63
Huysmans, Joris Karl, 47-48, 62
Hylé, 102
Idolatry, 76, 135
Illuminati, 80, 119, 141
Independent Group for Esoteric Studies, 62
India, 99-100, 135
Indo-European Awakening, 146
Inquisition, 36
International Order of Kabbalists, 59
Irenaeus, Saint, 152
Irwin, Francis O., 50, 53
Isaiah, Book of, 94
Isis, 37, 60, 66, 77, 82, 93, 99, 129, 134, 136
Jackson, Thornton A., 85, 96
Janet, Pierre, 49
Jehovah's Witnesses, 133
Jerome, Saint, 53, 94
Jesuits, 41-42
Jesus Christ, 2, 8, 9, 12, 16-17, 22, 23, 26, 27, 30, 31, 32, 37, 38, 41, 48, 75, 76, 77, 78, 79, 80, 104, 105, 106, 107-08, 148, 151
Jews, Judaism, 36, 37, 38, 148
Jhourney, M. Alber, 46
Joachim of Floris, 48
Jobert, Madame, 16
Johannite Doctrine, 41-42, 48, 80, 81
John, Apostle, 17, 19, 25, 41, 76, 78, 80, 81, 94
Johnson, Andrew, 72-73, 92
Jones, Jenkins Lloyd, 147
Joseph, 17, 76, 83
Journal of Anthroposophy, 110
Judge, William Quan, 101, 103, 107, 134, 153, 162
Julian the Apostate, 79
Jung, Carl Gustav, 6, 30, 53, 122, 130, 152, 165
Kabbalah, 17-28, 41, 43-47, 51, 53, 55, 59, 62, 64, 65, 74, 75, 77, 78, 79, 80, 81, 82, 83, 94, 99, 102, 104, 111, 122, 123, 128-31, 135, 145, 146, 149, 152, 153-55, 158, 164
Kadosh, Rites of, 74, 92
Kant, Immanuel, 145
Karma, 109
Kellner, Karl, 119
Kelly, Gerald, 53
Kelly, Rose, 66
Kharouff, 46
Kheroub, 46
Kingsford, Anna, 53, 63
Kipling, Rudyard, 123
Kircher, Athanasius, 53
Kitagawa, Joseph, 161-62

Knights Templar
   see Templars
Koran, 46
Kratona Institute, 132
Kundalini (Serpent Power), 125, 167
Ku Klux Klan, 74, 87-89, 92, 96, 149, 163
Lacuna, Abbé, 61
Lacy, Thomas, 71
Land, Frank S., 165-66
LaRouche, Lyndon, 74, 87, 96
Le Populaire, 5
Le Gallois, 7
Leadbeater, C. W., 134
Leary, Timothy, 67
Lee, Robert E., 91
Legrand, Adoiphe, 7
Legrand, Clarisse, 7
Legrand, Madame, 7
Leigh, Richard, 166
Lejune, Father, 16
Leo XIII, Pope, 87
Lévi, Éliphas, 1-67, 68, 75-84, 92-97, 100-107, 110, 111-12, 114, 115, 117, 118, 121-31, 135, 139, 145-68
Lewis, Harvey Spencer, 117-18, 154
Lewis, Ralph, 117-18
Lincoln, Abraham, 72
Little, Robert Wentworth, 50, 114
Logos (Word), 80
Louis XV, King, 43, 104
Louis XVI, King, 60, 83, 95
Lucifer, 78, 86-87, 94, 96, 135
Ludwig Lodge of Berlin, 119
Lull(y), Raymond, 6, 46-47, 128

L'Univers, 5
Luther, Martin, 36, 37, 104
M.A.C., 31
Mackenzie, Kenneth Robert Henderson, 50-52, 63, 118
Magi, 12, 18, 26, 46, 75, 78, 79, 100, 127
Magic(k), 94, 122, 126, 127
Maitland, Edward, 53, 63, 65
Majumdav, 161
Manicheanism, 24
Marcuse, Herbert, 157
Marie Antoinette, 30
Martinists, 46, 62
Marty, Martin E., 147
Mary, Blessed Virgin, 2, 8, 27, 30, 151-52, 166
Masonic Grand Orient of France, 99
Masons, Masonic Lodge
   see Freemasonry
Mathers, S. L. M., 53-55, 66
Maurice, Thomas, 84
McIntosh, Christopher, 1
Memphis Appeal, 73
Memphis, Rite of, 99, 120
Mendès, Catulle, 15, 44
Mendès, Judith, 15
Mercavah, Church of, 123-24, 155, 163
Mercury, 79, 80
Mercury Publishing Company, 114
Mexican War, 71
Mexico, 110
Michilet, Victor-Emile, 46
Milton, John, 94
Miscegenation, 87, 97, 105
Misraim, Rite of, 120

Index

Mniszech, Comte Georges de, 15-16
Molt, Emile, 109
Montandon, James Ray, 130-31, 155, 163
Montandon, Luther Ray, 130-31, 144
Moore, Frances Adams, 166
More, Henry, 53
Mormonism, 133
Morris, Robert, 132
Moses, 17, 37, 38, 76, 83
Movement for Religious Renewal, 109
Muhammad (Mahomet), 38, 42, 60, 95, 148
Müller, Max, 146, 159
Muslims, Islam, 36, 37, 38, 105, 133
Mystery Religions, 24, 46
Nataraja (Cosmic Dancer), 155
National Assembly, 32
Native Americans, 71-72, 91
Nebuchadnezzar, 18
Neo-Orthodoxy, 162
Nephesh, 22
Nereus, 104
Neshemah, 22
New Age Movement, 91, 154, 166
New Age, The (journal), 90-91
New York Liberal Club, 134
Nibbas, 76
Nineteenth-Century *Zeitgeist*, 145-51, 159, 162
Nodier, Charles, 41
Occult Science, Occultism, 103-04, 137, 145, 159
Odin, 84

Olcott, Henry Steele, 45, 100, 105-07, 137, 153
Olivier, Monsignor, 5
Order of the Temple of Astarte (O.T.A.), 122, 131, 152
Order of the Temple of the Orient (O.T.O.), 56, 98, 108, 118-22, 131, 138, 141, 155
Oriflamma, 120
Orpheus, Orphism, 64, 79
Osiris, 12
Oversoul, 99, 134
Pages, Gabriel, Jogang
  see Taxil, Leo
Pan, 60, 76
Papal Infallibility, 86
Papus, 44, 48, 62, 119, 152
Paracelsus, 26, 100, 102, 127
Paraclete
  see Holy Spirit
Pascal, Edouard-Adolphe, 16
Patanjali, 128
Path, The, 101
Paul, Apostle, 19
Payne, Daniel Alexander, 161
Pea Ridge, Battle of, 71
Péladin, Adrien, 61
Péladin, Joséphin, 45, 48, 61
Penny, Edward Burton, 50-51
Pentagram, 26, 35, 127
Pharisees, 19, 27
Philip IV, King (Philippe le Bel), 60, 82
Philo of Alexandria, 92
Philosopher's Stone, 27, 42, 79
Philosophical Publishing Company, 114
Phylaxis Society, 96
Pike, Alfred W., 69

Pike, Albert, 53, 65, 68-97, 118, 129, 131, 136, 148, 150, 152, 155, 158, 159
Pike, Benjamin, 68-69
Pike, Lillian, 91
Pike, Mary Ann Hamilton, 71, 91
Pike, Sarah Andrews, 68-69
Pison River, 75, 93
Pistorius, John, 53
Pius VI, 83
Plato, 71, 92
Pleroma, 102
Plummer, George Winslow, 114-15, 118, 154, 167
Poe, Edgar Allen, 122
Poesnecker, Gerald E., 114, 154, 166
Postel, Guilloume, 6, 53
Postellus, Guielmus
 see Postel, Guilloume
Postmillennialism, 149, 151
Premillennialism, 149
Prince Hall (African American) Freemasonry, 33, 85, 87-89, 96-97, 164
Progressivism, 149, 151
Protocols of the Elders of Zion, 141-42
Pseudo-Dionysius the Aeropogite, 79
Psyche, 22
Pythagoras, 29, 75-76, 132
Quantum Physics, 155-56
Qur'an, 37, 63
Ragon, 52
Randolph, Pascal Beverly, 12-13, 35, 66, 112-14, 118, 154, 158, 166

Raschke, Carl A., 68, 87, 89
Rasputin, Grigory, 45
Rawson, Albert Leighton, 98-99, 132-33, 163
Rebelais, Francois, 6
Reconstruction, 149
Reich, Charles A., 157-58
Reincarnation, 109, 110, 134, 155
Remphan, 76
Reuchlin, Johannes, 53
Reuss, Theodor, 56, 65, 119
Revelation, Book of
 see Apocalypse
Revolution in Consciousness, 124-25, 129, 156-58
Revolution of 1848, 9, 31-32, 48
Richardson, James D., 74
Rimbaud, Arthur, 47
Robinson, John J., 68, 73, 90, 92, 94, 148
Roman Catholicism, 34, 36, 38, 41-42, 45, 58-59, 78, 80, 82, 86, 94, 97, 100, 104, 105, 128
Rose Cross, 111
Rosenkreuz, Christian, 111
Rosenroth, Knorr von, 33, 53, 55, 75, 92, 93
Rosetta Stone, 25
Rosicrucianism, 11-12, 17, 35, 39, 45, 50, 53, 59, 62, 63, 65, 81, 82, 98, 99, 108, 111-18, 119, 120, 131, 139, 142, 154-55
Rousseau, Jean-Jacques, 37, 82, 95
Royal Asiatic Society, 50
Rue de l'Ancienne Comedic, 29
Rue Saint-Jacques, 16
Runyon, Jr., Carroll R., 122

Index

Saint-Francois Xavier, Church of, 16
Saint Germaine, Count, 98
Saint-Nicholas de Chardonnet, 2-3
Saint Sulpice Seminary, 3, 9, 19
Salt, 80
Samaritan Doctors, 77
Sanhedrin, 104
Santa Sophia, 37
Sat B'hai, 63
Satan, Satanism, 60, 74, 76, 86-87, 96, 104
Schleiden, Hubbe, 135
Scholem, Gershom, 24, 146, 164
Schuré, Edoard, 53, 108
Scottish Rite Journal, 90-91
Scottish Rite of Freemasonry, 60, 71, 73-74, 85-87, 90-91, 95, 99, 120, 128, 150, 152
Seagar, Richard Hughes, 149, 161-62
Sephiroth, 17
Sepoher Toldos Jeshu, 104
Sepher Yetzirah, 19, 78
Sephiroth (Emanations), 75, 105
Septenary, 77
Serena, Mother, 114, 140
Seth, 17, 76
Seven Seals, 78
Seventh Day Adventists, 133
Sex Magic, 66, 120-21
Sexuality, 113, 119
Shamballah, 133
Shekhinah, 23, 38
Shiva, 155
Shriners, 99, 133, 150-51, 163-64
Siphra Dzeniuta, 47
Sixtus IV, Pope, 53

Smith, Joseph, 133
Societas Rosicruciana in Anglia, 50, 114
Societas Rosicruciana in America, 114-15
Societas Rosicruciana in Civitatibus Foederatis, 114
Socialism, 30, 51, 97, 102, 119, 134, 167
Socialist Labor Party, 134
Söen, Shaku, 167
Solomon, 12, 20, 22, 31, 41, 78, 80, 128, 148
Sota, 104
Sotheran, Charles, 99, 133-34
Southern Loyal Convention, 113
Spedalieri, Baron Giussepe, 58, 65
Speed, James, 72
Sphinx, 46
Spiritism (Spiritualism), 113, 114
Spiritus Sanctum (House of the Holy Spirit), 111
Sprengel, Anna, 52
Star, 75, 83
Steiner, Rudolf, 107-11, 115, 120, 138, 141
Stukely, William, 84
Sturzaker, D. L., 59
Sublime Prince of the Royal Secret, 95
Sufism, 63, 108, 164
Sulphur, 79
Surrealism, 49
Suzuki, D. T., 155-56, 161, 167
Swedenborg, Emanuel, 47, 51, 63, 82, 160-61
Swedenborg, Rite of, 99, 119, 120

189

Swedenborgian Church, 147, 160-61
Sword, 80
Symbolist Doctrine, 47
Synchronicity, 152, 165
Tantra, 108
Taoism, 156
Tarot, 24, 38-39, 44, 46, 50, 59, 61, 62, 64, 65, 87, 94, 122, 123, 128-31, 152, 155
Taxil, Leo, 86-87, 96
Templars (Knights Templar), 18, 41-43, 46, 50, 59, 60, 79, 80, 81, 82, 94-95, 97, 102, 120, 146, 152, 163, 165-66
Tentates (Teuth), 77
Thartac, 77
Thelema, 56, 58, 66
Theology of Numbers, 27
Theoclete, 81
Theon, Max, 51, 64
Theosophist, The, 100, 101
Theosophy, 35, 38, 44-45, 45, 51-53, 61, 63, 66, 98-110, 115, 117, 119, 120, 131, 132-38, 153-55, 163-64, 167
"13" Craze, 150-51
Thoth, 77
Tibet, 98
Tingley, Katherine, 134
Toleration, Religious, 96, 151, 164
Transcendentalists, 133
Tree of Life, 129, 155
Trinity, 48
Tristan, Flora, 5, 30
Trowel, 80
United Lodge of Theosophists, 134

Union League, 149
Van Mater, Kirby, 134-35
Vandertuin, Victoria E., 166
Vatican Council I, 86
Vatican Council II, 152
Vaudois, 95
Vedanta Society, 161, 163
Vedas, 51, 92-93
Verlaine, Paul, 47
Vienne, Council of, 41
Vivekananda, Swami, 161-63
Voltaire, François-Marie Arouet de, 37
Waite, Arthur Edward, 1, 17, 53-55, 59, 65, 66, 75, 119
Waite, Stand, 91
Waldorf Astoria Tobacco Factory, 109
Waldorf Schools, 109
Walkes, Jr., Joseph A., 87-88, 96
Wandering Jew, 95
Wattelet, Dr., 16
Watts, Alan, 167
Webb, Alexander Russell ("Muhammad"), 161
Weishaupt, Adam, 141
Wesak, 161
Westcott, William Wynn, 52, 54-55, 65, 119
Williams, Fannie Barrier, 161
Wirth, Oswald, 44, 61
Woodford, Adolphus F.A., 50, 52
Woods, Howard L., 88-89
World War I, 45, 48-49
World War II, 162
World's Columbian Exposition of 1893, 160

Index

World's Parliament of Religions
 of 1893, 137, 139, 147-49,
 151, 160-61, 163-64, 167
World's Parliament of Religions
 of 1993, 134-35
Wronski, Henri, 10, 33
Yeats, William Butler, 53, 65
Yoga, 119, 128
Yogananda, Paramahansa, 131,
 144, 163
York Rite of Freemasonry, 71
Yugoslavia, 141
Zaza, Lola, 58
Zen Buddhism, 155, 167
Zerubbabel, 41, 80
Zohar (Sohar), 17, 46, 78, 83, 127,
 146
Zoroaster, Zoroastrianism, 12,
 24, 148

About the Author

Robert L. Uzzel was born on 22 May 1951 in Waco, Texas. He graduated from Waco High School in 1969 and received an Associate of Arts degree from McLennan Community College in 1971. He received a Bachelor of Arts in Religion and Sociology in 1973, a Master of Arts in Church-State Studies in 1976, and a Ph.D. in World Religions in 1995 from Baylor University. He has done additional graduate work in Political Science at the University of Texas at Arlington.

Uzzel is an ordained elder in the African Methodist Episcopal Church. He has served as pastor of Texas A.M.E. congregations in Dallas, Fort Worth, Kaufman, Blooming Grove, and Maypearl. He currently serves as pastor of Wayman Chapel AME Church in Ennis.

Uzzel has taught courses in Religion, History, and Political Science at Paul Quinn College, Cedar Valley College, Mountain View College, Tarrant County College, Temple College, and Navarro College.

Uzzel's articles have appeared in a number of church and Masonic publications. For his Masonic writings, he received Certificates of Literature from both the Philalethes Society and the Phylaxis Society. He is a Fellow of the Phylaxis Society, a holder of the Dr. Charles H. Wesley Medal of History, and a member of the Society of Blue Friars.

Uzzel's first book *Blind Lemon Jefferson: His Life, His Death, and His Legacy*, was published in 2002. His second book, *Prince Hall Freemasonry in the Lone Star State: From Cuney to Curtis, 1875-2003*, was published 2004.

Uzzel is married to the former Debra Bass, a native of Fairfield, Texas. They have four children and seven grandchildren.

CPSIA information can be obtained at www.ICGtesting.com
Printed in the USA
LVOW041931030912

297195LV00002B/50/A